UNDERSTANDING
TAHRIR SQUARE

TO MY DEAR FRIENDS DAN AND BERT,
WHO HAVE BEEN FRIENDS FOR
TOO MANY YEARS TO COUNT.

FONDLY,

UNDERSTANDING TAHRIR SQUARE

What Transitions Elsewhere Can Teach Us about the Prospects for Arab Democracy

STEPHEN R. GRAND

BROOKINGS INSTITUTION PRESS
Washington, D.C.

The Brookings Institution is a private nonprofit organization devoted to research,
education, and publication on important issues of domestic and foreign policy. Its
principal purpose is to bring the highest quality independent research and analysis
to bear on current and emerging policy problems. Interpretations or conclusions in
Brookings publications should be understood to be solely those of the authors.

Library of Congress Cataloging-in-Publication data
Grand, Stephen R.
    Understanding Tahrir Square : what transitions elsewhere can teach us about the
prospects for Arab democracy / Stephen R. Grand.
       page   cm
    Includes bibliographical references and index.
    ISBN 978-0-8157-2516-9 (pbk. : alk. paper)
    1. Democratization—Arab countries. 2. Democracy—Arab countries.
3. Democratization—Cross-cultural studies. 4. Democracy—Cross-cultural
studies. 5. Arab Spring, 2010– 6. Arab countries—Politics and government—
21st century. I. Title.
    JQ1850.A91G73 2014
    320.917'4927—dc23   2013050930

9 8 7 6 5 4 3 2 1

Printed on acid-free paper

Typeset in Sabon

Composition by Cynthia Stock
Silver Spring, Maryland

"The work of freedom is never done."

Supreme Court Justice Anthony Kennedy

CONTENTS

Preface and Acknowledgments

This book—which seeks to garner lessons for the countries of the Arab Spring from the recent experiences with democratization of countries elsewhere around the globe—is the product of a long intellectual journey. It began in 1990, when, while researching my dissertation, I had the good fortune to live in Prague immediately after Czechoslovakia's Velvet Revolution. I became fascinated by the rapid political and economic transitions that were reshaping Czech society from day to day. With totalitarian regimes crumbling all around, it was a period when "people power" and civil society were widely celebrated. However, as a budding political scientist, I struggled to understand the precise connection between the two and democratization. Did every democracy require a Chamber of Commerce and a League of Women Voters to be successful?

It was during this period that along with my long-time friend and now Brookings colleague William Antholis, I helped establish and served as executive director of a nonprofit organization, the Civic Education Project, that sent Western-trained university lecturers to teach at and help rebuild social science departments in the former Eastern bloc. What struck me most about the experience was the profound difference in attitudes toward authority between East and West. In their first encounter with Western-style education, our Eastern European students found most revolutionary not the new Western texts that we provided but our more informal, horizontal style of teaching. Many reported that they had never before been asked their own opinions or expected to take responsibility for a project from beginning to end.

That made me curious about the connection between popular attitudes toward authority and democracy.

For the rest of the 1990s, I remained engaged in Eastern Europe, first as a staffer on the Senate Foreign Relations Committee, then as director of programs at the German Marshall Fund of the United States (GMF). In the latter role, I was heavily involved in grant making to new think tanks and civic groups throughout the region. I had the good fortune of being present at a gathering of Bulgarian, Romanian, and Slovak democracy activists (described briefly in the Slovak country case study in this book) that proved influential in the formation of the OK '98 civic movement, which helped oust Slovak strongman Vladimír Mečiar from office. We then recruited one of the OK '98 leaders, Pavol Demeš, to come work at GMF. He shared his experiences with the Croats and Serbs, in the latter case helping to shape the EXIT 2000 civic movement, which eventually unseated Slobodan Milošević. Working with these civic movements was one of the highlights of my career. I was captivated by how like-minded citizens were able to come together to challenge authoritarian and semi-authoritarian regimes. Later, I also watched with interest as these movements struggled to figure out their roles after the dictator had fallen—to determine the part that civic groups could and should play in consolidating democracy.

Thanks to an International Affairs Fellowship with the Council on Foreign Relations in 2002–03, I had the luxury of being able to step away to think and write for a year about the lessons to be learned from the transitions, successful and unsuccessful, in the former Eastern bloc and their implications for political change in the Middle East. The ideas generated during that period deeply inform this work, and the Slovak and Serb country case studies that appear in chapter 3 draw heavily from an unpublished paper that I wrote during that year.

Following two years as founding director of the Aspen Institute's Middle East Strategy Group, which worked on Palestinian-Israeli issues, I was invited to be the director of Brookings's Project on U.S. Relations with the Islamic World, housed within the Saban Center for Middle East Policy. It was a fascinating opportunity to immerse myself in an entirely different region of the world. Traveling from Cairo to Qatar to Karachi to Kuala Lumpur, I came to recognize over time that "the problems of the Muslim world" had far less to do with religion than with poor governance. And, as I had witnessed in Eastern Europe, citizen movements were already taking shape to push for change. Then, in early 2011, as I was beginning to write this book in earnest, the Arab

Spring erupted. A book that had been focused broadly on the problems of governance in the Muslim world was quickly transformed into one about the prospects for Arab democracy.

Writing about current events can be like trying to hit a moving target—one that seems to be moving especially rapidly in these tumultuous times. In the week or so before this book went to press, significant changes had already occurred in some of the countries that it covers: civic protests had ousted President Viktor Yanukovych in Ukraine, a corruption scandal had revived public demonstrations against Prime Minister Erdoğan in Turkey, large-scale public protests had erupted against President Nicolás Maduro in Venezuela, and the interim government in Egypt had resigned. None of these events, however, changes in any way the basic argument of the book. In fact, they are consistent with the pattern of events described in the country case studies presented here.

Many people gave me valuable advice and assistance in writing this book, although any errors and omissions are, of course, wholly my own. First, I would like to thank the many democracy activists, scholars, journalists, and politicians whom I met with during trips to Egypt and Tunisia in recent years. They are brave men and women who are living in a dangerous but pivotal moment in their countries' history, and I appreciate greatly how generous they were with their time and how freely they shared their ideas, opinions, and perspectives on the events unfolding around them.

Second, I would like to thank those who read and commented on various drafts of the book, including Daniel Byman (the Saban Center's director of research), Thomas Carothers, Ivan Krastev, Michael O'Hanlon (the Brookings Foreign Policy program's director of research), Ted Piccone (the Foreign Policy program's acting vice president), and an anonymous outside reviewer. Their advice was invaluable in shaping the final product.

Third, thanks go to my many wonderful colleagues at Brookings. For the last eight years, I have found Brookings to be an extremely collegial and stimulating intellectual home, and I want to express my deep appreciation to its president, Strobe Talbott, for making it such a place. Thanks also to Carlos Pascual and Martin Indyk, both of whom served as thoughtful and able vice presidents of the Brookings Foreign Policy program during my tenure. It was my good fortune to be housed in the Saban Center for Middle East Policy, which includes among its senior scholars some of the finest minds thinking about today's Middle East.

This book borrows heavily from my own chapter ("Democracy 101") in a volume entitled *The Arab Awakening: America and the Transformation of the Middle East,* which the center's scholars collectively wrote immediately after the Arab Spring. I want to thank in particular the Saban Center's former director, Kenneth Pollack (who, together with Daniel Byman, edited that volume), and its current director, Tamara Wittes, for their continual support, advice, and friendship. It was Ken who encouraged me to make the book a comparative study that was global in scope. That meant a far more ambitious research project than I had envisioned, but the hard work ultimately made for a much better book.

While director of the Project on U.S. Relations with the Islamic World, I was blessed with the best staff that anyone could wish to have. I had the good luck to have three stellar research assistants: Aysha Chowdhry, who supported and encouraged me through the book's early stages and planned and accompanied me on initial research trips to Egypt and Pakistan; Akram Al-Turk, who ably managed the research phase and critiqued early draft chapters; and Jomana Qaddour, who patiently and capably steered the book toward completion. Durriya Badani, my incredibly talented and dynamic deputy director, assumed day-to-day management duties so that I could disappear to do research and write. Other staff members over the years included Jacob Elghanayan, Duaa Elzeney, Rabab Fayad, Noha George, Rim Hajji, Neeraj Malhotra, and Christal Shrader. As they move on with their own careers, I am expecting great things. Thanks to a grant from the Ford Foundation, a steady stream of visiting fellows that included M. J. Akbar, Hisham Hellyer, Mehrangiz Kar, Mirette Mabrouk, and Mohammad Waseem provided me with ongoing tutorials about the Arab and broader Muslim worlds. The State of Qatar's Foreign Ministry generously supported much of the rest of the Project's activities, including the annual U.S.-Islamic World Forum.

I am indebted to Brookings Institution Press for all of its assistance. Eileen Hughes was the kind of editor of whom every writer dreams: thoughtful, meticulous, and swift and skillful with the pen. Susan Woollen oversaw the design of the terrific book cover. (In what may be a first for Brookings, I snapped the cover photo, while visiting Tahrir Square, on my own I-Phone 5.) I also greatly appreciate the assistance of the Brookings Library staff, most particularly Laura Mooney.

Finally, I would like to thank my wife, Paige Alexander, who has been a part of this journey every step of the way. Ever since our life together in Prague, our careers have intertwined in exciting ways. What a delight to have a soul mate who shares the same interests and passions. It is to her and our three almost perfect kids, Rachel, Carly, and Josh—whom we have had the great joy to watch grow up and who have helped us grow along the way—that this book is dedicated. May our children and our children's children live in a world ever more free and secure.

CHAPTER ONE

WHITHER THE ARAB SPRING?

It is a hard time to be an optimist about the Arab Spring. What started with the self-immolation of a Tunisian street vendor frustrated by the injustice and ineptitude of his country's corrupt leaders and then mushroomed into massive public demonstrations across the Arab world now seems to have degenerated into violence, instability, and chaos. Syria has been ripped apart by civil war. Bahrain's government continues its crackdown on its Shiite majority. Al Qaeda's presence in Yemen appears to be growing, as are secessionist pressures in the south of the country. Libya still grapples with lawlessness two years after the end of its civil war. Tensions between Islamists and secularists in Tunisia reached a boiling point in 2013. And, of course, following nationwide antigovernment protests in Egypt, a military-controlled transitional government has replaced the country's first democratically elected one.

This book nonetheless presents an optimistic assessment of the long-term prospects for the democratization of Arab countries. Drawing on the recent experience of a broad range of countries elsewhere in the world that embarked on their transition to democracy during what is known as the "Third Wave" of democratization,[1] this book seeks to show that the trials and tribulations of the Arab Spring are neither entirely new nor unique. They are instead part and parcel of the struggles often faced by countries in transition to democracy. And from those countries' experiences, it seeks to illuminate a path forward for the countries of the Arab Spring.

The Puzzle

A recent *Time* magazine cover captured well the status of the Arab Spring nearly three years on. Published shortly after the June 30, 2013, mass demonstrations in Egypt against then-President Mohamed Morsi—which ended with the military removing him from office—it featured a split screen superimposed on a photo of the crowds in Tahrir Square. The caption "World's Best Protesters" was printed on the left and "World's Worst Democrats" was printed on the right—and the image of the crowd on the right was shaded blood red.

This is the puzzle presented today by Egypt as well as the other countries touched by the Arab Spring. The citizens of the Arab world have finally found their collective voice. Long trammeled by years of autocratic rule, they now fill the region's squares, roundabouts, and boulevards with their protests, braving tear gas, truncheons, and even torture to make themselves heard. Yet what began with such great promise— with the youth of the Arab world spontaneously protesting in the name of freedom, dignity, and opportunity—has yet to produce a functioning democracy. Instead, it has deteriorated in many parts of the Arab world into a complex and at times bloody struggle between youthful revolutionaries and stalwarts of the old regime, Islamists and secularists, Muslims and Christians, Sunnis and Shia. The euphoria that accompanied the early protests in Tunisia and Egypt—in those heady days when it looked as if Arab youth were set to tear the region from its history— has given way to deep-seated pessimism. Libya, Yemen, Bahrain, and Syria degenerated into violence and even civil war while Tunisia and Egypt have struggled to overcome the legacy of authoritarianism, to write new constitutions, and to keep their newly elected governments on the democratic path. Moreover, pessimism turned to consternation as the so-called liberals in Egypt and, for a time, Tunisia looked to the military to save them from elected Islamist governments. Some commentators have compared the events of the Arab Spring to those of 1848, when the youth of Europe also took to the streets to protest tyranny. Yet for all the tumult and upheaval, in the end little changed politically, at least for a generation.[2] Others have drawn darker parallels with the French, Russian, and Iranian revolutions, in which more violent and extreme forces outmaneuvered nascent democratic movements.[3] The Arab region's democratic activists have been remarkably successful in mobilizing citizens to take to the streets and in tearing down a number of the region's most despotic regimes, but they have been far less successful in translating that revolutionary energy into lasting political change.

The popular revolts of the Arab Spring have left not democracy but a political vacuum in their wake. All kinds of forces—political Islamists, ultranationalists and violent sectarians, secular democrats, elements of former regimes, and al Qaeda and other violent extremists—are now vigorously competing to fill that vacuum. The disorder has been so pervasive that many across the region and in the West have expressed the wish that the Arab Spring had never happened and have called for an end to the civil disobedience roiling the region. They have come to view free assembly itself as dangerous, too fraught with the risk of instability. Shortly before the June 30 demonstrations in Egypt, for example, the then–U.S. ambassador to Egypt delivered a now-famous speech discouraging students from protesting in the streets.[4]

The puzzle is this: how could such widespread public demonstrations of citizens' hunger for change have produced so little change so far? In Egypt, for instance, how could a protest movement that reputedly collected an unprecedented 22 million signatures from citizens expressing no confidence in their elected president—and that mobilized those millions to take to the streets—have then ceded control of the country's transition to the military? How could the Egyptian people stage three popular revolts in the span of less than three years—against long-time strongman Hosni Mubarak, the interim military government, and Morsi's Muslim Brotherhood–dominated government—yet still end up well short of democracy? Throughout the region, the last three years have seen a remarkable outpouring of popular protest yet far fewer constructive steps to build successful new democracies.

This book attempts to explain that puzzle and propose a way forward by examining recent experiences with democratization in other regions of the world: in the former Eastern bloc; the Muslim-majority countries of Asia; Latin America; and Sub-Saharan Africa. The Arab world was not the first region of the world to embark on a transition to democracy but the last. Before the Arab Spring, some ninety countries across the globe had embarked on transitions to democracy since the mid-1970s.[5] What the experiences of those regions suggest is that much of the pessimism about the Arab Spring is unwarranted. Democracy takes time to take root, even under the best of circumstances. How the events of the Arab Spring play out—whether they lead to a more stable, prosperous, and democratic Middle East or something more sinister and tragic—is a story that is still unfolding.

The Rise of the Citizen and the Collapse of the Old Order

While it is still too early to predict the fate of Arab democracy, it is clear that there is no returning to the status quo ante. As much as some may wish, there is no putting the genie back in the bottle. Arab citizens are demanding a say in their own governance and are no longer willing to tolerate authoritarianism. For more than half a century, the Arab Middle East was ruled largely by autocrats whose reign over time became increasingly heavy-handed, unjust, and corrupt. While the old status quo may have served the perceived short-term interests of the United States—because it provided a modicum of stability in the region, ensured the flow of cheap oil from the Gulf, and protected America's most important ally in the region, Israel—it failed to meet even the most basic social welfare needs of the region's citizens, who increasingly chafed at the limitations imposed on their personal freedom and economic opportunities.

Then, on December 17, 2010, Mohamed Bouazizi, a Tunisian fruit vendor, set himself on fire and the old order suddenly began to unravel. As he lay dying in a hospital room, Tunisians angrily massed in the streets in protest. By mid-January 2011, as the popular protests continued to grow, Tunisian strongman Ben Ali was forced to flee into exile. The aura of invincibility that had long surrounded the region's dictators had suddenly been pierced, and the fear began to dissipate. Inspired by events in Tunisia, Egyptian activists who had long struggled against the Mubarak regime mobilized supporters to occupy Tahrir Square. The demonstrations soon spread to Alexandria, Giza, and Suez, then throughout Egypt. After more than two weeks of sometimes bloody demonstrations and counter-demonstrations in Egypt, Mubarak stepped down. The events in Egypt had ripple effects throughout the Arab world. Protests quickly spread to Yemen, Bahrain, Libya, Syria, Morocco, Jordan, and Oman, then throughout much of the rest of the Arab world. Rulers struggled to get ahead of the protests by proposing reforms, doling out cash benefits to citizens, deploying force, or trying some combination of the three.

The Arab world has been forever changed by these events. The "hour of the citizen," a term that the late Lord Ralf Dahrendorf used to refer to post-1989 Eastern Europe, has now arrived in the Arab Middle East.[6] Ordinary Arabs have finally found their voice and in important respects are now driving events in the region. They are demanding the right to choose their own political leaders, partake in certain basic freedoms, participate in their own governance, and craft societies that respect the basic dignity of all citizens. Any effort by the United States to reinstate the ancien régime would lead to greater upheaval and instability. Trying to repress this Arab civic awakening would not only be impracticable but also contrary to American values and interests. It is just such repression that has bred al Qaeda and other forms of extremism in the Arab world.

While the power of the citizen is indisputably on the rise, it is less clear what that will ultimately mean for the region's future. Countries in the region now appear to be following three different trajectories.[7] In one set of countries, including Tunisia, Egypt, Libya, and Yemen, citizens have succeeded in sweeping away the old order and ostensibly have begun to make a still fragile transition toward democracy. In the second set, the old rulers have succeeded to date in staying ahead of or suppressing the demands of their people by revamping the old order in ways that allow them to preserve, at least for now, their hold on power. This group includes not only the Gulf monarchies, which benefit from their oil and gas wealth to buttress their rule, but also Morocco and Jordan, which lack that wealth but share the legitimacy accorded to hereditary monarchies. In the third group, state and society are locked in a violent stalemate, even civil war, over the future of their country. Syria now falls into this category, as Libya, Yemen, and Bahrain once did; others, like Jordan (and possibly Bahrain once again), could yet meet this fate if change does not come quickly enough to satisfy their citizens' demands. What is not yet known is how successful the transition toward democracy will be in the first set, how far the democratic impulse will spread beyond those four countries, and how long the others can stave off citizens' demands for greater participation, accountability, transparency, and effectiveness in government. Will the future of the region bring democracy, continued autocracy, or ongoing civil war? The region remains in a state of flux. The Arab Spring has forever transformed the region's politics, yet its ultimate impact remains unclear.

Lessons from Elsewhere

What recent history shows is that democratization tends to be a lengthy process. It is far easier to unseat an autocratic leader (although events in Syria are demonstrating once again that even that is not a simple task) than it is to construct a new democratic order: "You can tweet a revolution, but you can't tweet a transition" to democracy.[8] Transitions rarely proceed in a smooth, straightforward manner; they almost always include sudden advances coupled with heartbreaking reversals. Often the reversals contribute in important ways to the political learning required to build a democracy. At root, democratization is a political process. It involves a fundamental shift in power from those governing to those governed—power that is never ceded freely, without at least a political struggle. Political power in a democracy derives in large part from the ability to organize—in order to mobilize supporters at election time, to corral votes in the legislature, and to govern effectively.

In this political struggle, the legacies of the past loom large and shape the constellation of forces involved today. In the Arab Middle East, the dysfunctions of former regimes, not the introduction of democracy, are primarily responsible for the polarization and violence now being seen.[9] The region's authoritarian leaders have inculcated throughout society a paternalistic pattern of behavior that influences human relations in general: from how a ruler relates to the ruled to how a parent relates to a child, a teacher to a student, and an employer to an employee. Moreover, they have instilled a xenophobic nationalism in the population that may take a generation to undo. They have strengthened and empowered the military and security services, generously funding and equipping these critical props to their rule to the point that these forces are now first among equals in many countries. At the same time, the region's autocrats pitted secularists against Islamists as a way of dividing the opposition to their rule. They generally clamped down tightly on the secular opposition, limiting its engagement in political life. They were unable to do the same as successfully with their Islamist foes because of the Islamists' tight connections to religion and religious institutions.

Consequently, three main camps now vie for power in the Arab Middle East: the security forces long associated with the ancien régime, the Islamists, and the secularists. The security forces inherited all of the firepower, but they are hindered by the problem of legitimacy because of their links to the old order. The Islamists were best prepared to participate in the first truly competitive multiparty elections in the region because, thanks to their history of political opposition to secular autocrats, they are the most organized and disciplined of the groups competing and have the deepest roots within society. The secularists are far weaker organizationally because they were rarely allowed to participate in politics before and because they are divided ideologically among liberals, socialists, communists, nationalists, and the like. At the moment, they may appear outmanned, out-organized, and outmaneuvered, but in numerical terms they probably represent the largest proportion of the population in most countries.

This book argues, drawing on the experiences of countries elsewhere in the world that transitioned to democracy fairly recently, that over the long term successful democratization requires the emergence of a political constituency that supports democracy. What citizens tend to seek when they embark on a democratic path are not just elections, but democracy in a much richer sense. They seek not just *electoral democracy*, in which periodic multiparty elections are held for political office under free and fair conditions, but democracy in the broader sense of *liberal democracy*. In the words of Robert Dahl, the latter includes "classical liberal freedoms that are a part of the definition of public contestation and participation: opportunities to oppose the government, form political organizations, express oneself on political matters without fear of governmental reprisals, read and hear alternative points of view." Those freedoms are what citizens want, along with the right to "vote by secret ballot in elections in which candidates of different parties compete for votes and after which the losing candidates peacefully yield their claim to office to the winners."[10] In a word, they desire a state that governs effectively and justly, according to the rule of law and with respect for individual rights and the will of the public.

Achieving those ends is often the work of not months or years but decades or more. Even the most established democracies, the United States being just one case in point, struggle continually to realize in full the "more perfect union" to which the U.S. constitution aspires. Building such a union requires the convergence of many factors. Among other things, it requires a well-crafted constitution that enumerates the rights of the citizen and divides power among different branches of government. It requires well-designed political institutions staffed by talented individuals. Effective political parties also are critical. Material support and incentives from the international community may be valuable. But this book argues that most of all, it requires public demand—the existence of an effective political constituency for democracy.[11] The best-designed and most well-intentioned political systems will fail to function as intended unless political leaders understand that there will be a price to pay if they violate the rules of the game—that the public stands ready to defend its hard-won freedoms. At the end of the day, democracy requires democrats.

To provide some historical perspective, in the ninety or so countries across the world that have embarked on a democratic transition since the mid-1970s, events rarely unfolded according to the highly idealized visions of how such transitions should proceed. The early optimistic hopes of the revolutionaries in the streets often were dashed as political realities set in. Democrats, liberals in particular, often found themselves isolated as demagogues, populists, ultra-nationalists, and religious zealots capitalized on citizens' insecurities and prejudices to gain power. In scant few of the countries was there a well-organized and politically popular liberal democratic party prepared to move the country forward rapidly. In many there were neither strong constitutional traditions nor robust political institutions for new political leaders to build on. Debate often raged over who had the right to participate in the new democratic system and how and by whom constitutions were to be written. Founding elections rarely proceeded without incident, and unscrupulous candidates sought to exploit ethnic, religious, or class differences to win office. Contrary to expectations, in only very rare instances did the transitions proceed neatly from a political opening (usually the fall of an authoritarian political leader) to free and fair elections and the rotation in power of competing political parties that used their time in office to expand democratic freedoms and strengthen the rule of law. Most democratic transitions were far messier, full of democratic reversals and even breakdowns. Democracy in the fuller sense described by Dahl emerged, if at all, only after a long, arduous process involving intense political struggle over power and the nature of the future state.

If this history is any guide, the Arab Middle East is likely to experience a lengthy period of uncertainty as citizens and their leaders struggle toward a new balance between state and society. There is likely to be not one constitutional crisis—like Egypt's massive public demonstrations of June 30, 2013, or President Morsi's emergency decree of November 2012, which greatly expanded his powers—but many. Understanding the momentous events unfolding in the region requires looking beyond the political headlines of the moment and taking a longer-term view. The success or failure of democratization in the region is unlikely to be determined by the results of a single election, a clause that does or does not get written into a constitution, or one supreme court decision. Nor will the possibilities for democratic change be limited by what has or has not proved possible in the region before. The ongoing political changes in the region must be viewed in the context of the broader historical forces that are rearranging the relationship between citizen and state across the globe. Put simply, the Arab Spring needs to be put into comparative perspective. That is what this book attempts to do.

The Path Forward

What recent history teaches is that the popular protests convulsing the Middle East are not the problem but the beginning of a solution to the democratic deficit plaguing the region. More Tahrir Squares are needed, not fewer. That is, rather than trying to drive citizens from the public sphere, the United States and others should help democracy activists in the region broaden and deepen the constituency for change that the protesters in Tahrir represent and make it more politically efficacious. The youth in Tahrir represent an exciting new generation; their values differ from those of their parents, and they are more empowered than their parents to bring change to the Middle East. Rather than turn its back on them, the United States should seek to expand their ranks by encouraging more such value change and greater personal empowerment and by helping to make them more effective political actors.

In every corner of the Arab world, one can find democracy activists who are desperately looking for ways to push their country into the twenty-first century. They are trying to harness the power of crowds, new communication technologies, and the support of the international community to move their country toward democracy. Like Nelson Mandela, Lech Walesa, and Vaclav Havel before them, they are risking their lives to pursue a new vision for their country, one grounded in democratic principles. They organized the protests in Tahrir Square in Egypt as well as those in Avenue Habib Bourguiba in Tunisia, Benghazi's Court Square in Libya, Change Square in Yemen, and elsewhere. They merit U.S. support. At times they have been overshadowed by those who practice violence, who exploit sectarian differences for political gain, who dream of theocracy, or who hope to return the generals to power. But they remain unbroken and unshaken in their commitment to peaceful, democratic change. The United States should help them broaden their base of support, strengthen their links to the rest of society, and learn to engage more effectively in the political process. Ultimately, they can help generate the public demand from below that ensures that democracy prevails and nascent democratic institutions function as intended.

As chapter 2 discusses in detail, the changes sweeping the Arab world are only one manifestation of broader forces that are altering the nature of politics around the globe. Rising living standards, more education, enhanced mobility, and the freer flow of information are changing the expectations of citizens everywhere about the proper relationship between the citizen and the state. As Zbigniew Brzezinski has observed, there is a "global political awakening" under way that is centered on issues of human dignity.[12] Democracy, once a political system practiced exclusively in a handful of Western (or Western-colonized) states, has become universally desired, to the point that a majority of citizens in almost every country in the world express a preference for it.[13]

But desiring democracy and realizing it are different things. While democracy as a norm has spread across the world relatively quickly, citizens are learning only more gradually how to put it into practice. They are discovering that achieving democracy requires more than just deposing a dictator, holding elections, and writing an effective constitution. Particularly at a time when new democratic institutions are just being formed, it requires citizens to be actively engaged in the political process, ensuring that the constitutional rules of the game remain inviolate. The key test of a democracy's durability is how citizens respond in those "constitutional moments" when the very foundations of democracy are under challenge. When a political leader suspends parliament or gets caught flagrantly taking a bribe in return for political favors—when the democratic rules of the game are being flaunted—do citizens take action to defend the rules or passively condone the transgression? In such moments, the fate of a democracy hangs in the balance and only its citizens can ensure that it endures.

If history counts for anything, in time a number of countries within the Arab world, though not all, will succeed in making the transition to democracy. So far, Tunisia, Egypt, Libya, and Yemen have embarked on that transition, albeit with substantial setbacks along the way. Others, like Jordan and Morocco, could yet do so, as could Syria and Iraq should they overcome the current polarization along sectarian lines.

How quickly and successfully any transition occurs depends in part on the regional security context in which domestic developments take place. Will the United States exercise leadership in stabilizing the Middle East, or will it leave the field to Iran and Saudi Arabia—the two major regional powers, besides Israel—to continue their proxy wars across the region? Will the sectarian polarization and political violence ignited by the Syrian civil war continue or be contained? Will the alarming military advances by al Qaeda offshoots throughout the region increase or be rolled back? Regardless, all of these countries will need time to develop the constitutional rules, the electoral processes, the democratic institutions, and, above all, the level of civic engagement that lead to consolidated and, it is hoped, liberal democracies. Over the long term, the prospects for success look brighter for a country like Tunisia, which has a relatively homogenous population, a shared sense of nation, a relatively educated population, a history of openness to the rest of the world, and a connected citizenry, than, say, Yemen, which has few of those traits. But only time will tell—the history of democratization is full of surprises.

The Purpose and Structure of This Book

This book is written for the Arab democratic activists struggling to bring democracy to their own country and for those in the West who support them. In the hope of enriching the collective understanding of the events of the Arab Spring, it tells the story of democratization in other regions of the world during the so-called Third Wave. It does so in the conviction that we can learn from the experiences of other nations that have attempted to transform their political system into a democracy. Their culture, history, and socioeconomic conditions may differ, but broad common patterns can be discerned that help make the unfamiliar familiar. Many of the issues that Arab democrats are now grappling with are broadly similar to those that their counterparts in other regions of the world once faced: how to create effective transitional governments, how to overcome the polarization of society that undermines democracy, how to deal with nondemocratic actors, what the proper place of the military is in new democracies, and how to move from protest to politics. From the struggles of citizens to advance the cause of democracy in other countries, powerful lessons can be gleaned to assist those in the Arab world struggling to achieve the same end.

The book focuses in particular on the role that citizens play in consolidating democracy. The role of civil society in a democracy has often been celebrated, but how it plays a part in developing and strengthening democracy has not been well understood. As mentioned, the book makes the case that it is often pressure placed on government leaders by citizens and civic groups that ensures that nascent democratic institutions function as intended. If people are to be truly sovereign, they need to demonstrate to political leaders that it is they, the people, who wield ultimate power. Their chief weapon against the coercive apparatus of the modern state is their sheer numbers; when broad sections of a society rise up against the state, even the most authoritarian government must take heed. As was the case in the Third Wave countries, an extended tug-of-war between state and society is now under way in the Arab world over where power resides. It will take sustained effort on the part of the population to wrest control of the "deep states" that their authoritarian leaders have forged over the course of the last half-century.[14] It is the citizens of the Arab world and their newly found collective power that offer the greatest hope for the future of democracy in the region.

This book's argument harks backs to a very old one. The careful separation of powers—a division of executive, legislative, and judicial powers among competing bodies that creates "an invitation to struggle"—is often regarded as the genius of the American political system.[15] But its founders understood equally well that liberty's ultimate defense was an enlightened and engaged citizenry. James Madison, the visionary architect of the U.S. Constitution, wrote: "The advancement and diffusion of knowledge . . . is the only guardian of true liberty."[16] He noted further that "to suppose that any form of government will secure liberty or happiness without any virtue in the people, is a chimerical idea."[17] Similarly, Thomas Jefferson wrote confidently to a friend in 1789 about the decision to revise the Articles of Confederation and move toward a federal government: "Wherever the people are well informed they can be trusted with their own government; that whenever things get so far wrong as to attract their notice, they may be relied upon to set them to rights."[18]

It was people power that set off the dramatic revolutions that upended the old order in the Middle East, and people power will be required to ensure that the dreams of those revolutions are eventually realized. The story of democracy's advance across the globe is one of profound attitudinal changes and fierce political struggles for power. This book looks at that story, region by region, to see what it may have to say about the Arab Spring.

Chapter 2 provides an overview of the attitudinal changes that helped produce the Third Wave of democratization and that are now influencing political events in the Arab Middle East. The four chapters that follow chapter 2 tell the story of democratization efforts in other regions of the world. Chapter 3 focuses on the Eastern bloc—Eastern Europe and the former Soviet Union—because in many respects Eastern Europe's popular revolutions resemble the bottom-up political uprisings now convulsing the Arab world. Chapter 4 focuses on Muslim-majority countries in Asia, which bear some cultural and religious similarities to the Arab world and have much light to shed on the often debated issue of the relationship between Islam (and, more aptly, *political* Islam) and democracy. Chapter 5 looks at the democratization experience of Latin America, where often societal polarization has been high and militaries have played an important role in governance. Chapter 6 looks at that of Sub-Saharan

Africa, where, although politics has long been dominated by political strongmen, positive changes are afoot in a number of countries. These chapters examine how the Third Wave of democratization played out in each region and the consequences that it ultimately had for the region's politics. Each includes four country case studies—two of countries that were relatively successful and two that were less so—in order to ground the discussion in the concrete experiences of particular countries. Chapter 7 summarizes the key lessons that emerge from the democratization experiences of countries elsewhere for the countries of the Arab Spring. Chapter 8 looks at the key strategic challenges faced by democratic activists in most, if not all, transitions and tries to provide guidance, based on experiences in other regions, on how activists might address them. Chapter 9 concludes the book with a set of detailed policy recommendations on how the United States might best assist democratic activists struggling to bring democracy to the Arab Middle East.

CHAPTER TWO

DEMOCRACY'S
LONG ARC

Democracy, though conceived by the ancient Greeks, is largely a modern phenomenon. From the time that human beings began to gather together in large settlements—to erect towns and cities populated by more than a single clan or tribe—political power tended to be concentrated in a single individual. History is replete with kings and queens, emperors and empresses, caliphs, kaisers, khans, maharajas, emirs, sultans, shahs, and tzars. Whether they claimed legitimacy on the basis of divine right, hereditary succession, or brute force, power lay in their hands. Hierarchical arrangements may have allowed them to delegate some of their earthly authority to subordinates—princes, dukes, barons, or sheikhs—but the sovereign retained ultimate decisionmaking power. There were, of course, notable exceptions across history, instances of aristocratic or democratic rather than monarchical rule: the ancient Greek city-states, the Roman Republic, the northern Italian city-states, the trading states of the Hanseatic League, and the Swiss Confederation, among others. Those political entities tended to be small enough in geographic terms that citizens and their political leaders knew one another and often were relatively short-lived.

Popular notions about politics began to change, albeit slowly, with the dawn of the Enlightenment. In the cafés of Paris and the coffeehouses of Scotland, the doctrine of the divine right of kings began to be challenged by new ideas, based on human reason, about the rights of man. The revolutionary ideas of Locke, Montesquieu, Rousseau, Hume, and Kant have over time transformed the world. They informed the American and French revolutions, and they have influenced other popular movements since then.

There were three significant waves of democratization in more recent times. The first ran from the 1820s, when the United States extended the political franchise to all free white men, to the rise of fascism in Europe a hundred years later. The second began with European decolonization following World War II and lasted through 1962. The "Third Wave" of democratization started in 1974 on the Iberian Peninsula with the transitions to democracy in Portugal and Spain, followed by the transition in Greece in 1975.[1] The wave then expanded to Latin America and parts of East Asia. The fall of the Berlin Wall in 1989 precipitated a series of popular revolutions in Eastern Europe, which resulted in the fall of communism and the eventual disintegration of the Soviet Union. Democratic fervor spread thereafter to Sub-Saharan Africa, hastened by the end of the cold war and the collapse of apartheid in South Africa. The popular uprisings in the Arab world may herald a fourth wave.[2]

Before the Third Wave began in the mid-1970s, only about 40 countries were considered to be democratic—mostly countries in Western Europe and North America and a handful of states that those countries had formerly colonized or occupied.[3] When Freedom House conducted its first annual survey of freedom around the world in 1972, it categorized 44 of 155 countries, or a little more than a quarter, as "free" and 69 of 155, or just shy of a half, as "not free." Democracy was long considered to be the product of cultural values unique largely to the West or to the attainment of a certain level of per capita income.[4] By the time the Third Wave crested in 1999, however, 120 countries—from cultures all around the globe, at all levels of wealth—could be said to be electoral democracies. The same year, Freedom House categorized 85 of the 192 countries that it surveyed, or nearly half, as "free," but only 47 of 192, or a quarter, as "not free"—a striking shift over the course of less than 30 years.[5] Of the 36 countries with the lowest human development scores in the world, 13, or just over a third, were considered either to be democratic or to have embarked on a transition to democracy.[6] Moreover, with the fall of communism, totalitarianism was swept largely into the dustbin of history. Today North Korea and possibly Cuba are the only remaining totalitarian states, whereas just over 20 years ago such states covered nearly half the globe. There are no empires. With the notable exceptions of tiny Brunei and Swaziland, there are no ruling monarchies left outside the Arab Middle East.[7]

Changing Attitudes toward Authority

Underlying the remarkable political changes over the last 30 years have been dramatic attitudinal changes among the world's people. In the span of just a few decades in some parts of the world, citizens' views toward political authority have altered significantly, hastened, no doubt, by rising living standards; advances in technology; acceleration of contacts across borders, societies, and civilizations; and rising levels of literacy and educational attainment.

These changes in political and social attitudes have been documented most thoroughly in the World Values Survey, conducted by Ronald Inglehart at the University of Michigan and colleagues. The survey—which has been undertaken since 1981 in a multitude of countries (now ninety-seven) in every region of the world—charts the profound shift in many societies from what it terms "traditional" values to "secular-rational" values and from "survival" values to "self-expression" values. Like other modernization theorists before them, Inglehart and his colleague Christian Welzel contend that the switch from agrarian societies that "emphasize religion, national pride, obedience, and respect for authority" toward more urban, industrial settings prompts a realignment of values that favors greater "secularism, cosmopolitanism, autonomy, and rationality."[8] Likewise, the advent of post-industrial societies, with their high levels of wealth and extensive social welfare systems, has created a sense of "existential security" that has led to a shift in emphasis from survival values like "order, economic security, and conformity" toward self-expression values like "participation, subjective well-being, trust, tolerance, and quality of life concerns."[9]

Several things are especially striking about the survey results. First, attitudes toward authority have tended to cluster along civilizational lines: citizens' responses to the survey can be differentiated consistently across time by the cultural region in which they live. Differences across countries—for example, between Switzerland and Saudi Arabia—are much more pronounced than those within countries—for example, between a Swiss aristocrat and a Swiss pauper. National culture, while changing in important ways, remains the primary definer of difference. As figure 2-1 shows, countries can be grouped roughly by region according to where they fall on the traditional-secular spectrum of values and the survival–self-expression spectrum.

Second, Inglehart and Welzel find a strong correlation between self-expression values and various measures of the strength of civil society, the extent of civil rights and political liberties, the quality of democracy, and the effectiveness, transparency, and accountability of government.[10] The prevalence of self-expression values appears to be a strong predictor of a

Figure 2-1. *The World Values Survey Cultural Map, 2005–08*

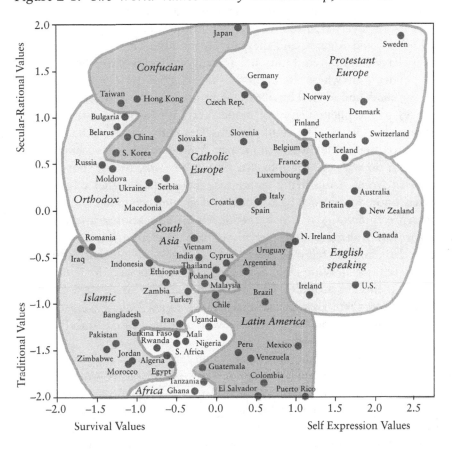

Source: Ronald Inglehart and Christian Welzel, "Changing Mass Priorities: The Link between Modernization and Democracy," *Perspectives on Politics*, vol. 8, no. 2 (June 2010), p. 554. Reproduced with permission.

robust civil society, active citizen participation, and effective democracy. In the view of the authors, "Modernization favors democracy because it enhances ordinary people's abilities and motivations to demand democracy, exerting increasingly effective pressures on elites."[11]

Third, in just a few short decades, the attitudes of citizens in many non-Western regions of the world—Eastern Europe and East Asia—have converged markedly toward those in Western Europe and the United States along both spectrums. Fourth, attitudes in the Arab Middle East and the broader Muslim world have, at least until recently, changed the least. The World Values Survey data are thinnest in this region of the world—the only Arab countries polled in the survey are Jordan, Egypt, Morocco, and Algeria, and they are recent additions—but respondents there have emphasized traditional and survival values more heavily than respondents anywhere else in the world.

Inglehart and Welzel attribute the attitudinal changes found in their survey to the phenomenon of modernization—in particular, to higher standards of living. The authors themselves note, however, that it is difficult to disentangle the causal factors. Attitudinal changes seem to have more to do with factors that are *associated with,* though not entirely derived from, rising living standards: factors like higher educational levels, more knowledge-based jobs, and greater economic security. For instance, individuals with higher levels of educational attainment—regardless of income level—are more likely to exhibit tolerance toward and trust in their fellow citizens.[12] In the view of Inglehart and Welzel, economic development *can* bring certain socioeconomic changes, which then alter attitudes. But it does not *always* bring such changes. The authors themselves concede that if per capita income were the only determinant of democracy, "then Kuwait and the United Arab Emirates would be model democracies."[13]

They also do not consider the possibility that other exogenous factors could produce the same socioeconomic changes, irrespective of changes in per capita income. Globalization, for instance, can also provide greater access to information and education, greater mobility, more knowledge-based employment, and greater exposure to the outside world—all of which should spur the same kind of attitudinal changes. Cell phone and Internet usage, for example, has spiked dramatically throughout the developing world in recent years. Cell phone penetration is now greater in Libya (173 lines per 100 residents) than in the United Kingdom (132 per 100); in Egypt, it is on a par with that in the United States (85 and 90 lines per 100 residents, respectively).[14] Internet penetration levels are far lower than in the advanced industrial world, but growing exponentially (Tunisia had 39 percent penetration in 2011 as opposed to 10 percent in 2006; Egypt had 36 percent penetration in 2011 as opposed to 11 percent in 2006).[15] The youthful crowds that filled the squares of the Arab world in early 2011 suggested the profound impact that such technologies can have on political values. When individuals suddenly are able to compare their lot with that of people in other countries, it can dramatically alter how they see the world.

Increased Support for Democracy

The profound shift in attitudes regarding the individual and his or her relation to political authority documented by the World Values Survey appears to coincide with increased public support around the world for democracy. The available data suggest that worldwide public support for democracy continues to be robust, even as dissatisfaction with the actual performance of many democracies, emerging and established, continues to grow.[16] In public opinion surveys, the majority of citizens in almost every country polled expressed a preference for democracy over other forms of government.[17]

The Arab world is no exception. When asked in a recent Arab Barometer survey whether "democracy, whatever its limitations, is better than any other political system," large majorities of respondents in all eleven Arab countries polled (including Egypt, Tunisia, and Yemen) either agreed or agreed strongly.[18] The degree of support, which ranged from 72 percent in Saudi Arabia to 90 percent in Tunisia, was comparable to or greater than that in other world regions (perhaps because of democracy's absence in the Arab world) and corresponded with the findings of numerous other surveys of Arab opinion conducted since 2000.[19] At the same time, depending on the country polled, anywhere from around a quarter to more than half of respondents disagreed or strongly disagreed with the statement "Men of religion should have no influence over the decisions of government." Yet this and other surveys of Arab public opinion seem to show that neither personal religiosity nor a preference for some form of *Islamic* democracy diminishes in any significant way support for democratic norms and values.[20] When asked in another survey to identify "two countries where you think there is the most freedom and democracy for their own people," Arab respondents overwhelmingly listed the main Western democracies.[21]

As an idea, democracy remains in ascendance and has acquired the status of a near-universal norm. That represents a dramatic shift from the twentieth century when other political models— socialism, authoritarianism, and even totalitarianism—held broad political appeal in various corners of the globe. China's single-party model of economic development may appeal to some—just as the idea of a return to an Islamic caliphate has captured the imagination of a very small, extreme minority of Muslims—but it is democracy that majorities in countries around the world now view as the only legitimate way to order society.

That does not mean that democracy faces no challenges. The Great Recession has taken its toll on democracy's reputation around the world.

As in the past, tough economic times have made governing more difficult for political leaders in both emerging and established democracies. The economic recession has been accompanied by a mild political recession: for the last seven years, Freedom House has recorded slightly more declines than advances in its annual survey of freedom in countries around the globe. The number of countries classified as "free" grew slightly, from 85 of 192 countries in 1999 to 90 of 193 in 2006, and it has remained around that level ever since; the number of countries classified as "not free" has hovered around 47 since 1999.[22] Part of the slowdown in democracy's spread appears to be due to the harsher economic environment, but part might also be attributable to the greater savvy of the world's remaining dictators, who have developed ever more cunning strategies for parrying democratic challenges to their rule.[23] It also bears mentioning that democracy's image in much of the world has been tarnished by the post–9/11 crackdown on civil liberties in the United States, the association of U.S. democracy promotion efforts with the controversial U.S. invasion of Iraq, and the recent political gridlock in the United States and other advanced democracies. However, the Egyptian youth who flooded Tahrir Square demonstrated that democracy is an idea that still resonates deeply and widely around the globe.

From Attitudinal Change to Revolt

What has the evolution in political attitudes meant for politics and the spread of democracy? There is often a lag between a population's broad embrace of democratic concepts and meaningful political change. Debates about democracy may be in the air for a long time within an authoritarian state before any kind of collective action to reform or change the system occurs. The reasons are many: lack of historical precedents; the difficulties inherent in collective action; the power of the modern state and its ability to appease, divide, or pacify dissenters; and, above all, fear felt by ordinary citizens. Modern states have developed elaborate national security apparatuses that often are employed to spy on and even eliminate regime opponents. In recent decades, the Arab world witnessed many regimes "upgrading" their particular brand of authoritarianism by ostensibly granting citizens greater freedoms while at the same time expanding the reach of their intelligence services and the lethality of their domestic security forces.[24] A common refrain of citizens during the Arab Spring was that finally the barrier of fear that had long prevented them from standing up to their governments had been shattered.

Scholars continue to debate the question of why citizens eventually revolt. One precipitating factor seems to be a deeply felt sense of injustice; in that case, grievances may be based on the perception that the dominant group within society has violated the implicit or explicit norms that hold society together.[25] One group, it is believed, has taken more than its fair share. Other triggers may include revelations of pervasive corruption or human rights abuses, gross mismanagement of the economy, the inability to deliver the most basic services, or any number of other failings. During the Third Wave, the spark in Latin America was severe mishandling of the national economy and human rights abuses by military governments; in Eastern Europe, it was the mounting inefficiencies and injustices of communist governments; in Africa, it was the excesses and hold on office of the "big men" who dominated politics post-independence; in Asia, it was in several cases the Asian financial crisis; and in the Arab world, it was the endemic corruption of long-standing autocratic regimes and their inability to deliver even the most basic of services.[26]

When citizens finally revolt, their sheer numbers are sometimes sufficient to topple repressive regimes. The modern state, with its extensive intelligence services, sophisticated police, and high tech weaponry, is well equipped to suppress or weather the protests of disgruntled citizens. However, when broad segments of the population, representing diverse socioeconomic groups and regions, take to the streets and question the legitimacy of the regime, they can pose a far more daunting challenge to its stability. Such protests may create fissures within the ruling elite, strengthening the hand of soft-liners advocating reform, or they may overthrow a regime outright. In this way, transitions to democracy are generally ushered in.

Democratic breakthroughs, when they finally occur, often have ripple effects far beyond their borders. During the Third Wave, those breakthroughs tended to take place in geographic clusters: Latin America, Eastern Europe, Africa, and parts of Asia. Both a demonstration and a diffusion effect appeared to contribute to the spread of democratic fervor from one country in a region to others. When one country experienced a democratic breakthrough, many of its neighbors tended to follow suit, eventually. Language and culture seemed to play a role. When one country overthrew a dictator, citizens in other countries who spoke a common language—or who had at least linguistic and cultural commonalities—were more likely to hear about it, consider the example provided by their neighbor to be relevant to their own condition, and feel empowered to take action because of it. Improvements in communication technologies appear to have only accelerated those effects.

Political Change in the Arab World

In the Arab Middle East, political change began much as it did in the closed societies of the former Eastern bloc. The Arab popular revolts of 2011 did not start with someone putting up a Facebook page any more than the popular revolutions that convulsed the Eastern bloc two decades earlier began with televised images of the fall of the Berlin Wall. Both had historical antecedents. In both cases, the regime had visibly failed to rule justly and adequately address the needs of its citizens over time. In both, technological change gradually eroded the regime's monopoly on the flow of information and hence its control of the national narrative. Those changes enabled citizens to see for themselves, more vividly than ever before, how their society compared with that of others. At the same time, a new generation came of age that was better educated, more exposed to the outside world, and more tightly networked than its parents' generation—and it had higher expectations. Through trial and error, citizens began to learn how to challenge the regime collectively and finally make their voices heard. Once citizens in one country in the region discovered how to use people power to take on the regime, those in other countries quickly began to try the same tactics on their own government. And, in both regions, events began to "snowball."[27]

However, democratic breakthroughs, when they did occur, did not lead immediately and ineluctably toward the creation of vibrant democratic political systems. There are some similarities between the conditions that facilitate successful popular revolt and those required for successful democratization, but they are far from identical. Revolt is generally spontaneous, reactionary, and short-lived, and its success hinges on the mobilization of broad segments of the population against the regime. Democratization, on the other hand, requires a positive political vision, not of what was but of what could be. It takes much longer to evolve, and it includes not only free and fair elections but also the creation of democratic political institutions and an accompanying democratic political culture. It requires clear political ideas about how society could be better ordered and the organizational power to see them realized. And it entails a much longer-term engagement of citizens, not only to help enshrine those ideas in a concrete set of political institutions but also to ensure that the institutions function as intended—that they indeed reflect the will of the people and safeguard their individual rights as citizens. To that struggle I now turn.

CHAPTER THREE

THE FORMER
EASTERN BLOC

Comparisons are often drawn, with some merit, between the Arab Spring and the collapse of communism in the Eastern bloc. The revolts that convulsed Eastern Europe and parts of the former Soviet Union in 1989 and 1991, respectively, and those that shook the Arab world in 2011 were similar in nature. All were largely spontaneous, largely nonviolent popular uprisings that helped topple some, but not all, of the repressive regimes in their respective regions. These bottom-up, citizen-driven revolts transformed politics in both the former Eastern bloc and the Arab world forever.

The two regions were also similar in the nature of the regimes that existed prior to the popular uprisings. Like those in the Eastern bloc, the societies and economies of the Arab world were stagnant, relatively closed, and state dominated. While there was a great deal of variation across each region in terms of the character of the regimes—some more liberal, others more highly bureaucratic, others more personalistic, and still others more rigid and repressive—all were highly centralized, hierarchical, top-heavy states that over time had become brittle and unresponsive to the needs of their citizens. In both regions, regimes had long ago lost any dynamism, sense of shared purpose, popular appeal, or political legitimacy. In most cases, they were economically stagnant and politically bankrupt.

On balance, the totalitarianism of Eastern European communism may have intruded in the lives of ordinary citizens more than the authoritarianism of the Arab world, but if so, it was only a matter of degree. Arab autocrats developed their own security police and extensive network of spies and informants in order to maintain tight control over society, although none came close to matching the former secret police, the *Stasi*, in East Germany, where it has been estimated that as many as one citizen in ten was an informant.[1] The argument could be made that Qaddafi's eccentricities were as harmful to the citizens of Libya as Ceausescu's were to Romanians and that the social restrictions and degree of ideological indoctrination in place in Saudi Arabia were similar to those in the Soviet Union (though perhaps not as extensive as under Stalin's rule). In both regions, the state's role in society was pervasive and generally pernicious.

Nonetheless, there are also significant and profound differences between the two regions, and any analogies must be drawn with care. Many Eastern European countries, for instance, had a past democratic tradition that they could look back to for inspiration and guidance in crafting new institutions. The states of the Eastern bloc were also part of the last empire in the world. The Eastern European satellite states—with the possible exceptions of Yugoslavia, Romania, and Albania—and the constituent republics of the former Soviet Union were not fully sovereign, independent states; they were political dependencies that had been installed by the center, the Politburo in Moscow, and they relied on its political, economic, and military support for their very existence. When it became clear that Mikhail Gorbachev would not intervene to prop up these regimes in the face of domestic popular unrest, the whole communist edifice of power collapsed quickly, rather like a house of cards.

By contrast, the Arab regimes, particularly since the Soviet Union's collapse, have not had a common external patron propping them all up. They are sovereign and independent states that generally have had to rely on their own resources for survival. Rather than being constituent parts of an empire, they are for the most part remnants of an empire's collapse—successor states of the former Ottoman Empire and products of the British or French colonial rule that followed. They have had to grapple with many of the complicated legacies of empire—poorly drawn borders, ethnic and religious diversity, post-colonial mindset, and so on—but their struggles have been largely their own. Hence, the revolutions in Tunisia and Egypt did not result in the collective collapse of all Arab regimes. Instead, the winds of change generated by the Arab Spring buffeted each differently, depending on its particular history, ethnic mix, and political structure—and, above all, the resources and determination of its ruler.

In many cases, Arab leaders have had substantial internal resources at their disposal. Many Arab rulers have become astoundingly wealthy because of the discovery of significant oil and natural gas reserves within their country's borders. They have not needed to tax their citizens in order to function; instead, they have had the luxury of being able to dole out money to key constituencies to maintain their grip on power. The United States also has been an important source of external support to many Arab states. Over the years, it provided significant military and financial assistance to some of the less wealthy Arab autocracies (Egypt, Jordan, Morocco) while offering arms sales and security guarantees to their wealthier counterparts (Saudi Arabia, United Arab Emirates, Kuwait). U.S. assistance, however, has never come close to the scale of the political, economic, and military support that Moscow provided to its dependent satellites.

Many Eastern European states also have benefited since the end of the cold war from their close proximity to Western Europe in terms of trade and investment links and their prospects for eventual membership in Western institutions like the European Union and NATO. The potential for political, economic, and security integration with the West provided a strong incentive for some Eastern European countries to implement far-reaching reforms. The Arab world does not have any such regional institutions that might attract them toward and help anchor them in a new political, economic, and security order.

The Antecedents of Change

In both the Eastern bloc and the Arab world, when change came, it came suddenly, convulsing the region. Change occurred because ordinary citizens in both regions had grown disenchanted with their leaders and took to the streets in protest; they, not the elites, were the primary driver of change. It was public demand, manifested by demonstrations of people power in the streets, rather than bargaining among elites (as in Portugal and Spain) that was pushing regimes to democratize.[2]

In both, the success of demonstrators in one country emboldened those in others. Suddenly, the veneer of invulnerability and unshakeable stability that regimes had long maintained cracked in the face of popular uprisings. Citizens discovered that the collective fear that had long gripped society and kept citizens quiescent had dissipated, and in its place was a new sense of empowerment and possibility. Rulers fought back, often resorting to brutal force in a bid to retain their grip on power. As they did, they often forfeited any remaining legitimacy that they had among their people.

However, media reports notwithstanding, the popular revolutions in both the Eastern bloc and the Arab world developed over a long period of time. As cataclysmic as these revolutions were when they finally erupted, they had historical antecedents. The story of political reform in the Eastern bloc did not begin with the dramatic scenes, televised around the world, of Germans tearing down the Berlin Wall any more than the story in the Arab world began with spontaneous street demonstrations in Tunisia and Egypt. In both regions, dissent had been building for a long time.

The first serious challenges to Soviet control in Eastern Europe emerged in the 1950s. Large worker strikes occurred in Poland and East Germany in 1954, and the latter were quelled only after the Red Army intervened militarily. Two years later, Hungary was convulsed by a full-scale popular revolt when hundreds of thousands took to the streets to push for reform. When the reform-minded government of socialist leader Imre Nagy dared to go so far as to propose removing Hungary from the Warsaw Pact, Khruschev ordered troops to crush the revolt and installed a new government more compliant with Moscow's wishes.

Twelve years later, the Soviets were forced to intervene again to suppress a similar reform movement in Czechoslovakia. The Prague Spring began in January 1968 when reform-minded Alexander Dubcek took the position of first secretary of the Czechoslovak Communist Party. Dubcek permitted implementation of sweeping political and economic reforms to address the shortcomings of a centrally planned economy that was visibly stagnating and a one-party state that had come to be seen as stifling the human spirit. Czechoslovak citizens responded enthusiastically to Dubcek's liberalizing reforms and the promise of "socialism with a human face." Through the spring and summer of 1968, free speech flourished, a number of new independent newspapers and periodicals were founded, and a rich cultural renaissance occurred. That proved threatening to the Soviets, who worried that the infectious spirit of freedom might spread to the other satellites. After a series of tense negotiations between Dubcek and Moscow, a Soviet-led invasion took place on August 21, 1968. Dubcek was deposed and the hard-liner Gustav Husak installed in his place. Dissent was not confined to the Eastern European satellite states. Within the Soviet Union itself, a small circle of intelligentsia—writers, scientists, musicians, and former political prisoners—spoke out against the human rights abuses perpetrated by the communist regime. Their critiques became all the more pointed after Stalin's death, when Kruschev permitted greater dissent.

Despite the authorities' efforts, they were never able to quash dissent entirely. Small groups of intellectuals refused to bend in the face of Soviet military intervention in satellite countries and brutal internal crackdowns at home. Brave individuals—like Adam Michnik, Jan Patocka, Vaclav Havel, and Bronislaw Geremek in Eastern Europe and Aleksandr Solzhenitsyn, Andrei Sakharov, Yelena Bonner, and Natan Sharansky in the Soviet Union—kept the flame of dissent alive. Although they represented a broad range of political viewpoints—from reformed communists to socialists, classical liberals, progressives, Christian Democrats, and hard-core nationalists—they were united by their fierce opposition to the existing communist regime. Through their writings and other creative works, they continued to challenge communist regimes throughout the region. They dared, as Vaclav Havel famously observed, to "speak truth to power."[3] Drawing inspiration in part from the counterculture that had emerged in the West in the 1960s, they sought to establish an alternative lifestyle of their own, beyond the reach of the state—to live, in Adam Michnik's words, "as if we were free."[4]

As the centrally planned economies of the Eastern bloc began to sputter in the 1960s and 1970s and the human rights abuses committed there became more broadly known, public opposition began to grow. The calls for reform became more widespread and incessant. Dissent was most pronounced in the parts of Eastern Europe that abutted the West—Poland, East Germany, Czechoslovakia, and Hungary—where proximity afforded citizens the opportunity to compare their living standards and freedoms with those on the other side of the Iron Curtain. Nowhere was the problem more acute for the Soviets than in Berlin, where in earlier years East Germans had been able to wander at will into the neighborhoods and shops of West Berlin as well as escape to the West—an anomaly that the Soviets sought to address in 1961 by constructing the Berlin Wall. Even after construction of the wall, East Germans could still catch glimpses of what was happening on the other side of the wall and follow West German radio and television.

An even more debilitating long-term problem for the Soviets was the proliferation of modern mass communication technologies. The use of radios, televisions, tape recorders, mimeographs, Xerox machines, videocassette recorders, and the like threatened to undermine the regime's monopoly on information—its ability to control the narrative. In the 1950s the United States began beaming—along with its existing Voice of America broadcasts—Radio Free Europe news programs to Eastern

Europe and similar Radio Liberty programs to the USSR, mostly via short-wave. The British Broadcasting Corporation and Germany's Deutsche Welle did the same. Later, dissidents were to create underground publishing houses by using mimeograph or Xerox machines, often smuggled in by sympathetic Western organizations, to replicate banned materials. So-called *samizdat* literature—self-published copies of a writer's work—was surreptitiously passed from person to person like contraband. The danger that all of these technological innovations posed to communist regimes was that they enabled citizens to compare their situation with that in other countries. Again, the problem was most acute in East Germany, where West German television could be easily accessed and, of course, understood by local audiences.

As was often the case later in the Arab world, many Eastern bloc dissident groups were widely discounted at the time as irrelevant, as lone wolves or eccentrics disconnected from the broader societies in which they lived. But they kept alive the flame of dissident during very dark periods in their country's history. And, with time, they helped to educate their fellow citizens by example, through their critique of the status quo and the sacrifices that they were willing to make in the name of freedom. Gradually, almost imperceptibly, public opinion began to shift.

Eastern Europe Stirs

Leadership changes in Moscow and the West were to hasten the pace of change. The Social Democrats came to power for the first time in the Federal Republic of Germany in 1969, with Willy Brandt as chancellor. Brandt's "Ostpolitik"—his pursuit of normalized relations with the East—led to renewed cultural and economic links across the Iron Curtain in the 1970s. The resulting expansion of contacts and relaxation of tensions between East and West Europeans heightened awareness among East Europeans of the gap emerging between capitalist and socialist societies.

At the same time, both Richard Nixon and Leonid Brezhnev saw advantages to reducing the level of hostilities between the two superpowers. Détente produced a series of high-profile summits and arms control agreements. The convening of the Conference on Security and Cooperation in Europe led eventually to the signing of the Helskini Accords in 1975, which provided dissident movements in the Eastern bloc with an unexpected yet critical boost. In essence, the Helsinki Final Act traded U.S. recognition of Europe's existing borders and agreement that they could be changed only by peaceful means (what came to be known as

Basket 1) for Soviet agreement to respect certain basic social and political rights (Basket 3). (Basket 2 included economic and science and technology cooperation.) The Soviets signed the accords because they believed that they could pocket the U.S. concessions on security—which they highly valued—while ignoring the part on social and political rights, which they believed to be meaningless because the accords lacked any mechanism for enforcement. However, dissidents in the East and governments and advocacy groups in the West quickly seized on the social and political rights clauses as a now internationally accepted set of moral standards that they could hold the Soviets accountable for ensuring. Helsinki Watch citizen groups sprang up to monitor compliance with the agreement and to criticize human rights practices in the Eastern bloc. In 1977 in Czechoslovakia, 242 intellectuals signed Charter 77, a document that called on their government to live up to the human rights commitments enshrined in the country's constitution and the various international agreements to which it was a party, most notably the Helsinki Accords. The Charter 77 movement was to become an umbrella under which Czech and Slovak opponents of the communist regime would loosely unite.

At just about the same time that the Charter 77 movement was organized in Czechoslovakia, the Workers' Defense Committee (KOR) was being established in Poland. A precursor to Solidarity, KOR was created by a group of Polish intellectuals to give aid to workers who had been jailed by the regime for participating in labor protests. KOR's creation was a watershed in Polish opposition politics in that it united for the first time intellectuals and workers, two groups that had long been wary of one another. When intellectuals had joined students in protests against the regime in 1968, the working class had not supported them; then, during the worker strikes of 1970, it had been the intelligentsia who stood aside. In addition to supporting the families of jailed workers, KOR sought to stimulate the creation of "autonomous organizations" throughout Polish society. Its activities included establishing an underground publishing house and a "Flying University," which taught clandestine courses to university students about freedom and democracy.

In 1978, Poles were buoyed by Cardinal Karol Wojtyla's surprise appointment as Pope John Paul II. The following year he paid a return visit to his homeland, where his masses were attended by ecstatic throngs, further stirring Polish national feelings while reinforcing the independent power and moral force of the Catholic Church. The next year saw major worker protests, spurred by government-imposed price hikes; they began in Gdansk and centered in the towns and cities of Poland's Baltic coast, where residents had long had greater contact with the outside world. When the government tried to crack down on the protests, they soon spread throughout the nation, mobilizing millions of workers.[5] In late August, an agreement was hammered out in the shipyards of Gdansk between the government and striking workers that recognized the right of workers to form independent trade unions. Solidarity (Solidarnosc, in Polish) was created as an umbrella organization uniting independent trade unions to advance the rights of workers, with the union leader Lech Walesa as its head. Within a year, it had a membership of some 9.5 million people, representing one in every three Polish workers.

Solidarity's growing strength and activism made the communist leadership and its allies in Moscow nervous. In October 1981, the moderate Stanislaw Kania was forced out as party leader and General Wojciech Jaruzelski was made prime minister. Under increasing pressure from Moscow, he declared martial law in December 1981 and had an estimated 40,000 to 50,000 Solidarity activists rounded up and jailed. Solidarity was forced underground, but the strikes and demonstrations continued, and Jaruzelski introduced wide-ranging economic reforms in an effort to buy social peace.[6] Despite the determined government clampdown, Solidarity's activities persisted, public resistance to martial law mounted, and independent organizations multiplied. Martial law was formally ended in 1983, but many of the restrictions on political freedoms continued, and state and society remained in an uneasy standoff.

Gorbachev and the Revolutions of 1989

In 1985, the Soviet Politburo named Mikhail Gorbachev as general secretary following the death of Konstantin Chernenko. Gorbachev was a lifelong communist and party apparatchik who had worked his way up from provincial party leader to become the youngest member of the Politburo before being tapped to lead the Soviet Union. Unlike his predecessors, he was convinced that the Soviet system was badly broken. In his view, the problems with the system were not merely economic and technical but existential and moral. He believed that if communism was to survive, it needed to be dramatically reformed in order to regain the support of citizens. The full extent of the far-reaching reforms that Gorbachev was contemplating was not immediately apparent, but by 1987 the twin policies that were to define his leadership—perestroika ("restructuring") and glasnost ("openness")—had taken form. What the new Soviet approach meant for Moscow's Eastern European satellites became evident only over time as Gorbachev, encouraging their leaders to implement significant political and economic reforms of their own, began to signal that Moscow would no longer be willing to intervene militarily to prop up unpopular regimes.

In Poland, the tense struggle between the Jaruzelski government and Solidarity continued into the latter half of the 1980s. Gradually it became clear to the general that the opposition movement had become too big to suppress by force. In 1988, he invited Solidarity to engage in roundtable talks. After two months of negotiation, it was agreed that elections would be held and Solidarity would be allowed to contest a limited number of seats in the Sejm, the lower house of the Polish parliament. In June 1988 elections, Solidarity dealt the government a surprising and resounding defeat. Solidarity won all 161 of the Sejm seats for which it was allowed to compete and 99 of 100 of the seats in the newly created Senate. In many other cases, voters simply crossed out the name of the lone communist candidate for the Sejm seats that Solidarity had agreed not to contest; as a result, Solidarity's support was required to get those candidates seated. In August, the communists bowed to the inevitable and invited Solidarity to form a government, with Jaruzelski remaining on as president.

Important changes also were under way in Hungary. Up to 100,000 demonstrators massed in the streets of Budapest on the March 1989 anniversary of the 1848 revolution, and the Communist Party there was soon engaged in roundtable talks of its own with opposition forces. By May the authorities began dismantling the Hungarian section of the Iron Curtain—the barbed wire fencing that separated Hungary from Austria and the West. July witnessed the reburial of Imre Nagy and four other heroes of 1956 at a ceremony attended by more than 100,000 Hungarians. By October, the Communist Party had changed the name of the country to the Republic of Hungary (from People's Republic of Hungary), agreed to allow the opposition to hold seats in parliament, and renamed itself the Hungarian Socialist Party.

In East Germany, Protestant church leaders, beginning in Leipzig, had been organizing protest marches every Monday evening all summer and into the fall. The largest was a protest in Leipzig on October 9, 1989, that drew a crowd of some 70,000 people, which grew to 120,000 the following week. On October 7, at a ceremony marking the anniversary of the founding of the German Democratic Republic, Gorbachev privately told the East German general secretary, Erich Honecker, that he could not count on Soviet troops to back him up. Meanwhile, East German refugees were streaming through Czechoslovakia to Hungary, taking advantage of the country's now open border to slip into the West. Refugees also occupied the West German embassy in Prague, seeking safe passage to the West. By October 18, with Moscow's encouragement, the more moderate Egon Krenz had replaced Honecker.

Another large demonstration took place in Berlin on November 4. By then, the protesters' cries of "We are the people" had been transformed into "We are the nation." East Germans were no longer clamoring for reform of the East German state but for reunification with West Germany.[7] On November 9, tens of thousands converged on the Berlin Wall after an erroneous report circulated that East Germans would be given unlimited access to the West. The East German border guards did not move to intervene and, as a worldwide television audience looked on, joyous citizens from East and West Berlin began to dismantle the wall that had long divided them.

Events in Czechoslovakia then moved quickly. On November 17, thousands of students took part in a long-planned march in Prague to mark the fiftieth anniversary of the murder of a Czech student by the Nazis. Such marches had been organized before, but this one turned violent as police tried to break it up with truncheons as the crowd neared the city center. Public outrage was ignited by scenes of police brutally beating students as well as by rumors (later proved untrue) that one of the students had been killed. A country that had appeared somnolent since the Soviet invasion of 1968 suddenly came to life. Massive demonstrations followed in Prague, where the air filled with the sound of hundreds of thousands of citizens jingling their keys overhead to symbolize their yearning for freedom.

The demonstrations quickly spread to other cities, including the Slovak capital of Bratislava. One rally followed another, with some 800,000 gathering in massive Letna Field, overlooking Prague, on November 25. The decisive event, though, proved to be a two-hour general strike on November 27, when an estimated three-quarters of all workers in Czechoslovakia walked off the job. The strike temporarily paralyzed the behemoth industrial factories that were the backbone of the country's economy. Intellectuals and workers, who as in Poland had long stood apart, had finally found common ground in opposing the regime.

Ten days after the start of the "Velvet Revolution," it was over. On November 28, the Communist Party agreed to relinquish power. By late December, Vaclav Havel, the quirky playwright who had dared to speak truth to power, was being sworn into office as the first president of a noncommunist Czechoslovakia. He presided over a broad caretaker government made up of intellectuals, communist moderates, and representatives of other major societal groups that was charged with revamping the country's constitution and preparing for multiparty elections in June.

The Aftermath of 1989

The dramatic changes that had swept over Poland, Hungary, East Germany, and Czechoslovakia in the span of just months were to have ripple effects throughout the rest of the Eastern bloc and the Soviet Union itself. But at least initially, only in the Baltic States did the ensuing changes turn out to be as peaceful and as hopeful as the changes in those four countries.

To the south, communist leaders sought to get ahead of events and co-opt any possible revolutionary fervor among their citizens. In late December 1989, the eccentric and megalomaniacal Romanian leader Nicolae Ceausescu, who had built his rule on a cult of personality, organized a mass rally of the faithful in downtown Bucharest to reinforce his grip on power. Just a few days earlier, the military and secret police had violently broken up a large demonstration in the city of Timisoara to protest the government's sacking of a dissident ethnic Hungarian pastor, and hundreds of people had been killed or wounded. Partway through Ceausescu's speech, several people began to shout "Ceausescu the Dictator!" while others chanted "Timisoara!" and the rest of the crowd soon joined in. A visibly shaken Ceausescu and his wife sought refuge in the Communist Party headquarters. About 100,000 demonstrators assembled in University Square, and mass protests and violence ensued throughout Bucharest. When Ceausescu sought to address the demonstrators again the following day, they stormed after him. He and his wife narrowly fled by helicopter, but they were subsequently hunted down by the military, summarily tried, and executed on Christmas Day.

A new political organization quickly emerged calling itself the National Salvation Front (NSF), composed largely of Communist Party apparatchiks. In the May 1990 elections, which were marred by fraud, the party won 70 percent of the vote and its leader, Ion Iliescu, a former Central Committee member, was proclaimed president. When, in response, further demonstrations broke out in Bucharest, the party is believed to have bused in truncheon-wielding miners from the Jiu Valley to quell them. Whether and to what extent Iliescu and his NSF colleagues engineered Ceausescu's removal from power and manipulated the country's transition toward democracy remains a subject of debate to this day.

Further south in Bulgaria, the end of the communist era was even more clearly stage managed by party apparatchiks. In November 1989, just as the Berlin Wall was coming down, the country's communist leadership arranged for the ouster of First Secretary Todor Zhivkov by forcing a vote in the Politburo. In January 1990, it changed the party's name to the Bulgarian Socialist Party and initiated roundtable talks with the Democratic opposition. The Socialists then narrowly won a majority of the vote in parliamentary elections that June.

The revolutionary ferment convulsing the region was to have far darker consequences further west, in Yugoslavia, where a number of ethnic and national groups lived closely intermingled. From its founding in the aftermath of World War II, Marshal Tito had ruled the Socialist Federal Republic of Yugoslav with a strong hand and had adroitly balanced the needs of the country's various constituent communities. He had sought to plaster over centuries of violent ethnic and religious tension among those communities (which had made "Balkan" not only a geographic label but also a synonym for disintegration and chaos) with a supranational Yugoslav (literally, "South Slav") identity that he hoped would replace the others. Through the force of his personality and with a good bit of coercion, Tito was relatively successful: internecine conflict ceased, a modicum of harmony prevailed, and intermarriage among the various ethnic and national groups became commonplace. But the system relied on Tito's strong hand and charismatic leadership to function. When he died in 1980, the whole Yugoslav project slowly began to unravel.

After his death, the leaders of the country's constituent republics began to jockey for power. In 1987, the Serbian youth leader Slobodan Milosevic paid a highly emotional and controversial visit to Kosovo Polje, the site of an epic fourteenth-century battle between Serbs and Albanians. Kosovo had once been the historic heartland of the Serb people but now was inhabited predominantly by Kosovar Albanians. Milosevic told the assembled crowd of ethnic Serbs to stand their ground, declaring that Kosovo would always be an integral part of Serbia and Yugoslavia. The speech solidified Milosevic's reputation among Serbs as a crusader for their rights within the federation. By May 1989, Milosevic had become president of the Republic of Serbia, within Yugoslavia.

The revolutions in Central Europe only hastened the slow disintegration of the Yugoslav federation set in motion by Tito's death. Milosevic is alleged to have orchestrated a series of street demonstrations that helped unseat several provincial leaders, who were then replaced by Milosevic's cronies. By January 1991, Milosevic had effectively dissolved the Yugoslav League of Communists, making him the most important political leader in Yugoslavia. Along with his allies, he was able to push through a series of constitutional changes that stripped Kosovo of the autonomy that it had acquired under Tito and made it once more a part of the Republic of Serbia. Kosovar Albanians took to the streets in protest. In July, the Kosovo Assembly declared Kosovo an independent republic, though still within Yugoslavia. The following month, Serbs living within the Republic of Croatia, encouraged by Milosevic, began to take up arms against their Croat neighbors. By the following year, Macedonia, Croatia, and Slovenia had all declared their independence and Yugoslav army troops, at Milosevic's direction, were battling against Croatia alongside Croatian Serb irregulars in Krajina and Eastern Slavonia. By 1992, the fighting had spread to Bosnia-Herzegovina, as ethnic Serbs there reacted to Bosnia's declaration of its own independence.

The Soviet Union's Demise

The collapse of communist rule in Eastern Europe had profound consequences for the Soviet Union itself. Long latent national movements within the constituent parts of the Soviet Union were quick to resurface. Beginning in the 1960s, Georgian nationalists had begun to campaign for restoration of the republic's sovereignty, and Soviet troops opened fire on a Georgian nationalist demonstration in April 1989. In February 1988, Nagorno-Karabakh, which contained an overwhelmingly Armenian population but was administered by Azerbaijan, asked to become a part of Armenia. The following year, assemblies in Armenia and Nagorno-Karabakh voted for unification.

In January 1990, just two months after the fall of the Berlin Wall, Mikhail Gorbachev traveled to Lithuania to try to dissuade local leaders from declaring independence. The following month, Sajudis, the Lithuanian independence movement, won local elections there. A declaration of independence ensued in March, which Moscow refused to recognize. Estonia followed suit in May, as did Latvia, although Latvia included a transition period. In August, on the fiftieth anniversary of the Molotov-Ribbentrop Pact between Nazi Germany and the Soviet Union, citizens from Estonia, Latvia, and Lithuania joined hands to form a human chain that stretched across the three Baltic republics to highlight to the world their lack of freedom. That July, the Ukrainian parliament adopted a declaration of state sovereignty, which was followed a year later by a formal declaration of independence.

Meanwhile, in October 1990, multiparty elections to the national assembly in Georgia—the first such election within the Soviet Union—brought a resounding victory for nationalist forces. Georgia declared its independence in April 1991, with the longtime dissident and nationalist Zviad Gamsakhurdia elected president the following month. After clashing with Moscow over Abkhazia and South Ossetia, Gamsakhurdia was ousted in a coup d'état in late December 1991, just as the Soviet Union was dissolving, sending the country into civil war. Further south, the long-simmering dispute between Armenia and Azerbaijan over Nagorno-Karabakh erupted into outright war in 1991.

In addition to stirring up secessionist fervor in the Soviet republics, the popular revolutions in Eastern Europe were to have seismic effects back in Moscow. If reform were to be permitted in the Soviet satellites, logic dictated that it should be allowed within Russia and the rest of the Soviet Union as well. In February 1990, Gorbachev proposed, and the Soviet Central Committee approved, a motion that the "leading role of the party be eliminated." That May, Boris Yeltsin, the popular former head of Moscow's Central Committee, was elected the first president of the Russian Federation. In August 1991, stalwart communists opposed to Gorbachev's policy of perestroika launched a coup attempt against him, detaining the general secretary at his country dacha in the Crimea and surrounding the Russian White House, the seat of the Supreme Soviet. Yeltsin led the resistance to the coup, marshaling crowds to defend the parliament building and delivering a defiant speech perched on the top of a tank.

While the coup failed, it laid bare where power now lay within the Soviet system. It was Boris Yeltsin, president of the Russian Federation, not Soviet general secretary Gorbachev, who now held the real power. The Russian Federation gradually began assuming control of the various Soviet ministries. When Ukraine voted for its independence three months later, in December 1991, the whole Soviet system had largely lost its raison d'être. By the close of the year, Gorbachev had resigned and the Soviet Union had been disbanded. Each of the former Soviet republics soon became an independent state within the loose framework of the Commonwealth of Independent States.

After the Revolutions

As communism collapsed, the region saw a series of "founding elections" take place, first in Eastern Europe, then in the former Soviet Union. In

Central Europe, elections ended up being largely free and fair contests, with international observers often helping to ensure their integrity. In Hungary, the Hungarian Democratic Forum, a coalition of center-right parties, won a majority of the vote following two rounds of balloting in March and April 1990. In March, East Germans went to the polls, although unlike in the rest of Eastern Europe, the issue at stake was not who would lead in the post-communist era but whether and how fast reunification with West Germany would occur. The East German reform parties were swiftly pushed aside by the traditional West German political parties, with the Christian Democrats emerging as victors. That June, Civic Forum, the opposition movement in the Czech Republic that had emerged out of the Velvet Revolution, and the Public against Violence, its counterpart in Slovakia, cruised to an easy victory over a highly discredited Communist Party. And in December, Lech Walesa was elected president of Poland, in the first truly free-and-fair election contest in that country, one without electoral quotas.

Further south, the results were more ambiguous. In Romania, as mentioned, the National Salvation Front, composed largely of former regime insiders, hastily organized presidential and parliamentary elections for May 1990, which they were able to win handily but amid accusations of widespread fraud and harassment. In Bulgaria, the Bulgarian Socialist Party, the successor to the Communist Party, won a narrow majority in that country's June parliamentary elections. The parliament later named the intellectual Zhelyu Zhelev—the leader of the noncommunist opposition, the Union of Democratic Forces—as president, although constitutional changes made the following year were to circumscribe his powers substantially.

In the Yugoslav Federation, the republic-level elections revolved around the question of nationhood and independence, and candidates (often former communist apparatchiks) representing ethno-national parties performed strongly. Nationalism and independence also provided the frame for elections in the Baltic States. Here, however, independent intellectuals became the first presidents of Estonia and Latvia, benefiting from their lack of association with the former Soviet regime. Nationalist considerations also were in play in the rest of the Soviet Union. Former dissident intellectuals with strong nationalist credentials were elected president in Georgia (Gamsakhurdia) and in Armenia (Levon Ter-Petrosyan), as was Leonid Kravchuk, the former chairman of the Supreme Soviet who had embraced the nationalist cause, in Ukraine. In Azerbaijan, the former anti-Soviet dissident scholar Abulfaz Elchibey was elected president in June 1992, but he was muscled aside the following year by the former longtime regional Communist Party boss Heydar Aliyev, who had restyled himself as a champion of Azeri nationalism. In the former Central Asian republics, which lacked any prior experience as nation-states, the Soviet Union's collapse triggered a scramble for control among former regime insiders that had much less to do with nationalism than with power politics. The old communist power structure remained more or less in place, albeit with the thin veneer of pseudo-democratic practices.

To a great extent, the initial power transitions and the founding elections in each country of the Eastern bloc were a harbinger of what was to follow. Where the public had played an important role in the transition from communism and the first post-communist elections were relatively free and fair, countries tended to proceed along a path toward liberal democracy. That was manifested most clearly in Central Europe, where the populations vividly demonstrated their opposition to the Soviet-backed communist regimes that had ruled them for half a century by protesting in the streets in large numbers for days, weeks, and even months. The exception was Slovakia, which had not had nearly as robust an opposition movement as its Czech cousin. Following its "Velvet Divorce" from the Czech Republic in 1993, its populist leadership helped turn the country once again toward authoritarianism.

Where the opposition movement was weaker, where citizens had not massed in large numbers to demonstrate their power, and where the break with the communist past consequently was not as decisive, a country's political fate proved more uncertain. Countries that did not experience a decisive shift of power away from the totalitarian-era elites toward the population at large ended up being more vulnerable to capture by the elites. In Romania and Bulgaria, communist elites dispensed with Ceausescu and Zhivkov but managed to retain their own hold on power. In Central Asia, the existing communist leader simply took over or was replaced by another former communist insider, albeit with a pledge to lead the new country toward democracy.

Where the primary issue that had mobilized the people was independence rather than democracy, a country faced a similarly uncertain fate. In Yugoslavia, nationalist politics soon splintered the federation and plunged the region into ethnic warfare. Nationalist politicians in places like Ukraine, Georgia, Armenia, and Azerbaijan successfully steered their countries toward independence, but their commitment to democratic principles and individual rights turned out to be far less exemplary.

A Second Round of Democratization

The late 1990s saw a second round of democratic movements emerge in several former Eastern bloc countries that had missed out on the first. It began in Romania and Bulgaria, where civic activists experimented with various mobilization techniques to try to engage local citizens more actively in political life, ostensibly on a nonpartisan basis. In Bulgaria, activists first devised a U.S.-style primary election to allow citizens to determine the next opposition candidate for president. The primary winner, attorney Petar Stoyanov, went on to win the presidency in November 1996. They then organized mass rallies to protest the rampant inflation and otherwise dismal economic conditions confronting the country. A civic campaign to increase turnout in the following year's parliamentary elections swept the opposition Union of Democratic Forces into power. A similar civic campaign in Romania finally brought the democratic opposition, led by University of Bucharest president Emil Constantinescu, to power in 1997, breaking the stranglehold on Romania's political life of the National Salvation Front and its offshoots. Afterward, the Bulgarian and Romanian activists shared their experiences with Slovak activists, who then shared their experiences with other Eastern European civic activists, sowing the seeds for what came to be known as the "colored revolutions" in many other parts of the former Soviet bloc.[8]

The experiences of these second-round countries seem of particular relevance to the countries of the Arab Spring because democratization proved to be a far more difficult and extended struggle than in, for example, Poland or the Czech Republic. The case studies that follow look at four of the second-round countries: two that have proceeded on relatively democratic paths (Slovakia and Serbia) and two where democracy has proved more elusive (Ukraine and Belarus).

Slovakia

Slovakia proceeded down a path very different from that taken by its Czech cousin immediately following their Velvet Divorce in 1993. With national politics dominated by the charismatic nationalist leader Vladimir Meciar, the country gradually turned toward authoritarianism and closer ties to Russia. Only after a concerted civic campaign by the country's nongovernmental organizations to engage the public more actively in the 1998 elections did Slovakia return to the democratic path. Fifteen years later, it continues to struggle with corruption, economic populism, and ethnic differences, but it is now firmly rooted in Western institutions and all political forces appear to be committed to playing by the democratic rules of the game.

THE RISE OF VLADIMIR MECIAR

Following Czechoslovakia's Velvet Revolution in 1989, Meciar quickly emerged as the most popular politician in the Slovak half of the country, in part because of his appeals to Slovak nationalism and his opposition to the economic "shock therapy" being pushed by the Czechs. He was first named Slovak prime minister in June 1990, following the strong performance of his Public against Violence movement (VPN, the Slovak equivalent of the Czechs' Civic Forum) in the first post-1989 elections in what was still Czechoslovakia. The leaders of his own party removed him from his post in April 1991 because of his increasingly nationalist and populist behavior, such as playing on Slovak anti-Czech chauvinism to win public support. Meciar left VPN and created the Movement for a Democratic Slovakia (HZDS), a political party uniting Slovak nationalists and ex-communists. The party won a plurality of the vote (37 percent) in the 1992 elections, and Meciar was elected prime minister for a second time. His deep personal and ideological differences with the Czech prime minister, Vaclav Klaus, a professed free-market liberal, soon led to an agreement between the two to split the country peacefully, on January 1, 1993.

Though hailed by many as the father of the newly independent Slovak state, Meciar was removed from his post once again in March 1994, when defections from HZDS and its coalition partner, the ultranationalist Slovak National Party (SNS), cost him his parliamentary majority. Following a brief grand coalition of all Slovak non-HZDS and SNS parties—with the tacit support of parties representing Slovakia's sizable ethnic Hungarian minority—Meciar's HZDS once again took a plurality (35 percent) of the vote in the September 1994 elections. After forging a coalition with SNS and the left-leaning Association of Workers of Slovakia (ZRS), Meciar returned as prime minister for yet a third time.

He spent the next four years aggressively consolidating his control over the country. He employed the power of his office to bend key state institutions, including the security services, the state-run media, and even the judiciary to his will. He waged a lengthy battle to oust—and, when that failed, to marginalize—Slovak president Michal Kovac. During a night wryly referred to as the "Night of Extended Democracy," HZDS parliamentary deputies seized on a walkout by the opposition to push through a host of legislative changes. Subsequently, Meciar's more ambitious efforts to switch from a proportional to a majority electoral system and to install a presidential system of government in Slovakia failed only because of a lack of sufficient votes in parliament.

Meciar was ruthless in his attacks on opponents, real and imagined. He routinely harassed the political opposition, accusing them publicly of being "insufficiently Slovak" and traitors to their own country. At every turn, he sought to intimidate and harass the independent press. For instance, his government proposed an exorbitant increase in the value-added tax on newsprint as a way of driving many of the independent dailies and weeklies out of business. Moreover, HZDS deputies rewrote the election law to prohibit independent radio and television outlets from offering any coverage of the elections. The Hungarian minority in Slovakia was singled out for especially harsh treatment, accused of being a "fifth column" of Hungary. The Meciar government pushed measures to limit the use of the Hungarian language in schools, road signs, and official government business.

At the same time, the government tightened its control over the economy. HZDS officials were inserted on the boards of the country's most profitable state-owned enterprises, but the majority of state-owned enterprises were privatized and at times the process was used to dole out favors to political friends. In return, business leaders helped finance the party's operations and a host of satellite organizations—youth groups, cultural foundations, professional associations, and even universities—that were set up to promote the party's nationalist ideology and crowd out its mainstream counterparts.

By late 1997, Slovakia seemed locked in Meciar's authoritarian grip. Increasingly Meciar and his government blatantly disregarded the rule of law, simply ignoring several Constitutional Court decisions that were not to their liking. When President Kovac's son was abducted, the government interfered in the investigation and a key witness was mysteriously murdered. When, in accordance with the constitution—and in response to a vote of parliament and a citizen petition—Kovac announced a dual referendum on NATO membership and the direct election of the president, the government had the ballots reprinted, with the latter issue dropped from consideration. A spate of bombings and mob-style killings in Bratislava, the capital, heightened fears that the country was descending into lawlessness.

For those who hoped for a democratic Slovakia, the situation seemed dire. Once a leading candidate for NATO and EU membership, along with the Czech Republic, Hungary, and Poland, Slovakia now appeared to be in danger of being shut out of the West altogether. Elections were expected by the following September—the month that the Meciar government's four-year mandate expired—but the political opposition was badly divided. Polls showed the country split between older, more conservative voters in the country's rural villages and towns, who remained loyal to Meciar, and younger, better educated voters from Bratislava and other urban centers, who tended to support opposition parties. The latter were deeply disaffected by political developments in their country and pessimistic about the possibilities for change. Many recent university graduates were leaving the country in search of better prospects in the West. Even if Meciar allowed the upcoming elections to be free and fair—a prospect that increasingly seemed open to question—there was deep skepticism that the democratic opposition could prevail.

CIVIL SOCIETY RESPONDS

Then the country's civic sector decided to get in the game. A rich and vibrant assortment of civic organizations had sprung up in Slovakia since 1989, supported in large part by Western governments and private foundations, but they had largely stayed out of politics until that point. The country's many talented civic leaders thought of themselves as continuing to practice the kind of "anti-politics" counseled by Czech dissident Vaclav Havel during the communist regime—creating through their work a virtuous parallel world free of the moral ambiguities associated with politics.

But the excesses of the Meciar government gradually propelled them toward political action. Environmental groups fought the government's plans to build a nuclear power plant in Mochovce and a massive dam across Tichy Potok. Cultural groups waged a Save Our Culture campaign to protest government interference in cultural affairs. In 1996, the nongovernmental organization (NGO) sector as a whole came together to fight a government-sponsored draft law on the grounds that it threatened to destroy the sector's independence by requiring foundations to register with the Ministry of the Interior and NGOs to report all large donations that they received. Civic groups also played an important role in the petition campaign for a referendum on direct election of the president and then in the boycott that ensued when the government struck the item from the ballot. Each of those actions gave the NGO sector much-needed experience in organizing itself and growing confidence in its political strength.

At a December 1997 meeting in Vienna, Western donors introduced some of Slovakia's most influential NGO leaders to a few of their

Bulgarian and Romanian counterparts. Drawing on their own recent experiences, the Bulgarians and Romanians argued that as civic leaders, the Slovaks had a moral obligation to become engaged in their country's democratic process. They told the Slovaks about the nonpartisan "civic" campaigns that they had successfully waged during their own countries' recent elections. The Bulgarians and Romanians made the Slovaks realize that the time had come to take political action and provided them with some real-life examples of how it could be done.

In March 1998, Slovak NGOs announced the formation of Civic Campaign '98, which was known by its Slovak initials as OK '98. It had three broad goals: to educate citizens about the parties and their positions on key issues, to encourage them to go to the polls and vote, and to monitor the election process to ensure that it was free and fair. Under the umbrella of OK '98, Slovak civic groups organized more than sixty different nonpartisan campaigns of various sorts—generally targeting specific geographic regions or demographic groups—that sought to engage citizens more actively in the election process. They received financial backing from the U.S. government, other Western governments, and private foundations. Various NGOs organized discussion groups, video presentations, cultural events, websites, and publications. The most prominent initiative, "The Way for Slovakia," was a fourteen-day march through 850 villages and towns across Slovakia to inform citizens about the issues and encourage them to vote. An MTV-style Rock the Vote campaign with the slogan "Don't let others decide your fate" featured rock concerts and a bus caravan through Slovakia's major cities that attracted thousands of Slovak youth. A group called Hlava (Head) ran a series of catchy television and radio spots featuring famous Slovak actors and athletes urging citizens to exercise their right to vote, each with the common tagline of "I vote, therefore I am." Another staged a political cabaret in communities around the country. The Association of Expert Seniors organized discussion forums for older voters. The country's leading think tank produced a slew of election-related materials, including an analysis of the different parties' platforms that was distributed throughout the country and two television documentaries on the election process. Besides these very visible nationwide efforts, a myriad of smaller civic organizations undertook more homegrown initiatives to educate and mobilize citizens within their own locality. Generally the target audiences of all these activities were first-time voters, women, the handicapped, or the Roma minority.

Meanwhile, important developments were taking place on the political front. After years of bickering, in July 1997 the country's opposition political parties forged an agreement to run as a bloc in the upcoming elections. The Slovak Democratic Coalition (SDK) comprised five ideologically disparate political parties, ranging from the conservative Christian Democratic Movement to the more liberal Democratic Party and Democratic Union to the Social Democratic Party and the Greens. When, in an effort to thwart their cooperation, Meciar revised the election law so that each party in a coalition was required to receive 5 percent of the vote for the coalition's votes to count, the SDK formally merged to become a united political party. Despite the coordination problems inherent in bringing together ten disparate parties under one umbrella, the SDK ran an aggressive election campaign. Nonetheless, it paled in comparison to the effort undertaken by the NGOs, which had greater organizational resources, deeper networks in society, and, in many respects, more credibility with voters.

As spring merged into summer, concern grew that, regardless of the final vote, Meciar would manipulate the election results in order to declare himself the winner. For months he had played a canny cat-and-mouse game with the Organization for Security and Cooperation in Europe, publicly impugning the credibility of the organization and hinting that he might not allow its election observers into the country while being careful not to close the door completely on its participation. In response to concerns about possible voter fraud, the Association for Fair Elections, a Slovak NGO, organized a project called Civic Eye to recruit and train independent domestic election observers. In all, approximately 1,750 volunteers—mostly young people—signed up, although only half were able to staff polling stations on election day because the government refused to accredit them. At the same time, the Anton Tunega Foundation trained members of the official election commission and local polling station committees in election monitoring. A new media watchdog group, MEMO '98, monitored how the electronic and print media covered the pre-election campaign, publishing regular reports that carefully documented the extent of the pro-HZDS bias in the official media.

On election day, in September 1998, the Slovak Democratic Coalition (SDK) claimed a significant victory. Meciar's HZDS received 27 percent of the vote (down 8 percent from 1994) while the SDK received 26.3 percent (up just over 4 percent from its constituent parties' combined performance in 1994). But with only the Slovak National Party (9.1 percent) willing to go into coalition with it, HZDS was incapable of forming a new government. The SDK then was able to forge a four-party coalition government with the Hungarian Coalition Party (7.6 percent), the Party of the Democratic Left (14.7 percent), and the Party of Civic Understanding (8.0 percent), which gave it 93 of the 150 seats in parliament. Voter turnout was a remarkable 84 percent of eligible voters, up by nearly 9 percent from the 1994 election and far higher than post-1989 election turnout in neighboring Poland, Hungary, or the Czech Republic. The participation of eligible first-time voters was estimated to be over 80 percent, up from roughly 60 percent in 1994, with exit polls confirming that this cohort of voters overwhelmingly supported the democratic opposition.

The OK '98 campaign is widely credited with having altered the entire psychology of the campaign by convincing citizens that their vote mattered and that they were not powerless in the face of an increasingly repressive regime. In the absence of a strong political party apparatus, it was civic organizations that were able to reach out to citizens—particularly younger citizens—and get them to the polls. They created a culture of dissent that suddenly made it acceptable to voice criticism of the regime. They provided citizens with a way of getting involved and of demonstrating their concern for their country, which over time, as more and more people joined in, became infectious and acquired a momentum of its own.

AFTER MECIAR

Slovakia has made important advances since 1998, but it also has faced its share of challenges. The new coalition government under prime minister Mikulas Dzurinda revived economic reforms, sought to strengthen the judiciary and address corruption, and set the country on a path toward EU and NATO membership, both of which were finally achieved in 2004. In the country's first direct presidential elections in 1999, Rudolf Schuster, the mayor of Kosice and a former communist, handily defeated Meciar. Meciar's HZDS party again won a plurality (19.5 percent) of the vote in the 2002 elections, but with no other major party willing to form a coalition with it, Dzurinda was able to assemble a center-right coalition that allowed him to continue in office and push forward with economic reforms. Those painful measures revived economic growth in the country, and the GDP growth rate climbed steadily from 0 percent in 1998 to a peak of 10 percent in 2007.[9] At the same time, Meciar's HZDS began to fracture during the party's time in opposition. His former HZDS ally Ivan Gasparovic challenged him for the presidency in 2004 and defeated him, 60 percent to 40 percent.

Public dissatisfaction with the hardships associated with economic reform led to the collapse of the Dzurinda government in 2006. In early elections, the new left-wing Smer (Direction) Party—led by populist politician Robert Fico—won a plurality, receiving 29 percent of the vote, while Dzurinda's Slovak Democratic and Christian Union Party received 18 percent. Fico assembled a governing coalition that included the far-right, anti-Hungarian Slovak National Party and the far-left HZDS (though without Meciar in the cabinet). The government performed better than its critics' worst fears. It generally maintained Slovakia on the path of reform that had been established by Dzurinda's government, allowing Slovakia to be the second Central European country after Slovenia to join the Eurozone in 2009. Nonetheless, corruption and lack of transparency remained a problem. Fico's government nearly fell over revelations of corruption in the Slovak Land Fund. Fico also was criticized for filing repeated libel suits against prominent media outlets, which was seen as a heavy-handed attempt to silence his detractors within the media.

Fico's Smer Party again won a plurality (35 percent) of the vote in the 2010 parliamentary elections, but with Meciar's HZDS party failing to gain even enough votes to enter parliament, it lacked the support needed to forge a coalition government. Instead, Iveta Radicova of the Slovak Democratic and Christian Union Party became prime minister by forging a center-right coalition. Her government lasted a little more than a year before controversy over Slovakia's contribution to the Eurozone bailout led to a vote of no confidence. Early elections in 2012 returned Fico as prime minister, with his party holding a majority of the seats in parliament.

CONCLUSION

Despite concerns over where Fico might lead Slovakia, the country has progressed markedly since the dark days of Meciar's semi-authoritarian rule. Slovakia is a stable democracy, firmly anchored in the European Union and NATO. An active civic sector continues to push for greater transparency, accountability, and public participation in governance. Meciar's popular support has dwindled to the point that he no longer presents a viable political threat. Even though other populist politicians, like Fico, continue to win elections, they have moderated their rhetoric and policies to align with the views of a Slovak public that overwhelmingly sees the country's future in the West rather than the East and as a democracy rather than an autocracy. It is unlikely that Slovakia's increasingly educated and urbane citizens will allow the country to revisit its troubled past.

Serbia

In Serbia, democratic activists soon appropriated many of the civic mobilization techniques that had been employed by the Slovaks, which were to prove invaluable in helping the democratic opposition finally succeed in its decade-long struggle to unseat Slobodan Milosevic.

THE STRONGMAN OF THE BALKANS

Many Western policymakers in the late 1990s were of the view that Serbia was a kind of "civic dead zone"—bereft of strong civic institutions and democratically minded citizens. How else could one explain a society that permitted its political leaders to drag it into three calamitous inter-ethnic conflicts—first in Croatia, then in Bosnia-Herzegovina, and finally in Kosovo? In fact, Serbia had an increasingly rich variety of independent associations and interest groups. Because Milosevic had enjoyed broad popular support among Serbs in the early years of his rule (he won the 1990 elections for the Serb presidency by a landslide), his regime was relatively permissive in allowing independent organizations to operate—even if many were closely watched and occasionally those perceived as unfriendly were brutally harassed.

Over the years, there were several important, if ultimately unsuccessful, popular challenges to Milosevic's rule. In March 1991 there were large anti-Milosevic demonstrations in downtown Belgrade that were halted only after a brutal crackdown by the Yugoslav army. The following year, 840,000 people signed a petition calling for Milosevic's removal from office. Throughout the Yugoslav wars of the 1990s, many Serbian men evaded conscription into the army, and groups like the Center for Anti-War Action staged frequent demonstrations against Serb participation in the conflicts.

However, the most significant civic protests against the Milosevic regime during the 1990s were those following the municipal elections of November 1996. The Zajedno coalition of opposition forces won control of forty-one municipalities, including Belgrade, but Milosevic refused to recognize the results and had local courts annul them. That set off mass demonstrations in Belgrade and Nis, which quickly spread to forty-five other towns in Serbia. Parts of Belgrade were soon in open revolt, with thousands jamming the public squares each day, blowing whistles and waving flags to show their defiance of the regime. But the protests were largely an urban, middle-class phenomenon, drawing for the most part students, professors, and white-collar professionals from Belgrade. Milosevic was able to split the opposition when he acceded to its most immediate demand by recognizing, in February 1997, the election results. The attendance at the daily rallies dropped off until the opposition, concerned that it had lost momentum, canceled them entirely. By early spring, the civic rebellion was dead. By summer, two of the key Zajedno leaders—Zoran Djindjic, the head of the Democratic Party and newly installed mayor of Belgrade, and Vuk Draskovic, the head of the more nationalist Serbian Renewal Party (SPO)—were once again feuding openly. Soon Draskovic was allying the SPO with the Socialists to remove Djindjic from the Belgrade mayor's office.

The period immediately after the 1996–97 civic protests saw a marked increase in civic activity. A host of new NGOs focused on environmental issues, women's rights, and human rights, and community action groups sprang up, not only in Belgrade and other major Serbian cities but even in smaller villages and towns. Belgrade-based civic groups like Civic Initiatives, the European Movement, and the Center for Anti-War Action turned their energies toward the Serbian heartland, convinced that the failure to unseat Milosevic in 1996–97 showed the need to broaden the base of support for democracy. Through their activities, they sought to teach democratic values, deepen their networks, and support the emergence of indigenous civil society groups in the more rural villages and towns of Serbia.

The NATO bombings that were launched in response to Milosevic's murderous war in Kosovo put many of their activities on hold, particularly those conducted in areas outside Belgrade. Milosevic seized on the state of emergency as an opportunity to crack down on his internal critics. The regime's security forces closed down the independent radio station B-92 and ransacked the headquarters of other civic groups. Moreover, at a time when Serbia was under direct foreign attack, many civic activists regarded it unpatriotic, not to mention dangerously imprudent, to question their government. Some joined their fellow citizens in the anti-NATO protests on Belgrade's bridges and in public squares, while others went underground and waited out the war.

Along with the physical and economic devastation that it wreaked, the war had profound psychological effects. Many Belgrade-based civic and opposition leaders emerged from the war despondent. The country had sunk so far that they were convinced that the only way that Milosevic was ever going to be removed was through a bloody civil war. But the perspective was somewhat different outside the capital. Whereas

Belgrade experienced a near-total information blackout during the war, local independent media continued to function in opposition-controlled cities, offering a welcome antidote to the surreal triumphalist propaganda being churned out by state-run sources. As the opposition used its governing authority to assert greater autonomy from the Belgrade regime, a sense of civic self-confidence began to arise in those cities. Meanwhile, change was afoot in eastern and south central Serbia, traditional Milosevic strongholds. The two regions had provided a disproportionate share of the young men sent to fight the UCK (Kosovo Liberation Army) rebels in Kosovo. As the toll of dead and wounded mounted, residents became increasingly embittered and angry with Milosevic and his regime. Protests by reservists and their families became a frequent occurrence.

DISSENT GROWS

In this changed atmosphere, a new student movement known simply as "Otpor," from the Serbian word for "resistance," emerged as a direct challenge to the Milosevic regime. A half-dozen students at the University of Belgrade had come together to form Otpor in December 1998, but it was only after the 1999 war that its activities began to attract notice. Frustrated at the failure of past student activism to elicit fundamental change, the organizers took the Yugoslav communist guerilla movement against Nazi occupation in World War II as their organizational model. Otpor was structured as a series of small cells connected only loosely to one another. Decisions were taken by a handful of operatives at the top, whose identities remained concealed. The role of spokesperson rotated every fortnight among some of the younger activists so that the police had a hard time knowing whom to arrest.

The founders envisioned Otpor's principal task to be political marketing: to sell to ordinary Serbs the possibility of resistance, using the same modern-day communications techniques employed in the West to market consumer products. They took as their symbol a black, upraised fist—an ironic twist on the bloody white fist that had become the Milosevic regime's symbol. Crisp, spray-painted images of the fist soon began to proliferate on street corners, the walls of buildings, and in public squares. Each Otpor cell organized meetings, rallies, and concerts to press the group's cause. The events were used as a vehicle for enlisting new "recruits," who, after being trained, formed new cells. Care was taken to ensure that each new event was bigger than the last, in order to convey the impression of ever-increasing public support for change. In one of its more memorable acts, Otpor organized a massive New Year's concert in

Belgrade to mark the millennium. When the time came for the celebration to begin, the audience was treated instead to a somber video presentation of the atrocities committed by Serbs in the wars of the preceding decade. Following the presentation, the organizers told the assembled youth to go home because there was no reason to celebrate what had been one of the darkest periods in Serbian history.

Surveys conducted at the time showed widespread public dissatisfaction with the situation in the former Yugoslavia and a sharp decline in Milosevic's popularity. But they also showed low levels of public trust in all the major political parties and a quite sizable bloc of voters (roughly 40 percent in one survey) who were unsure for whom they would vote in the next election. Despite widespread hunger for change, a substantial majority of Serbs viewed themselves as powerless to alter the situation and regarded Milosevic as the politician most likely to win any future election.

THE 2000 ELECTIONS

In that environment, Milosevic took a calculated gamble. He pushed through constitutional changes that enabled him to run for a second term and legislative changes that altered the election rules in his favor. Then, in late July 2000, he called snap elections for September 24 for local offices, the parliaments of Yugoslavia's remaining constituent republics (Serbia and Montenegro), and his own post of Yugoslav president, even though his term did not expire until the following May. He undoubtedly wagered that with the economy faltering and fuel shortages expected for the upcoming winter, the sooner the elections were held, the better. The announcement had been preceded by a crackdown on independent media outlets in Belgrade in mid-May, when the regime had taken over the offices of the independent radio station B2-92 (the successor to B-92, whose management had been purged by the regime earlier), Radio Index, and the tabloid newspaper *Blic*.

Under pressure from civic leaders and their own regional party officials, opposition politicians had been negotiating for months in an effort to unite under a common banner to fight Milosevic. Now, with the encouragement of the same groups, they chose to press ahead and contest the elections. Eighteen opposition political parties came together to form the Democratic Opposition of Serbia (DOS). Crucially, Zoran Djindjic, the most prominent politician within DOS, stepped aside to allow a relative unknown, Vojislav Kostunica, to run against Milosevic as the DOS candidate for Yugoslav president. Public opinion polls showed that the quiet and unassuming Kostunica, a constitutional lawyer who was untainted by any past association with Milosevic or the West but who had strong nationalist credentials, had the best chance of unseating Milosevic in a head-to-head race. Vuk Draskovic remained the one hold-out, threatening to boycott the elections, but the rest of the opposition opted to push ahead without him.

A broad range of Serbian nongovernmental organizations, using the Slovaks' OK '98 campaign as a model, had formed the civic campaign Exit 2000 to coordinate their election-related efforts. With just weeks to go before the elections, they hastily put together a myriad of nonpartisan activities designed to better inform Serb voters about the elections, their rights as voters, and the positions of the different political parties and to get as many voters as possible to the polls on election day. There was an unparalleled outpouring of civic energy and creativity as civic groups throughout Serbia mobilized their networks in an effort to reach potential voters from every conceivable constituency and locality. The U.S. Agency for International Development and its grantees provided significant financial and technical support. The think tank G17 PLUS produced and distributed widely a publication entitled "Program for a Democratic Serbia," which outlined a vision for a new Serbia and informed citizens of their rights as voters. Civic Initiatives blanketed the country with stickers, T-shirts, grocery bags, leaflets, and posters that reminded citizens to vote. The European Movement conducted an ambitious campaign to educate young voters about their civic responsibilities. The Blue Rider Group organized discussions for women at cultural events on the importance of voting. Complementing those and other nationwide campaigns were more focused efforts by local and regional civic groups. In Kragujevic, volunteers of the Alternative Culture Center went door to door to explain their voting rights to peasants and internally displaced Serbs. In Vrsac, the Union of Small and Medium-Size Entrepreneurs sought to motivate entrepreneurs, their families, and employees to get to the polls. In Novi Sad, the group European Vojvodina sought to make the same case to farmers.

Alongside and in coordination with the extensive NGO effort, Otpor launched two election-related campaigns of its own that targeted younger voters in particular. The first was a political marketing campaign designed to pierce the aura of invincibility surrounding the Milosevic regime and to encourage citizens to resist. Otpor activists distributed more than 2 million posters, T-shirts, and leaflets featuring the Otpor fist accompanied by the slogan "He's finished." The second was a get-out-the vote campaign with the more upbeat message "It's time." Some of the country's best-known rock stars criss-crossed the country, staging concerts in more than twenty-five cities and appealing to first-time voters to go to the polls. Throughout the run-up to the elections, Otpor activists, who now numbered well over 20,000, endured extensive harassment and even torture and imprisonment by the authorities. In September, five activists were detained by police in the southern Serbian town of Vladicin Han, hung by their legs from the ceiling, and badly beaten. The bravery of these and many other Otpor activists encouraged ordinary citizens to join in public opposition to the regime.

To an even greater extent than in Slovakia, the opposition was concerned about electoral fraud—that the regime would simply steal the elections. With U.S. assistance, the Center for Free Elections and Democracy (CeSID)—an NGO formed by a small group of students and faculty at the University of Belgrade Law School in 1997—spearheaded a massive election monitoring effort, the centerpiece of which was an elaborate parallel vote count. CeSID recruited and trained thousands of Serbs unaffiliated with any political party to observe polling stations on election day. The volunteers, working in parallel with DOS election observers, relayed the results from individual precincts to CeSID computers in Belgrade, where the election totals were analyzed and tabulated. Multiple redundancies were built into the system to make it difficult for the police to halt the effort. DOS ran a similar vote count of its own.

In the early morning of September 25, 2000, only hours after the polls closed, the opposition was able to announce that Vojislav Kostunica had won a majority of the vote for Yugoslav president, receiving 56.8 percent of the ballots cast; Milosevic got 34.2 percent. In absolute terms, Milosevic had received slightly more votes than the ruling parties had received in the 1997 Serbian parliamentary elections, but turnout was 15 percent higher. First-time voters, who numbered roughly 400,000 and voted overwhelmingly for Kostunica, provided a substantial portion of the margin of victory. When the preliminary results were announced, thousands streamed into Belgrade's Terazija Square to celebrate.

Milosevic and the state-run Federal Election Commission were slow to respond. First, a regime spokesman claimed that Milosevic was in fact in the lead. His statement was then amended to suggest that Kostunica was leading but had failed to obtain the requisite majority. Finally, on September 27, the Federal Election Commission announced its "official" results—Kostunica, 48 percent; Milosevic, 40 percent—and set a run-off election for October 8.

A small group of representatives of DOS, Otpor, and the NGOs carefully coordinated the democratic opposition's response. Kostunica flatly refused to take part in any run-off election, arguing that he had won outright and threatening a general strike. A wave of protests, which began inauspiciously with a sparsely attended rally in downtown Belgrade, gradually gained momentum and spread throughout the country. Schools shut down, taxi drivers walked off the job, businesses closed, roads were blocked, and several state-run media outlets abandoned their pro-government line and began to report on the situation objectively. A key development was the seizure of the Kolubara coal mine, which fueled half of the country's electrical needs, by 13,000 striking miners on September 29. When police were sent to intervene on October 4, thousands of Serbian citizens showed up to defend the miners.

The denouement came on October 5. In a carefully planned set of maneuvers, five convoys set out from the opposition strongholds of Cacak, Nis, Subotica, Mitrovica, and Pancevo in the direction of Belgrade, picking up supporters along the way. State security forces placed barricades across the roads in an effort to stop them, but the marchers were undeterred. They used the trucks and forklifts in their convoys— and even at times their bare hands—to clear the route. As they drove into Belgrade, they were joined by hundreds of thousands of cheering residents of the city. The marchers surrounded key symbols of Milosevic's rule: the federal parliament, the state television agency, the Socialist Party headquarters, and the main police station. The largest crowd had assembled around the parliament, which they began to storm around mid-day. The police repeatedly repulsed the crowd using tear gas, but then a worker from Banovo Brdo steered his bulldozer to the front of the crowd, scooped up a dozen marchers, and lifted them to an open first floor window. The parliament now belonged to the opposition. The state television agency soon was overtaken as well. Milosevic called on the army to use deadly force to disperse the protesters, but faced with a massive public uprising, the commanders on the ground ignored his orders.

The next day, October 6, 2000, Slobodan Milosevic went on Serbian television and conceded defeat. Kostunica was sworn in as Yugoslav president and Djindjic as prime minister of Serbia. On June 28, 2001, Milosevic was extradited to The Hague to stand trial for crimes against humanity.

THE AFTERMATH

Serbia has struggled since 2000 to put its troubled past behind it. The Djindjic government sought to implement institutional and economic reforms that would put Serbia on a path to EU and NATO membership. Tragically, in March 2003, a former Milosevic-era Special Forces officer with ties to organized crime gunned down Djindjic. As the nation mourned, Kostunica replaced Djindjic as prime minister; Boris Tadic was elected president of the Republic of Serbia the following year. Montenegro declared its independence in 2006, prompting new elections. Although the Serbian Radical Party won a plurality (28.6 percent) of the vote, anti-Milosevic forces were able to cobble together a governing coalition with Kostunica again as prime minister, largely because the Serbian Radical Party's likely coalition party, Milosevic's former Socialist Party of Serbia, polled only 5.7 percent.

In 2008, Kosovo unilaterally declared its independence, triggering a government crisis over how to address the issue. In new elections, Tadic's Democratic Party won a commanding plurality of the vote (38.4 percent) and formed a governing coalition that included a newly reformed Socialist Party of Serbia as a partner. The government continued with a reform agenda, strengthening its NGO legislation by finally passing the Law on Associations, which provided a clearer legal framework for the formation and operation of NGOs, and expanding autonomy for the province of Vojvodina. At the same time, it cooperated more fully with the International Criminal Tribunal for the Former Yugoslavia and improved relations with its neighbors. It also formally submitted Serbia's application for membership in the European Union.[10]

Serbia was hit hard by the global recession and the European financial crisis. GDP growth, which had averaged more than 5 percent a year since Milosevic's fall, suddenly dipped into negative territory in 2008–09,[11] and unemployment eventually reached 25 percent.[12] In the May 2012 presidential elections, Tomislav Nikolic of the Serbian Progressive Party, a reformist offshoot of the ultranationalist Serbian Radical Party, narrowly defeated the incumbent Boris Tadic, who had been tainted by rumors of corruption and political favoritism. In the parliamentary elections that took place at the same time, Nikolic's party captured a plurality (24 percent) of the vote and forged a governing coalition with the Socialist Party of Serbia, naming Ivica Dacic, the head of the Socialists and Milosevic's wartime spokesman, as prime minister.[13]

CONCLUSION

As in Slovakia, both new leaders in Serbia have renounced their ultranationalist pasts and pledged to work toward integrating their country fully into Europe.[14] To date, they have cooperated closely with the European Union in trying to negotiate an agreement over Kosovo. Many Serbian democracy activists have forlornly concluded that this is what successful democratization looks like: your extremist foes of the past are in power but have so moderated their positions that they are implementing your reform agenda. But only time will tell what Nikolic and Dacic's leadership means for Serbia's future. Serbia has come a long way since the Milosevic era, but the ghosts of that era still haunt its politics today.

Belarus

Within Europe, Belarus has become the anomaly—the region's sole remaining dictatorship. While its neighbors to the west—Latvia, Lithuania, and Poland—fought fiercely to attain their independence from Moscow during the Gorbachev era and have since become vibrant democracies, dynamic market economies, and full members of the North Atlantic Treaty Organization and the European Union, Belarus has been ruled for the last 19 years by the strongman Alexander Lukashenko, who continues to function at times as a satrap of Russia.

BECOMING A NATION

There are many reasons, besides its geographic proximity to Russia, that Belarus remains an outlier in Europe. Belarus was long a part of other national projects—for example, the medieval state of Kievan Rus, the Polish-Lithuanian Commonwealth, and the Soviet Union—but it has only recently become its own country. Only a quarter of the population speaks Belarusian as a first language; most of the rest speak Russian. A landlocked region at the former Soviet Union's periphery, isolated by forests, marshes, and hills and devastated by two world wars, Belarus was until recently quite poor, with just a small intelligentsia and masses of peasants and urban workers.[15]

Although Belarus has remained the last authoritarian outpost in Europe, shifting social and economic conditions hold the prospect for change. For much of its recent history, Belarus was viewed, along with Ukraine, as "little Russia"—the westernmost appendages of the Big Bear. Although Gorbachev's perestroika and glasnost policies brought major change to its neighbors, they did not bring major change to Belarus. "There was no confrontation with tanks as in Red Square, no defense of the television tower as in Vilnius, and no overwhelming referendum favoring independence as in Ukraine."[16] Belarusians largely remained loyal to the Soviet Union.

In the new political environment created by Gorbachev, a small group of intellectuals did begin to initiate a renaissance in Belarusian culture and language, primarily to emphasize to Belarus's own population as well as the Russians that Belarus had its own identity and history. Twenty-eight Belarusian writers, for instance, signed a letter to Gorbachev decrying the declining use of the Belarusian language.

Two other events were even more critical in forging an independent Belarusian identity. The first was the nuclear disaster at Chernobyl in 1986, following which an estimated 70 percent of the radioactive contamination ended up in Belarus. The second was the discovery by an archeologist in 1998 of mass graves near Minsk of Belarusians who had been murdered during Stalin's Great Terror. On learning of the discovery, the population took to the streets in outrage. A number of small youth groups, cultural organizations, and historical societies sprang up that year to promote Belarusian identity, including the Martyrology of Belarus, a society that sought to use the massacre to awaken within the public a Belarusian national consciousness. From the latter group emerged the Belarusian Popular Front (BPF), with Zenon Poznyak, the archeologist who had discovered the mass graves, as its president. The group was quite small (50,000 members by the end of 1989) and composed almost exclusively of intellectuals and youth, but it was to lead the country's push for independence.[17]

In 1990, elections were held for the first time for the Supreme Soviet. Opposition groups won twenty of the twenty-two Minsk seats, but they did far less well outside the capital. Overall, the communists won 49 percent of the seats and two satellite parties won another 19 percent. That July, the government adopted the Declaration of State Sovereignty, although it was never submitted for popular referendum as in many other republics. In August 1991, formal independence was declared. That December Boris Yeltsin, Leonid Kravchuk of Ukraine, and Stanislav Shushkevich, the new Belarusian chairman of the Supreme Soviet, signed the Minsk Accords, thereby dissolving the Soviet Union and creating in its stead the Commonwealth of Independent States, to be headquartered in Minsk.[18]

Shushkevich and the new prime minister, Vyacheslav Kebich, a conservative communist, developed an intense rivalry that dominated political life and inhibited reform. The former curried the favor of industrial and business leaders, while the latter appealed to the intelligentsia and nationalists. Finally, in January 1994, Shushkevich was ousted from his post following a parliamentary vote of no confidence after he was charged with corruption. A new constitution was prepared that gave substantial powers to the country's president, on the assumption that Kebich would win that office. However, the July elections produced a surprise: a little-known populist politician named Alexander Lukashenko, who had directed a state farm before being named to parliament, won 45 percent of the vote in a crowded field of six candidates that included Shushkevich and Kebich. Lukashenko used his position as chairman of a parliamentary committee investigating state corruption to tarnish his rivals (it was he who had lodged the corruption charges against Shushkevich) while burnishing his own credentials as a crusading reformer. He called for closer ties with Russia and claimed to have been the only deputy to vote against the dissolution of the Soviet Union. He appealed to ordinary citizens with his youthful charm, folksy manner, and mixed Russian-Belarusian dialect. He handily defeated Kebich in a run-off election, securing 80 percent of the vote, to become president. Although it was not immediately apparent, Lukashenko's election effectively put an end to Belarus's brief experiment with democracy.[19]

LUKASHENKO TAKES OVER

Once in office, Lukashenko initially continued to portray himself as a reformer and flirted briefly with Western-style reform programs. He secured a loan from the International Monetary Fund, and Belarus joined NATO's Partnership for Peace program. By temperament and opportunity, however, Lukashenko was drawn eastward, toward Russia. Yeltsin badly needed his support as he sought to win his own reelection bid and was willing to invest heavily in Belarus in return.[20] Following protests over dairy prices, Lukashenko went on television to condemn his own government's reform policies. "We will build what we know," he declared, meaning that the country would return to a planned economy.[21]

As he was abandoning market reform, he was also beginning a series of crackdowns that would put an end to political reform as well. His government started to censor the country's newspapers. When deputies of the Supreme Soviet complained, Lukashenko proposed dissolving the body and then called for a referendum to let the people decide the matter. Several deputies went on a hunger strike in protest, but they were removed from the parliament by regime forces.[22]

From 1995 to 1996, Lukashenko held a series of referendums and elections and issued decrees that put him firmly in charge. He disbanded the Supreme Soviet and replaced it with the National Assembly, which was made up of his supporters. He cowed the Constitutional Court into submission and reworked the constitution, extending his own term for another five years. An effort to impeach him by opposition deputies was derailed with a duplicitous maneuver in which a high-level Russian delegation pretended to mediate an end to the conflict; Lukashenko then reneged on his side of the bargain. He shut down independent newspapers and harassed the opposition, establishing pseudo-opposition parties of his own. He extended his control over the state security services, the state-owned media, and the election commission.[23] In 1998 he forced twenty-two foreign embassies out of a posh suburb of Minsk by shutting off their water and electricity and then moved his supporters into the suburb. A number of key opposition figures fled to the West.

Lukashenko continued to edge the country closer to Russia. As Yeltsin's health and popularity deteriorated, Lukashenko aspired to succeed him as the head of some kind of Russian-Belarusian confederation. The parliaments of both countries ratified the Act of Union in 1997, but Lukashenko hesitated to incorporate Belarus's six provinces into the Russian Federation, clearly not wanting to give up his autonomy. The country, nonetheless, remained heavily dependent on Russian raw materials and energy resources.

In 1999, when Lukashenko's term in office had officially expired, protesters took to the streets. Many regime opponents were beaten or jailed. During that time, several prominent political figures with whom Lukashenko had clashed simply disappeared. The opposition boycotted the 2000 parliamentary elections, which were deeply flawed procedurally, leaving the country with a "puppet parliament" composed almost completely of Lukashenko supporters.[24]

A COLORED REVOLUTION?

As the 2001 presidential election approached, the anti-Lukashenko forces were buoyed by the fall of Milosevic in Serbia. They hoped that they could mimic the Serbian opposition's success in uniting around a single candidate for president and that the NGO sector could employ the same voter education, get-out-the-vote, and election monitoring strategies that had been used so successfully in Serbia, Croatia, Slovakia, and Ukraine to create civic movements for change.[25] The Belarusian opposition received technical assistance from activists from many of those countries and generous Western financial support for the election effort.

The opposition did succeed in uniting around a single candidate, Uladzimir Hancharyk, the head of the Belarusian Federation of Trade Unions. He spoke Russian and had been a former communist party apparatchik, so it was hoped that he would be acceptable to Moscow. The federation also represented 4.5 million workers and possessed a strong organizational base from which to run a nationwide campaign. But the opposition took until three weeks before the election to decide upon Hancharyk, and only then did he present his political program to the nation. He proved to be an uninspiring candidate, and his campaign team, a group of unimaginative former apparatchiks, mounted a lackluster effort.

Far more impressive was the NGOs' campaign team, with which Hancharyk's team barely consulted. Under the collective banner of "Vybiray!" (with the double meaning of "vote" or "choose"), more than 200 groups organized election-related events and distributed nonpartisan informational materials, targeting in particular young, educated urban voters. Post-election surveys found that the campaign reached nearly half of its target audience, and turnout was far higher than in the 1994 elections.[26]

Lukashenko deftly employed the full powers of the state to ensure his reelection. His message to voters was that even though the economy remained weak and the population impoverished, he had protected them from the misguided shock therapy demanded by the West, which had wreaked such havoc in Russia and Ukraine. He instructed his subordinates to increase salaries and pensions just prior to the election. He encouraged additional candidates to join the race in order to confuse voters. He harassed opposition campaign workers and NGO activists and cut off their telephone, Internet, and satellite communications on election day. The state media covered his campaign activities almost to the exclusion of all others. He prevented observers from the Organization for Security and Cooperation in Europe from arriving to monitor the election until just days before the election and after early voting already had taken place, when it is believed that most of the vote tampering occurred.[27] On election day, observers were kept at such a distance that they could not see the ballot boxes, and the final tallying of votes was conducted behind closed doors, with only members of the Lukashenko-appointed election commission and local government officials in attendance. The Central Election Commission declared that Lukashenko had won with 75.6 percent of the vote, while the opposition argued in vain that he had in fact failed to secure a majority of the votes and that a run-off was required. Neither the United States nor the European Union recognized the election as legitimate, and the West broke off many of its ties to the country.[28]

Lukashenko continued his crackdown on opposition groups. He prevented any major protest demonstrations from occurring immediately following the vote. Moreover, approximately 350 NGOs were stripped of their registration between 2003 and 2005, and in their place Lukashenko created a number of GONGOs (government-organized nongovernmental organizations), which purported to perform the same functions but were tightly connected and loyal to the government.[29] Between 2003 and 2005, the number of independent newspapers fell from fifty to eighteen.[30]

At the same time, relations with Russia under Putin deteriorated. Putin had less interest than Yeltsin in any closer integration with Belarus. Moreover, Russian business interests like Lukoil and Gazprom, which had helped with Lukashenko's reelection campaign, were angered that the promised quid pro quo of greater investment opportunities in Belarus had never materialized.[31] In 2002, Putin called Lukashenko's bluff on integration by proposing the creation of a "single state" with a common currency, parliament, and president (who clearly would be Putin)—a proposal that Lukashenko had no choice but to reject.[32] Nevertheless, the close economic ties between the two countries helped revive the moribund Belarusian economy. With its pipelines supplying vital Russian natural gas to Western Europe and Russia providing it generous loans and subsidies, particularly for oil and natural gas, Belarus was able to share significantly in the Russian energy boom that began in 2000. Between 2001 and 2005, GDP growth averaged 7.5 percent a year, boosting Lukashenko's sagging popularity.[33]

Lukashenko used the 2004 Chechen terrorist attack on a school in Beslan, North Ossetia, as a pretext for extending his term. He went on television immediately after the tragedy, brazenly boasted that "over these ten years no Belarusian has become a victim of a terrorist attack," and announced a referendum as part of parliamentary elections the following month to enable him to serve a third term. With the economy booming, the opposition divided, and Russia distracted, the measure officially passed with 88 percent of the vote (though a private exit poll suggested that Lukashenko may have actually fallen short of the required majority of all eligible voters.)[34]

For the 2006 presidential elections, the opposition once more tried to unite around a common candidate. After much bickering and several rounds of balloting, the Coordinating Council of Democratic Forces narrowly selected the Belarusian-speaking civic activist Aleksandr Milinkevich as their candidate—after the second-place, rightist-nationalist candidate Anatol Liabedzka, who was a favorite of BNF (Belarusian Popular Front) veterans, angrily withdrew his support for Milinkevich. The communists, nationalists, and liberals—not to mention Russian speakers and Belarusian speakers—had once more found it difficult to make common cause. Lukashenko again inserted into the race a loyal opponent of his own choosing (Siarhei Haidukevich) to confuse voters, while a fourth candidate, dark horse Aleksandr Kazulin, the rector of Belarusian State University, emerged seemingly out of nowhere as the favorite of many of the Russophile elite and perhaps even the Kremlin.

The national committee that was set up to coordinate Milinkevich's opposition campaign badly lacked resources, and its members had difficulty agreeing on tactics. Eventually the group settled on branding its effort the "Denim Revolution," in the spirit of the "Rose Revolution" in Georgia and the "Orange Revolution" in Ukraine.[35] Its approach had two drawbacks. First, it meant that the group's organizational energies would be devoted less to winning the election (which Lukashenko was unlikely to allow anyway) than to the protests afterward. However, the legitimacy and effectiveness of the post-election protests in Ukraine and Georgia had hinged on the perception that the elections had been stolen outright. Second, it left the opposition vulnerable to charges of colluding with outside elements. Many in the former Soviet Union, including Vladimir Putin, viewed the so-called "colored revolutions" as the work of a Western conspiracy to instigate regime change throughout the region. Lukashenko had warned in 2005: "In our country, there will be no pink or orange—or even banana—revolution."[36] His political handlers maligned Milinkevich, who had Polish roots, as a "foreign stooge bent on social chaos."[37]

Lukashenko's regime had also learned important lessons from the revolutions in neighboring states. The intelligence services infiltrated the youth group Zubr, which had been modeled on the Serbian youth group Otpor. They carefully monitored social media to determine when and where opposition groups would be gathering. Fake leaflets were planted and then uncovered at the NGO Partnerstva ("Partnership") and cited as evidence that the group intended to declare victory for Milinkevich on election night regardless of the results; the group's leaders were jailed and brought to trial. Mimicking the civic campaigns elsewhere in Eastern Europe, the regime staged a six-week-long rock tour across the country dubbed "For Belarus!" to woo undecided voters. It also developed fake exit polls of its own to counter those of the opposition. Meanwhile, the expansion of early voting and the continued tallying of votes behind closed doors provided the regime the leeway to manipulate the vote count as needed. Immediately following the elections, the Central Election Commission declared Lukashenko the winner, with 83 percent of the vote, while Milinkevich's received 6 percent and Kazulin 2 percent. Independent polling firms encountered such interference in conducting their work that the true vote count is unknown.[38]

This time, thousands flocked to October Square in downtown Minsk on the night of the election. The protests continued for a week, with opposition youth setting up tents in the square. Rumors spread that Lukashenko was in seclusion after suffering a nervous breakdown. But the protests, while reaching into the tens of thousands, never achieved sufficient critical mass to pose a real threat to the regime. Little by little, the security services cut off supplies to those encamped in the square and jailed those who tried to leave. Finally Kazulin, who had played a more aggressive role in leading the demonstrations than the more timid Milinkevich, was arrested and the protest petered out.[39]

CHANGING GEOPOLITICS

Soon after the elections, Russia announced that it would gradually eliminate its subsidies for natural gas sold to Belarus. A separate dispute followed over the fees to be paid on Russian oil flowing by pipeline through Belarus to be refined and sold on Western European markets. In retaliation, Belarus began siphoning oil from the pipeline for its own use. Russia responded by turning off the pipeline. The "energy wars," Lukashenko claimed, cost Belarus $5 billion (10 percent of GDP).[40] A more critical point was that Russian support, which had long propped up the Belarusian economy, was gone.

Lukashenko was able to turn, at least for a time, to the European Union for economic support. Following the 2006 elections, the EU determined that its policy of isolating Belarus was not working and decided instead to "seek to expand its links with Belarusian society and its leverage on the regime." It supported the new, Warsaw-based radio station, European Radio for Belarus, and the first independent Belarus satellite channel, BelSat. It incorporated Belarus into a number of its technical and financial assistance programs, including by making it a member of the Eastern Partnership Initiative in 2009. Faced with the cut-off of Russian subsidies, Lukashenko had no choice but to engage with the EU as well as to reorient the economy more along market lines. The change in course had benefits for Lukashenko: millions of euros in EU assistance began to flow to Belarus; by 2008 the EU had become Belarus's largest trading partner; borrowing from the International Monetary Fund and other external sources increased markedly; and foreign direct investment mushroomed between 2006 and 2009 from $351 million to $4.8 billion. At the same time, in large part because of those changes, Belarusian society began to change in important ways. The economy began to open up and businesses began to look westward for markets. Cultural links with the EU grew. In 2010, more than 4 million foreigners visited Belarus and the number of private citizens traveling from Belarus to the EU grew to 3 million, from 1.6 million in 2006. Nineteen percent of the population had access to satellite television, and 1.6 million Belarusians were getting news and information from the Internet.[41]

Nonetheless, in many ways the 2010 elections looked like a rerun of the 2006 contest. Once again, the opposition had difficulty uniting, and nine opposition candidates entered the race for the presidency. Once again, coverage of Lukashenko dominated the state media. Once again, the elections were neither free nor fair. Once again, Lukashenko claimed victory, with 80 percent of the vote, while probably garnering closer to a bare majority. Once again, protesters took to the streets of Minsk, and once again, they were beaten and jailed. Seven of the presidential candidates were arrested.

The elections soured the EU's relationship with Belarus. Both the EU and the United States responded with sanctions, just as the downturn in the world economy was creating economic hardship in Belarus. The regime has continued to crack down brutally on internal dissent, forcing its opponents to find creative, often surreal, means to press their cause: silent protests in which participants simply walked up and down a prede-termined street, demonstrations by stuffed animals, and even an airdrop of teddy bears by a group of enterprising Swedes.

CONCLUSION

Lukashenko remains firmly in control in Belarus, but shifting attitudes among its citizens suggest that even the reign of "the last dictator in Europe" will not last forever. In a March 2011 poll, 72 percent of respondents thought that life was better in neighboring countries; 50.5 percent preferred membership in the European Union to integration with Russia, up 21.5 percent from five years before; and more than half expressed a desire to emigrate.[42]

Change will undoubtedly come to Belarus as citizens become more educated and exposed to the outside world, particularly those in more rural areas outside the capital of Minsk. To date, the country's political elites, who have been badly divided by ideology and language, have been more an impediment to change than a catalyst for change. The story of Belarus's post-independence politics shows the difficulties of creating new professionalized political parties. Political change in Belarus is unlikely to come through the efforts of opposition political parties, which have been driven largely by the politics of personality and have been unable to unite, but from civic movements from below. The valiant efforts of civic activists to challenge the Lukashenko regime so far have often come up short because of the gap between the Minsk elite and ordinary Belarusians, who are divided not only by geography and education but also by language. The many public demonstrations that have been held over the years against Lukashenko's continued rule have never reached the kind of critical mass that might pose an existential threat to the regime because they have never been able to unite the rural peasant, small-town merchant, industrial worker, and urban elite. Someday soon that may change.

Lukashenko has shown himself to be a wily politician. He has ably used deception and the state machinery to divide his political opponents and maintain his authoritarian rule. How long he can continue to do so, as Belarus's citizens become more integrated economically and culturally into Europe, remains to be seen.

Ukraine

Ukraine has made greater progress on the road to democratization than Belarus, but it nonetheless remains at best an electoral rather than a liberal democracy. The country's famed Orange Revolution helped topple the country's post-Soviet autocracy, but subsequent infighting among democratic forces once they were within government led to the eventual return to power of one of its more controversial and authoritarian figures, Viktor Yanukovych. He has reversed many of the liberalizing reforms ushered in by the Orange Revolution and threatens to return the country to its autocratic past.

THE STRUGGLE FOR INDEPENDENCE

Ukraine differs from Belarus in possessing a distinct and deeply felt historical national identity. A largely flat, lowland area at the crossroads of East and West, Ukraine (which means "on the edge" or "the border" in Ukrainian) has rarely over the course of modern history been independent; instead, it has been passed back and forth between Russia to the east and Poland and Lithuania to the west. In January 1918, immediately following the Bolshevik Revolution, Eastern Ukraine proclaimed its independence. The following year, upon the collapse of the Austro-Hungarian Empire, it declared a union with Western Ukraine. Soviet troops occupied Kiev in 1919, and Eastern Ukraine became one of the four founding constituent republics of the Soviet Union. Western Ukraine was incorporated into the Soviet Union following its military victory in

World War II. Initially the Soviets adopted a policy of indigenization to give the republic a more Ukrainian face. Most business was conducted in Ukrainian, most of the schools conducted classes in Ukrainian, and more than half of government officials in the republic were ethnic Ukrainians.[43]

Long considered the breadbasket of Europe because of its vast wheat production, Ukraine became integral to Stalin's forced industrialization plans. The country became the Soviet Union's primary source of coal, iron ore, and pig iron, and by the late 1930s it was a leading European industrial center, manufacturing more metal and machines than Italy and France. However, the single-minded focus on industrialization came at the expense of agricultural production. Peasants were being forced off their land into inefficient collectivized farms and compelled to meet unrealistic production quotas or face punishment, even death. Grain that was badly needed on the home front was being exported to fund the heavy industrialization program. The result was the Great Famine of 1932–33, in which as many as 5 million Ukrainians starved to death. The causes are believed to have been as much political and ideological as economic: the famine helped the Soviet leadership eliminate the more nationalistic Ukrainian peasantry, which had resisted collectivization. The Soviets forcibly requisitioned much of their harvest for export, which is why so many starved; in many cases, entire villages were wiped out, which then were repopulated by Russian transplants. The memory of the famine was seared on Ukrainians' collective national consciousness forever after.[44]

In the 1960s and 1970s, a group of Ukrainian writers and artists began to campaign for greater human and national rights within Ukraine. Many of the so-called "shistdesiatnyky" (the "sixties") were arrested and jailed (Ukrainians formed the largest bloc of Soviet political prisoners) but later re-emerged as important political figures in the 1980s and 1990s.[45] The Chernobyl disaster, which released into the atmosphere about a hundred times the radiation produced by the U.S. bombings of Hiroshimo and Nagasaki, contributed further to Ukrainian grievances. Ukrainians felt that the Soviet authorities had shown blatant disregard for the welfare of the people by failing to alert them to the dangers to which they were being exposed until a full ten days after the catastrophe. Chernobyl "traumatized the population, and then galvanized it."[46]

In the new atmosphere of glasnost, introduced by Mikail Gorbachev in 1986–87, a Ukrainian nationalist movement began to take shape. At the 1986 congress of the Ukrainian Writers' Union, two of Ukraine's leading literary figures (Oles Hanchar and Ivan Drach) gave speeches calling for a national revival. In 1988, the Ukrainian Helsinki Union was formed with Levko Lukyanenko, who had been a political prisoner for 26 years, as its president. Many of the same intellectuals created the Ukrainian Association of Independent Creative Intelligentsia, with the objective of spurring a cultural renaissance. In Lviv, university students formed the Lion Society (Tovarystvo Leva) to revive through cultural, environmental, and intellectual activities a sovereign Ukrainian state. In Kiev, students established Hromada ("Community"), named after the Ukrainian cultural societies of the nineteenth century, to pursue similar objectives. The latter, together with the environmental organization Green World Association, held a 10,000-person demonstration in Kiev in the fall of 1988 opposing nuclear power and calling for the resignation of the hardline, pro-Russian first secretary of the Ukrainian Communist Party and the formation of the Ukrainian Popular Front. Religious groups joined the national effort, pressing for the re-legalization of the Ukrainian Greek Catholic Church and the revival of the Ukrainian Autocephalus Orthodox Church, both of which had been liquidated by Soviet authorities in favor of the Russian Orthodox Church. In 1988, 20,000 to 50,000 people assembled outside Lviv University to support creation of the National Front, but the authorities sent in security forces to break up the gathering.[47]

In February 1989, many of these groups came together to form Rukh (Popular Movement of Ukraine for Perestroika), which was modeled on the Estonian and Latvian Popular Fronts and Lithuania's Sajudis. The movement's program called for reform of the socialist system and the creation within the Soviet Union of a sovereign Ukrainian republic with control of its own industries and resources, but it stopped short of an outright declaration of independence. It further indicated that Rukh would nominate its own candidates for the upcoming elections.[48]

In March 1989, the first popular elections were held for the Congress of People's Deputies. While a third of the seats were allocated to Communist Party members, in theory the rest were open to all; however, the authorities employed a variety of tactics to try to keep Rukh members off the ballot. The election results represented a moral victory for Rukh in that several of its members won seats in Kiev and Western Ukraine and voters in some cases simply struck off the names of the Communist Party officials who ran unopposed, preventing them from receiving the required majority of all votes cast. The vote made manifest the geographical differences that were to define Ukrainian politics going forward: Rukh performed extremely well in Kiev and in Western Ukraine, where more of the people spoke Ukrainian and were historically oriented toward the West, but far less well in the industrialized and Russophile east. There were strikes and demonstrations in the east too, but they tended to be more economic than national in nature.[49]

In January 1990, on the anniversary of Ukraine's 1918 declaration of independence, Rukh organized a demonstration of 450,000 Ukrainians linking hands from Lviv to Kiev. That March the Democratic bloc, composed of forty parties, won 25 percent of the seats in the Ukrainian Supreme Soviet, claiming strong majorities again in Kiev and Galicia and gaining a few seats in the eastern cities of Khrkiv and Donetsk. However, they received very few votes east of the Dnieper River, which divides the two parts of Ukraine. In local elections, Vyacheslav Chornovil, one of Rukh's leaders, became the head of the Lviv regional council, which he proclaimed an "island of freedom." With the nationalist cause gaining momentum, many began to desert the Communist Party, and its power ebbed. In July, the still communist-dominated Supreme Soviet voted overwhelmingly in favor of the Declaration of Sovereignty, which called for a legislatively, economically, and militarily independent Ukraine within the framework of a reformed Soviet Union.[50]

KRAVCHUK LEADS THE WAY

Amid crackdowns by nervous Communist Party authorities and counterdemonstrations by pro-independence students, workers, and intellectuals, Leonid Kravchuk—the chairman of the Supreme Soviet and the most senior Ukrainian official—emerged as a pivotal figure. He embraced the call for Ukrainian sovereignty while reaching out to the Kremlin to find some sort of compromise that would maintain the federation with Russia and the other Soviet republics. In November 1990, he negotiated a treaty with Boris Yeltsin that would continue close relations between Ukraine and Russia in a variety of areas. Gorbachev, still intent on preserving the Soviet Union, called for a popular referendum on the issue of whether the Soviet republics would remain part of the Soviet Union, but six of the Soviet republics, intent on independence, declined to participate. Kravchuk had Ukraine take part, but he arranged for Ukrainian voters to be asked, in addition to the question "Do you support the preservation of the Soviet Union as a 'renewed federation of equal sovereign states?'" a second question: whether they wanted Ukraine to continue to be part of the Soviet Union on the basis of the Declaration of Sovereignty. Gorbachev's proposal implied a continuation of a Moscow-dominated union, albeit in improved form; Kravchhuk's formulation suggested a sovereign Ukraine continuing a relationship with the other Soviet states but on the basis of equality. In a March 1991 vote, both measures passed in Ukraine by wide margins (the first by 70 percent and the second by 80 percent), leaving the true will of the people on this issue altogether muddled.[51]

Then, that August, the abortive coup against Gorbachev took place. Three days after the coup attempt unraveled, the Ukrainian Supreme Soviet approved the declaration of independence. The following week the Communist Party was disbanded, but because the independence vote had enjoyed the begrudging support of Communist Party deputies, no measures were passed to decommunize the Ukrainian state or society. On December 1, 1991, a popular vote was held to endorse the country's declaration of independence and Kravchuk was elected president, with 62 percent of the vote. He swept all the major regions in the country except the west, where Rukh leader Chornovil was the favorite.[52] On December 8, Yeltsin, Kravchuk, and Shushkevich of Belarus met and agreed to disband the Soviet Union while creating the looser Commonwealth of Independent States in its stead.

Kravchuk had skillfully steered Ukraine's diverse factions toward an eventual consensus on independence, bringing along the warier eastern and southern regions as well as his fellow communist apparatchiks. He managed Ukraine's departure from the Soviet Union while maintaining amicable relations with Russia. He saw to it that the new Ukrainian state developed all the formal trappings of a proper nation: the blue-and-yellow flag, the old anthem, the trident as the state emblem, Ukrainian as the official language (although the use of Russian continued as well), a small diplomatic corps, and a new army. He negotiated with Russia and the West over the disposition of the 200 nuclear missiles left on Ukrainian soil, insisting on financial assistance and security guarantees in return for their removal, and he negotiated with Russia over the disposition of the Black Sea fleet, which was headquartered in Crimea.[53]

What Kravchuk lacked was a domestic agenda. He was focused on building a nation-state and was much less interested in reforming the economy or building democratic institutions. He was content to preside over an independent Ukrainian state that looked and functioned much like its Soviet precursor. However, with the collapse of the former Comecon trading system, intraregional trade decreased significantly, and Ukraine's industrial production plummeted, the economy collapsed, and hyperinflation ensued.[54] On the political side, corruption continued unchecked, the media continued to be heavily state controlled, and little dissent was tolerated. Public disillusionment grew as living standards fell and little else seemed to change.[55]

KUCHMA TAKES OVER

Presidential and parliamentary elections were held in 1994. Leonid Kuchma emerged as the major challenger to Kravchuk. Kuchma had run a massive state-owned firm in Dnipropetrovsk that produced Soviet intercontinental ballistic missiles and had then served as prime minister from 1992 to 1993. He courted Russian-speaking voters in the east and the south with his opposition to many aspects of Kravchuk's Ukrainianization program. The National Democrats in parties like Rukh confronted a dilemma. They had generally supported Kravchuk as president because he had ably steered Ukraine to its centuries-long goal of independence, but his failure to liberalize the economy and politics had tarnished their reputation as well as his among the public. Yet Kuchma—who was neither a Ukrainian nationalist (he could not even speak Ukrainian well) nor a democrat—presented an even less appealing alternative. Ultimately Ruhk opted to back Kravchuk rather than run a presidential candidate of its own, but it did not matter. Kuchma defeated Kravchuk, 52 percent to 45 percent, in the second round of voting. His Communist Party eventually took 97 of the 415 seats in parliament while Kravchuk's Center Party took 37 and Rukh took a meager 29, with other parties associated with the former regime and independents capturing much of the remainder. Kravchuk's last and perhaps most important contribution to Ukrainian democracy was to leave the office of president peacefully.[56]

President Kuchma initially surprised many who had expected him to take the country back toward Russia and old-style communism. With the economy reeling, he threw his support behind an ambitious economic reform program underwritten by the International Monetary Fund. His government succeeded in getting inflation under control and implementing a mass privatization program, which shifted much of the economy into private hands. The measures were enough to stem the economy's free fall, but because Soviet-era price controls, regulations, and red tape remained in place, they were not enough to spur growth.[57] He courted the West and expressed a desire for Ukraine to eventually become a member of NATO.

Kuchma fought a bruising battle with parliament to win passage of a new constitution. It strengthened the powers of the presidency—powers that many hoped Kuchma would use to bypass an increasingly recalcitrant parliament and speed economic reform. But Kuchma's enthusiasm for reform had waned, and he opted instead to use his newly acquired authority to move his friends—what came to be referred to as the "Dnitropetrovsk clan"—into positions of power. The economy continued to be dominated by business oligarchs, many with close ties to Kuchma. Privatization and state corruption became a means of enriching political allies. Crony capitalism prevailed.[58]

On the political front, many democratic advances were reversed. Kuchma tightened the state's control of the media and intimidated his political opponents. Political and civil liberties were curtailed. Elections became less free and fair. Despite widespread public disillusionment with Kuchma, he was reelected in 1999, but only after one of his main challengers, Rukh leader Chornovil, died in a mysterious car accident and the elections themselves were compromised by widespread irregularities, including voter intimidation, ballot stuffing, and vote rigging.[59] By the decade's end, the country's GDP had fallen by 54 percent and polls showed that only 17 percent of Ukrainians believed that their country was democratic.[60]

Then came what would be known as the "Kuchmagate" scandal. Kuchma's political opponents released tape recordings that appeared to feature him ordering the murder of Georgii Gongadze, an Internet journalist whose decapitated body had been discovered in 2000, as well as engaging in election fraud and other major crimes. The revelations galvanized public opposition to Kuchma. Students, trade unionists, and some business leaders formed the "Ukraine without Kuchma" movement, which organized street demonstrations that were routinely broken up by the police. Gradually Yulia Tymoshenko, a former deputy prime minister, and Viktor Yushchenko, who had been dismissed as prime minister after trying to push through market reforms, emerged as leaders of the political opposition to Kuchma. Under the banner "Our Ukraine," Yushchenko ran in the 2002 parliamentary elections and his coalition won nearly a third of the party list votes, while the pro-Kuchma party, For a United Ukraine, won only 12 percent. However, the latter was more successful in single-mandate districts—in which the remaining half of the seats was allocated—where state resources and bribes could be more easily used to get its candidates elected. Anti-Kuchma groups mounted street protests denouncing the way in which the election was conducted, but the police repeatedly dispersed them. The end result was a divided parliament and the continuation of political tensions between pro- and anti-Kuchma forces.[61]

THE ORANGE REVOLUTION

The opposition was better prepared for the presidential elections that followed two years later, in fall 2004. Kuchma (and Vladimir Putin) threw his support behind Viktor Yanukovych, the former Donetsk regional governor, to be his successor. Yushchenko and Tymoshenko struck a deal: the former would run for the presidency on the combined ticket of the People's Power Coalition; in return, the latter would be named prime minister if the campaign succeeded. Drawing lessons from successful civic movements elsewhere in the region, the opposition adopted the neutral color of orange and the slogan "I believe, I know, we can do it!" to distinguish their campaign.[62] It trained election observers to conduct their own parallel vote count on election day. Drawing on activists who had honed their skills in past antigovernment protests, the opposition created its own extensive grassroots network to reach voters across the country in order to make up for the near-blackout of coverage of Yushchenko's campaign by the state-run media. Two months before the election, Yushchenko checked into a Vienna clinic with what appeared to be a bad case of food poisoning but was soon discovered to be dioxin poisoning—a revelation that only boosted the ailing candidate's public support.

In the initial round of voting, Yushchenko narrowly edged out Yanukovych, 39.9 percent to 39.2 percent. With neither candidate in a crowded field having secured a majority, a second round of voting was scheduled for three weeks later. In the meantime, most of the other losing candidates gave their support to Yushchenko. Following the second round of voting, the Central Election Commission announced unofficial results showing Yanukovych beating Yushchenko 49.5 percent to 46.6 percent. However, independent exit polls had Yushchenko ahead by 10 percent.[63] Yushchenko announced that the election had been stolen from him and called on his fellow countrymen to gather in Maidan Square (Independence Square). Led by the youth movement Pora, as many as 1 million orange-clad protesters, ranging from students to housewives, urban professionals, and industrial workers, poured into the square. Tents were pitched at one end, a big speaker's platform at the other. The stand-off, which quickly became known as the Orange Revolution, lasted seventeen days and gripped the entire nation, although it garnered greater support in the west than the east. Responding to an appeal from Yushchenko, on December 3 the Supreme Court declared the election results invalid and ordered the election redone. On December 26, the election was rerun, with thousands of foreign and domestic election monitors closely observing the process. Yushchenko defeated Yanukovych with 52 percent of the vote and became Ukraine's new president.[64]

AFTER THE REVOLUTION

The storybook tale of the Orange Revolution soon lost much of its luster. Yushchenko named Tymoshenko as prime minister. It became clear that the two had limited experience at governing and differing policy priorities: she was a Social Democrat intent on undoing the more corrupt business deals of the past while he had become a free marketer—with growing ties to the country's business oligarchs—who was keen to "bury the hatchet and forget where it lies."[65] The two quickly clashed. Yushchenko came out in opposition to Tymoshenko's plans to review thousands of privatization deals, boost social spending, and control meat and energy prices. He made his friend Peter Poroshenko head of the National Security and Defense Council and conferred on him the additional power to give directives to individual ministries, thereby circumventing the prime minister. Amid the uncertainty over economic policy, GDP growth began to fall by a percentage point a month before becoming negative in August 2005. Charges of corruption and bribery within the government were rife. Finally, in September Yushchenko sacked both Tymoshenko and Poroshenko, nominating Yuriy Yekhanurov, who had overseen the country's privatization process in the late 1990s, as Tymoshenko's replacement as prime minister. Yushchenko cut a deal with Yanukovych's Party of Regions (which included amnesty for past crimes) to get the nomination approved by parliament.[66]

In March 2006 parliamentary elections that were deemed "free and fair," Yanukovych's Party of the Regions won a plurality of the vote (32 percent), followed by the Tymoshenko Bloc (22 percent), Yushchenko's Our Ukraine (14 percent), the Socialists (6 percent), and the Communists (4 percent). Neither Yanukovych nor Tymoshenko could muster sufficient support to form a coalition government, and a lengthy stalemate ensued. Then in July, after considerable wrangling, the head of the Socialist Party, Oleksandr Moroz, who had long been a part of the anti-Kuchma opposition, switched his support to Yanukovych in return for remaining as speaker of the parliament.[67]

Yanukovych claimed that he was now fully committed to democracy and to Ukraine's integration into Western and international institutions. His return as prime minister, however, brought little progress toward reform. A number of government positions were once more doled out to members of his "Donetsk clan," who appeared to use public office as a means of personal enrichment. Several questionable privatization deals took place. The powers of the state were used to intimidate the media, political opponents, and small businesses. Yanukovych, who was supposed to leave foreign policy to Yushchenko as president, sought to court Putin's support. When Yanukovych coaxed (allegedly through cash payments) eleven members of Our Ukraine and the Tymoshenko Bloc to switch allegiance, thereby threatening to have enough votes in parliament to override a presidential veto, Yushchenko intervened by dissolving parliament and calling for new elections.[68]

The September 2007 parliamentary election results looked much like those from 2006, except the Tymoshenko Bloc boosted its share of the vote by more than 8 percent, enabling Tymoshenko to forge a narrow majority coalition with Our Ukraine and once more become prime minister. With the Orange Coalition once more in power, Yushchenko and Tymoshenko, as president and prime minister, resumed their self-defeating personal feud. Tymoshenko returned to office determined to govern more cooperatively and to adhere to market-based policies. She liberalized trade and completed the final steps for Ukraine's accession to the World Trade Organization and opened up negotiations with the European Union for a free trade agreement. She identified 19 large state firms for privatization and designated more than 400 other smaller firms for auction. However, Yushchenko had concluded from his past dealings with both Tymoshenko and Yanukovych that he had been too accommodating. He rejected the privatization plans, claiming that they resembled "a seasonal sale in a Kyiv department store." He also stymied Tymoshenko's attempts to permit private land sales and to remove the chair of the State Property Fund, a socialist adamantly opposed to the privatization of state assets. In 2008, as neighboring Russia and Georgia battled over South Ossetia and Abkhazia and the international financial crisis was devastating Ukraine's economy, Yushchenko, in what appeared to be a blood feud with Tymoshenko, began pushing once again for new parliamentary elections. She countered by pushing through parliament—with the support of Yanukovych's Party of the Regions—the Law on the Cabinet of Ministers, which drastically curtailed the powers of the president and effectively turned Ukraine into a parliamentary state. Yushchenko pulled Our Ukraine out of the governing coalition and issued a decree to dissolve parliament. When the maneuver was ruled unconstitutional, Yushchenko sacked the judge, whom the Council of Judges promptly reinstated, leaving the issue unresolved.[69]

Presidential elections were held in January 2010. President Yush-chenko finished fifth, with just over 5 percent of the vote. In the sec-ond round of voting, Yanukovych edged out Tymoshenko, 49 percent to 46 percent, in an election that met most international standards. Yan-ukovych has continued Ukraine's democratic backsliding, moving the country further away from the promise of the Orange Revolution. He pushed through a change in parliamentary procedure to allow deputies to change their party affiliation so that he could increase his governing majority. He replaced several Constitutional Court justices in order to get a favorable court ruling overturning the limits that had been placed on presidential authority. He got parliament to postpone local elections, then put in place new electoral rules that prohibited the kind of multi-party electoral blocs that had previously allowed Our Ukraine and the Tymoshenko Bloc to join forces.

When they finally took place in October 2010, the local elections rep-resented a step backward for the country in terms of electoral process: the government blocked certain candidates from running and prevented some observers from monitoring the elections. In the Kharkiv and Odessa mayoral races, the number of votes counted exceeded the number of bal-lots distributed.[70] In its annual survey of freedom around the world, Free-dom House downgraded Ukraine—which had been the only post-Soviet state other than the Baltic States to be designated "free"—from "free" to "partly free." Then in early 2011, the government filed criminal charges against Tymoshenko for abuse of office over a gas import contract that she signed with Russia in 2009. Both the United States and the European Union lodged complaints regarding the charges, arguing that the govern-ment was engaging in a selective and politically motivated prosecution. Despite Yanukovych's promises to the international community that the case would be resolved, Tymoshenko was convicted in September 2011 and sentenced to seven years in prison. The following year, she was charged with tax evasion and embezzlement in a 15-year-old case that had long ago been closed.

At the time of this writing, Yanukovych's government, in the face of heavy pressure from Russia, had scuttled a deal with the European Union to sign an association agreement that would have granted Ukraine privi-leged access to the European Common Market and other benefits, pro-vided that it released Tymoshenko for medical treatment in Germany and undertook other reforms. In response, tens of thousands of angry citizens, mainly students initially, poured into the streets of Kiev in protest. When the police used violent force to try to clear Maidan Square of protesters, the video images of police brutality galvanized hundreds of thousands more to take to the streets and to demand the government's resignation. Yanukovych cut a deal with Russia instead, under which Russia lowered the price of its gas exports to Ukraine and purchased $15 billion in Ukrainian government bonds to boost Ukraine's economy.[71] The protests only mushroomed, spreading to towns and cities throughout the country, including in the east. Feverish negotiations mediated by the EU sought to avert civil war as the protests entered their third month.

CONCLUSION

Regardless of how the latest events unfold, Ukraine can point to tangible achievements over the last two decades. The country won its independence after centuries of being the junior partner in other countries' national projects. Despite profound differences—linguistic, economic, and even national—between the largely Ukrainian-speaking west of the country and the largely Russian-speaking east, the country has held together and developed a true Ukrainian national identity. Crimea has remained a part of Ukraine, despite separatist tendencies in the early 1990s.

For all its messiness, democracy has put down important roots in Ukraine. The October 2012 parliamentary elections were deemed relatively free and fair, as have been most elections since 2004. With the notable exception of the 2004 elections, incumbents have stepped aside when they lost their bid for reelection. The Orange Revolution reinforced the norm that the will of the people as expressed through elections must be respected; it also gave ordinary Ukrainians the confidence that their voice mattered and provided useful experience and skills in civic activism. That said, politics remains an elite game, one played by a very small group of quite corrupt and inept political leaders. Ukrainian civil society has grown and developed, but it still has not managed to alter the fundamental nature of Ukrainian politics, which continues to be dominated by a handful of elites who pay lip service to the rule of law but often operate outside of it.

Ukraine's experience underscores the gap between the overthrowing of an authoritarian regime by a relatively small group of people and the more sustained effort and civic engagement required to build a vibrant democracy. Democracy requires a shared vision—a set of common understandings—of a country's political future and a willingness on the part of citizens to remain engaged to ensure that that vision is realized. Following the Orange Revolution, Ukrainians needed to continue to press their political leaders to change how politics was conducted, but beyond the major western cities, that did not happen. An enduring political constituency for democracy has not yet emerged in Ukraine, but it may in the future.

The task of democratization was made more difficult by the decision of political leaders early on not to dismantle the edifice of the former communist state. Building an independent nation took priority over democratization. Upon becoming Ukraine's first president, Kravchuk quite understandably determined that national unity and cohesion took precedence over decommunization. Therefore he did not purge the bureaucracy, or punish previous officials for crimes committed in office, or break up the tight clientelistic networks between the political and economic elite. The latter in particular have made the task of decentralizing and democratizing Ukraine all the more difficult. Ukrainians have shown their unwillingness to tolerate corrupt, authoritarian practices—and they may yet do so again—but they are still some way from being able to create and defend a liberal democracy.

Lessons from the Eastern Bloc

The popular revolutions and second round of political breakthroughs described above helped place certain countries on a path toward democracy, but they by no means guaranteed that those countries would succeed in reaching their destination. Democracy proved difficult to implement where democratic traditions were few. Even countries like Poland, the Czech Republic, and Hungary found the challenges involved in adopting liberal democracy daunting. They struggled with constitutional crises, parliamentary infighting, political scandals, glaring violations of minority rights, infringement on individual rights, and curtailment of freedom of the press.

As mentioned, more than 20 years after the collapse of communism, democracy has a mixed record in Eastern Europe and the former Soviet Union. Today, Freedom House categorizes only thirteen of the region's countries as "free," eight as "partly free," and seven as "not free."[72] Yet all had very similar institutions to start; all proceeded to craft what were, at least on paper, democratic constitutions; all put in place a set of putatively democratic political institutions, including elected parliaments and independent judiciaries; and all made some space for independent civil society groups and an independent media. But the results varied greatly.

While almost every country in the former Soviet Union has adopted the institutional forms of democracy, far fewer have acquired its substance. The Czech Republic, Hungary, and Poland, followed in short order by Slovenia and the Baltic States, moved quickly along the path toward liberal democracy—even if most have yet to attain that ideal fully (moreover, Hungary has experienced some troubling backsliding during Viktor Orban's most recent term as prime minister). They have put in place new democratic institutions, held several free elections in which power has been peacefully transferred from one set of political parties to another and back again, and maintained relatively good records in terms of safeguarding individual rights. Countries like Slovakia, Romania, Bulgaria, Croatia, Serbia, Georgia, and Ukraine belatedly began to move haltingly down the same path, some more successfully than others.

In contrast, many of the rest of the countries of the former Eastern bloc are at best illiberal democracies: while they may hold elections, they fail to safeguard the essential human freedoms of life, liberty, and property. The Central Asian republics, which had few democratic traditions let alone a common sense of nationhood, turned out to be among the most difficult cases. After independence, they reverted quickly to authoritarian, one-man rule, even while adopting the forms of democracy. Today, these countries possess many of the institutional trappings of democracy—elections, constitutions, parliaments—but they are neither liberal nor democratic. Individual rights are routinely trampled, the political opposition is harassed and jailed, and elections are rigged to the advantage of the incumbent. Autocratic leaders have used the forms of democracy to undermine its very substance, and passive populations have often allowed them to get away with it. These countries seem stalled in their transition toward democracy, occupying some sort of gray area between communism and democracy—what Marina Ottaway has labeled "semi-authoritarian regimes" and others have called "hybrid regimes."[73]

It is complicated to draw definitive lessons from the experience of the Eastern bloc with democratization simply because the outcomes in many cases were so over-determined. The countries that had the longest previous experience with democracy, were the wealthiest, had the most educated populations, and had the most exposure to the rest of the world were precisely those that were closest to Western Europe and had the most trade and contact with it. All of those traits made them the most logical candidates for NATO and EU enlargement. Conversely, the countries that were the poorest and had the weakest democratic traditions and the least educated populations tended to be those that were located farthest from the West and had the fewest links to it—making them the least likely candidates for NATO and EU enlargement. Not surprisingly, the first group tended to be relatively successful in developing consolidated democracies while the latter were not. It is very difficult to determine where causality lies.

However, the importance of the prospect of NATO and EU membership to eventual democratization should not be overstated. It is important to remember that most West European governments were initially opposed to expanding either organization eastward. Reportedly President George H. W. Bush promised Gorbachev, at the time of his agreement to Germany's unification, that as a quid pro quo NATO would not expand further east—a promise that was later broken. As it was, neither membership in NATO's Partnership for Peace nor the EU's association agreement was on offer until 1994, and the first Eastern European members were not admitted into NATO until 1999 and the EU until 2004. Therefore to argue that the prospect of membership is what drove certain countries to democratize is not wholly accurate.

The question of which countries would become members if either body were to enlarge was even less settled early in the post–cold war period. The behavior of the potential candidate countries ended up being critical in shaping the debate. Certainly Poland, Czechoslovakia, and Hungary were the most likely candidates for membership at the beginning, given their proximity to and historical association with the rest of Europe. Their admission into the EU and NATO was viewed by some as correcting the errors of history—undoing Stalin's artificial division of Europe after World War II—by returning these states to their rightful place within Europe. Beyond that, however, the contours of a new Europe in the aftermath of the fall of the Iron Curtain were largely undefined. Yugoslavia was an obvious candidate for membership, given its greater openness to and trade links with the West since the 1970s and its relatively advanced economy, but the disintegration of the Yugoslav Federation and the ensuing Balkan wars removed its successor states, with the exception of Slovenia, from early consideration. The Baltic States initially were regarded by many as off limits. They were considered part of Russia's sphere of influence, marking a "red line" that could not be crossed, but their exemplary economic performance and responsible domestic and foreign policies—combined with fierce political lobbying by their diaspora communities in the United States—made the once unthinkable thinkable.

Romania and Bulgaria seemed equally improbable candidates, given their geographic distance and relative underdevelopment, but with time they too would make themselves credible candidates for membership in both bodies. Ukraine seemed an even more unlikely candidate because of Russian sensitivities, its internal instability and backwardness, and its location, but that did not stop both Ukrainian and American political elites from at times making the case for its membership in NATO—a debate that continues to this day. Even Russian membership in NATO has been seriously debated at various times. The point is that the behavior of various former communist states was as important in determining which was considered for membership in NATO and the EU as the prospect of membership was in giving those states an incentive to behave in certain democratic ways.

What seems to have been an even more decisive factor in the prospects for democratization of Eastern bloc states was the presence or absence of a political constituency for democracy. Those countries that had a large and diverse subset of the population that opposed the existing communist regime and were able to organize themselves politically to confront the regime were generally able to topple it and make a decisive break with the past. In the tug-of-war between state and society, they pulled the rope decisively toward the side of society—toward giving the public a greater say in governance. Those societies that could not muster such opposition were more likely to have to muddle through with continued totalitarian, authoritarian, or semi-authoritarian rule. A political constituency for democracy seemed more likely to emerge in countries whose citizens were better educated, more exposed to the outside world, and more tightly connected to one another. Such a constituency was more effective as a political force if it included not only intellectuals but also other key segments of society—including workers, professionals, and elements of the security forces—and spanned beyond the capital to include cities and towns throughout a country.

The pace at which communism unraveled in the region was indeed breathtaking. However, as discussed here, the popular revolutions that swept Eastern Europe and parts of the former Soviet Union did not arise spontaneously. As in the Arab world, they built on a history of past opposition to the existing regime. Citizen dissatisfaction with the status quo had been percolating for a long time. Opposition groups had formed and repeatedly sought to challenge the regime. They had developed a forceful critique of their government, a vocabulary of dissent, and an alternative vision of their country's future that challenged the regime's narrative and undermined its legitimacy. While their early protests may not have been successful, activists learned through trial and error to bring citizens together in common cause. From those struggles, networks of like-minded citizens were formed.

When events in 1989 finally conspired to offer the opposition an opening to challenge the existing regime, important groundwork had already been laid. Like a snowball rolling downhill, popular uprisings, as in the Arab Spring, gained momentum as a myriad of networks, many forged in past struggles between state and society, joined together. The revolutions in Central and Eastern Europe were vivid demonstrations of people power. What proved decisive were not bargains struck among elites but bottom-up pressure for change from ordinary citizens. From Gdansk and Leipzig to Budapest and Prague, hundreds of thousands of people took to the streets and, through sheer force of numbers, brought long-standing communist regimes to their knees.

What seemed to tip the balance against those regimes was the mobilization by the opposition of vast segments of the population. The regimes could have handled a series of labor demonstrations or an uprising in one region of the country. What they were unprepared for—and likely could not have withstood even with Soviet military assistance—was having the entire country, citizens from every region and every socioeconomic class, rise up against them. No army or police force could long make war on the whole of society.

What happened after each country's founding elections proved as important as what preceded them. As Eastern Europe's new democratic leaders quickly discovered—and the events of the Arab Spring are demonstrating yet again—competitive elections are just one part of a vibrant liberal democracy. Hand in hand with elections must come the creation of independent legislatures and courts; the adoption of the rule of law, including protection of various individual and minority rights; and the development of an independent media and independent civil society. Those challenges extend well beyond an individual election cycle; indeed, they are the work of a generation. The former Eastern bloc countries that have succeeded in approximating liberal democracy in practice have been those in which citizens and citizen movements have remained engaged in political life after the country's founding elections. Those societies that have continually demanded of their political leaders accountability, transparency, and public participation in governance have over time come closest to achieving those aims.

CHAPTER FOUR

MUSLIM-MAJORITY ASIA

The Third Wave's effects, although significant, were more diffuse in Asia, a vast continent whose diverse nations make broad generalizations about their experience with democratization more difficult. Several important Asian countries began their democratic experiment well before the Third Wave. India was established as a parliamentary democracy on achieving its independence from Great Britain following World War II. Pakistan, on partition from India, also was founded as a democracy, although it has struggled through a series of military and civilian governments in trying to attain that ideal in practice. Following World War II, U.S. military leaders occupying Japan helped craft new democratic institutions that endure to this day. It could be argued that Turkey, which straddles Europe and Asia, began its long journey toward democracy during the Ottoman period, even before the founding of the modern Republic of Turkey in 1923.

The ripples of the Third Wave were first felt in Asia in the Philippines in 1986, when popular protests unseated strongman Ferdinand Marcos and demonstrated to the world the potency of "people power." In South Korea, the killing of a student in 1987 triggered mass demonstrations across the country that eventually compelled the ruling party to agree to direct presidential elections. Months of student-led demonstrations in Burma were brutally quashed by the military in 1988. Popular protests in China in 1989 were similarly halted by a bloody government crackdown in Tiananmen Square. Eight years later, the collapse of Thailand's currency, the baht, triggered a financial crisis that had political repercussions across Asia—the most notable being the fall of Indonesian dictator

Suharto and a democratic bargain in Thailand that helped push democracy forward in that country.

Because of the sheer complexity of studying democratic developments in a continent as large as Asia, this chapter focuses on the individual experiences of four important Asian Muslim-majority countries: Indonesia, Malaysia, Pakistan, and Turkey. These four cases were chosen not just because it helps to simplify a very complex reality but also because they are especially relevant to the Arab world. The Arab Spring has reignited debate over the relationship between Islam and democracy, and critics have asked whether Islam and democracy are in fact compatible. The early electoral success of Islamist groups in Tunisia and Egypt raises again the question of how such groups are likely to behave in a democracy (as well as provides a chance to see how they do in fact behave). The experiences of these four Muslim-majority countries (which happen to be among the most populous Muslim-majority countries in the world) promise to shed some light on these questions.

Of the four, two—Pakistan and Turkey—date the beginning of their experience with democracy back to the Second Wave of democratization, while the other two made their move toward democracy (tentatively, in the case of Malaysia) in the Third Wave. Indonesia and Turkey have made significant progress toward becoming consolidated democracies. Because its democratic experiments have been repeatedly interrupted by military rule, Pakistan has made much less progress, while Malaysia, which does not allow for truly free and fair elections, has yet to have a full democratic opening.

Turkey

Turkey is a case with special relevance to the Arab Spring. As youth throughout the Arab world took to the streets, many cited Turkey as a model of what they would like their country to become. Even though its population is not Arab, Turkey is 99 percent Muslim. It shares with other countries in the region an Ottoman heritage, and their geographic proximity has led to many cultural affinities. More important, Turkey offers for many a compelling example of how Islam (and arguably, even Islamism) and democracy can coexist. Turkey's AKP (Justice and Development Party)—a centrist party with Islamist roots (although it now prefers to describe itself as a "socially conservative" party)—has governed Turkey since 2002, garnering ever larger shares of the vote in the last three election cycles. In a state built on the Kemalist notion of radical secularism, the AKP is a religiously inspired party that, despite its brutal crackdown on protesters in Taksim Square in June 2013,[1] has largely lived within the democratic rules of the game.

Many have also held Turkey up as a possible model of the role that militaries can play in helping broker transitions to democracy. The myth, if not the reality, of the Turkish military is that it has remained above Turkish politics, in a caretaker-like role, intervening only when one party has strayed from the constitutional path and ensuring that all parties adhere to the Kemalist vision for Turkey's future. Some have suggested that Arab militaries could play a similar role in safeguarding the democratic transitions under way in the region.

The Roots of Turkish Democracy

Turkey's transition toward democracy has been an extended one. Even the question of when Turkey's transition began—and whether and when it ended—is difficult to answer with precision. Turkey has a very long tradition of constitutionalism and the rule of law. In 1839, as part of the Tanzimat (reorganization of the government or bureaucracy) during the final century of Ottoman rule, Sultan Abdülmecid issued an edict guaranteeing the life, honor, and property of his subjects and establishing their equality before the law, irrespective of their religious beliefs.[2] In 1878, the Ottoman Empire became the first Muslim state to promulgate a constitution, which included a partially elected legislative assembly. The constitution was suspended the following year but reinstated in 1908, and it remained in force until the dissolution of the empire after World War I.

Mustafa Kemal Atatürk founded the modern republic of Turkey in 1923, after an extended revolt that he and other junior officers launched against the remnants of the Ottoman Empire and the Allied powers over the territorial concessions made in the Treaty of Sèvres following World War I. Atatürk was determined to have the new state catch up to its more modern Western neighbors and was convinced that doing so required removing the "backward" vestiges of its history, including all the trappings of the former empire and its state religion, Islam. He abolished the caliphate, disbanded all religious orders, discarded the Arabic alphabet for the Latinate, and introduced new, more modern forms of dress.[3] The new Turkish state was built on Kemalist principles, which included nationalism, secularism, republicanism, and revolutionary social change. However, because of limited state capacity, the state's zealous modernization drive never took deep root beyond the two major urban centers, Ankara and Izmir:

Despite massive reforms, secular Kemalism barely infiltrated Turkish society at large. The rural and pious masses of Anatolia remained largely unaffected by the cultural engineering in Ankara, in contrast to the military, the bureaucracy, and the urban bourgeoisie, who embraced or adapted to Kemalism's superficial Westernization.[4]

The government's attempts to modernize, secularize, and homogenize Turkish culture were opposed from the outset by both Islamists and the Kurds, and in 1923 and 1938, the government had to forcibly suppress rebellions by each group. The growing divisions between the two Turkeys—a Western-oriented urban ruling elite and the more traditional and devout residents of small towns and rural areas—have shaped the country's politics to the present day.

In 1924, the Grand National Assembly ratified a second constitution that vested sovereignty in the people rather than God. The people were represented by elected members of the assembly, which became the supreme organ of the state. In fact, Atatürk's Republican People's Party (CHP) dominated the assembly, which elected him president of the republic. The new state was an authoritarian, single-party regime that allowed broad personal freedoms but severely restricted any organizations involved in politics, from labor unions to voluntary associations.[5] When Atatürk died in 1938, he was succeeded by Prime Minister Mustafa Ismet İnönü.

The Move toward Multiparty Elections

In 1945, as World War II drew to an end, several parliamentarians within the CHP began to push for political reform. The issue came to a head during the course of a heated debate over a government-sponsored land reform bill. Four members of parliament resigned in opposition to the bill and, with the blessing and encouragement of President İnönü, formed their own Democratic Party (DP). The following year, in the country's first competitive multiparty elections, the Democratic Party won 62 of 465 seats, amid charges that the government had engaged in election fraud. In its new role as the opposition within the assembly, the Democratic Party made electoral reform its rallying cry. In 1950 a new electoral law was passed that addressed many of its demands, including judicial supervision of the electoral process, secret ballots, and a transparent procedure for counting votes.

In the May 1950 general election, the DP won 53.3 percent of the popular vote and secured 408 seats in the assembly to the CHP's meager

69 seats. Its support base included the more rural constituencies that had opposed Atatürk's modernization drive. The new assembly elected Celal Bayar, a former prime minister, as president and Adnan Menderes as prime minister. In power, the DP focused on economic development, seeking to diminish the state's dominance of the economy and encouraging entrepreneurship and international investment. It presided over the country's admission into NATO in 1952. In the 1954 general elections, the DP added to its parliamentary majority, securing 57 percent of the vote and 502 of 541 assembly seats. The party appears to have understood its electoral landslide as giving it license to govern as it wished (a phenomenon not uncommon in other parts of the world, including, most recently, Egypt). It rammed through the assembly a bill that included reform of the civil service and state-run enterprises, in spite of protests by the opposition of undemocratic behavior. It passed increasingly restrictive legislation limiting press freedoms and the rights of the opposition. An economic crisis caused at least in part by the party's overspending forced it to institute price controls and currency restrictions. It won the 1957 general elections but by a far slimmer margin, taking 48 percent of the vote and 424 seats; the CHP received 41 percent of the vote and 178 seats. That only encouraged the ruling DP to behave in a more dictatorial fashion. The country's economic woes continued, and the government was forced to devalue the currency sharply. When in early 1960 a group of "political thugs" affiliated with the DP attacked CHP leader Inönü and other members of his party on a trip through Central Anatolia, the government declared martial law. When students demonstrated in protest in Istanbul, the police fired on them, killing one and injuring forty others.

The Military Intervenes

A group of mid-level military officers, convinced that the DP had moved the country away from Kemalist principles, then initiated a bloodless coup. They arrested the DP leadership and established the Committee of National Unity (CNU) to govern in its place. Six hundred DP officials were put on trial, and all but 100 were convicted of crimes against the state. Menderes, the former prime minister, and two associates were hung; President Bayar's sentence was commuted to life in prison. A constituent assembly drafted a new constitution, which strengthened personal freedoms but also created a National Security Council that gave the military a formal role in policymaking. The following year elections were held, with fourteen parties taking part. As was to happen in subsequent coups, the voters failed to give the military what it wanted and expected.

The Justice Party (Adalet Partisi [AP]), which was widely recognized as the successor party to the now outlawed DP and which continued to draw support from the more rural and conservative areas of the country, garnered 158 seats in the lower house to the CHP's 173 seats and 70 seats in the new upper house to the CHP's 36 seats. Neither major party could forge a government on its own, so after protracted negotiations that included an agreement on clemency for former DP officials, the two formed a coalition government, with the aged Inönü brought back as president. In 1962, several army officers, incensed by the lenient treatment given to the former DP regime and by its renewed role in political life through the AP, staged a revolt in Ankara, which was quickly crushed by the military.

In the 1965 general election, the AP won a majority of the vote and formed its own government with the youthful Süleyman Demirel as prime minister. His government, which had the backing not only of the conservative peasantry but also the business establishment, focused on developing the private sector and attracting foreign investment, but it also allowed for more open religious expression. In the wake of its election loss, the CHP was forced to rethink its political program and aligned itself more explicitly as a social democratic party, supporting a greater state role in the economy, greater attention to the social safety net, and, as before, secularism. Changes to the electoral laws in the 1961 constitution that lowered the threshold for representation in parliament allowed for the emergence, on the extreme left, of the Turkish Workers' Party, which favored the nationalization of the economy and closer ties to the Soviet Union, and, on the extreme right, of the ultranationalist Republican Peasants' Nation Party (later the MHP), led by the fiery Alparslan Türkes, one of the organizers of the 1960 coup. The party's youth division included a paramilitary group known as the Gray Wolves that violently attacked left-wing student groups. Such acts of violence became increasingly commonplace as the political upheavals of the 1960s that swept the United States and Western Europe also engulfed Turkey.

The Demeril government, which was returned to office by voters in the 1969 general elections, failed to stem the rise in political violence. The 1960s saw increasing radicalization in Turkish society, as elsewhere, from the emergence of revolutionary workers' movements on the left to nationalist paramilitary groups on the right. Both extreme left- and right-wing groups became engaged in a spiral of violent acts that included murder, bombings, kidnapping, and bank robberies. There were bloody worker revolts in Istanbul and Kocaeli. Peasants encamped on private farmland.

In 1971 the senior military leadership, having learned of a plot by some of the more radical junior officers to overthrow the AP government, decided to act. Rather than instigating a coup, this time the military published a memorandum alleging that Demirel's government had driven the country toward anarchy and that unless a "strong and credible" government could be formed to replace it, the military would be obliged to intervene.[6] Demirel resigned and a government of technocrats was installed. The new government stabilized the security situation and made amendments to the constitution that curtailed certain civil liberties deemed responsible for the growth of political extremism. That paved the way for new elections in 1973, in which the CHP won by a narrow plurality over the DP. A series of brief, weak coalition governments ensued with the CHP's Mustafa Bülent Ecevit alternating with the DP's Demirel as prime minister.

The late 1970s saw the reemergence of both Kurdish and Islamist political activism. Extremist political violence also returned, along with terrorism, but this time on a far larger scale. More than 5,000 people from all walks of life died in the escalating violence, which even the imposition of martial law failed to stem.[7] When in 1980 the two major parties remained deadlocked for six months over the choice of the next president, the military stepped in. The generals oversaw the rewriting of the constitution to place further restrictions on individual rights, strengthen the position of the National Security Council, and move the country toward a two-party political system.

In 1983, in the first post-coup elections, the new center-right Motherland Party won a plurality of the vote and the political maverick Turgut Özal, its founder, was named prime minister.[8] In many respects, his party drew from the same political base and shared the same ideological orientation as the now banned Justice Party and the Democratic Party before it. Özal redirected Turkish economic policy from import substitution toward exports, which spurred an economic revival, most notably in central Anatolia.

The prosperity of the 1980s soon gave way to the stagnation of the 1990s—what many have termed the "lost decade." The end of the cold war brought identity politics back to the forefront, pitting Kurds against Turks and Islamists against secularists. The PKK (Kurdistan Workers' Party) waged a full-scale insurgency in the southeast of the country, which was in part a response to the military's ban on the use of the Kurdish language and other cultural symbols and its brutal security measures.[9] Özal's government responded to the insurgency with an even harsher military campaign that depopulated entire villages and claimed the lives of many innocent civilians. Toward the end of his term, Özal, recognizing that military measures alone were not going to end the conflict, began to seek some sort of political accommodation. However, he died in 1993 and his successor, Tansu Çiller, returned to a strictly military approach to the conflict. Only with the capture of PKK leader Abdullah Öcalan in 1999 did the 16-year insurgency come to an end. Nonetheless, it did not resolve the Kurdish issue, which continues to haunt Turkish political leaders to this day.

The Rise of the Islamists

In 1994, the pro-Islamist Welfare Party, led by Necmettin Erbakan, won a stunning victory in the country's local elections, gaining control of the mayoralties of Istanbul and Ankara. The party was the ideological successor to the National Order Party and the National Salvation Party, both of which had been previously banned. The following year, in general elections, the Welfare Party, with the help of Kurdish voters, narrowly edged out the Motherland Party, receiving 21 percent of the vote. The Welfare Party forged a coalition with Çiller's True Path Party, and Erbakan became prime minister.

His tenure was brief. The military, convinced that secularism and the country's Western alliances were at risk, sought to force Erbakan out. The National Security Council presented the government with eighteen demands to limit the influence of political Islam. It mounted an "education campaign" in which key societal leaders were brought in for briefings on the Welfare Party and the risks posed by political Islam. With pressure from the military and the public mounting, the Erbakan government resigned just a year into its term and the Welfare Party was subsequently banned by the military.[10]

Rather than moving underground or turning to violence as other Islamist parties in more authoritarian settings have done, a younger generation of leaders began to steer the Islamist movement in a more pragmatic direction. After the Welfare Party's successor, the Virtue Party, was banned in 2001, Recep Tayyip Erdogan, who had served as mayor of Istanbul, formed the Justice and Development Party (AKP) as a "conservative democratic" party. The party's platform emphasized EU membership and social services to the poor. In the 2002 parliamentary elections, the AKP, which won 34 percent of the vote and two-thirds of the seats, became the governing party, with Erdogan as prime minister.[11] Its support appears to have come not just from the pious, the poor, and the provincial but also from a new class of wealthy Anatolian businessmen who had benefited from the country's export economy and from ordinary Turks who were fed up with the secular elite establishment. The previous year the country had experienced the most difficult financial crisis in its history, and wary foreign investors had withdrawn their capital, threatening the country's overly leveraged banks with insolvency. Only a rigorous economic stabilization program with the backing of international financial institutions helped save the country from economic collapse.

The AKP proved itself to be competent and pragmatic in governing the country. It implemented a broad range of reforms in the judiciary, in civil-military relations, and in human rights practices in order to qualify the country for membership in the European Union. It made food and housing, health care, educational grants, and basic infrastructure more available to poorer communities while enhancing minority rights. More important, it continued to nurse the Turkish economy back to health. Between 2002 and 2011, the economy grew at an average rate of 7.5 percent a year and the average personal income rose commensurately, from $2,800 per capita to around $10,000 per capita a year.[12]

In 2007, Erdogan's nomination of Abdullah Gul—the foreign minister and a cofounder with Erdogan of the AKP—as Turkey's next president brought tensions with secularists and the military to a boil. The CHP boycotted the vote in the assembly. The Constitutional Court was asked to rule on the constitutionality of the nomination, but the generals did not wait. In what has been described as an "e-coup," they posted on their official website a message warning that they were prepared to defend secularism if necessary. The court followed with its own decision a few days later, which put a halt to the nomination process.[13] Erdogan persevered. In keeping with the constitution, he called for early elections to resolve the deadlock. In the meantime, the AKP dismissed 160 parliamentarians and replaced them with individuals intended to appeal to diverse constituencies. Voters sided with the AKP in the dispute, increasing its share of the vote in parliamentary elections from 34 percent to 47 percent. Gul went on to be confirmed by parliament as president.[14]

The AKP has now been in power for more than a decade. In the most recent parliamentary elections, in June 2011, it increased its share of the vote yet again, to 50 percent. It charted a new, more muscular foreign policy for Turkey that made its leaders widely popular in the region and the broader Muslim world. Having successfully weathered the global economic downturn, the country was posting 8 percent to 9 percent economic growth rates until the turmoil in Syria and internal unrest slowed the economy. Along the way, the AKP has succeeded in reducing the military's influence in politics. In July 2011, the military chief of staff resigned following a dispute with Erdogan over staff promotions; the same day, the chiefs of all the branches of the armed forces requested early retirement. A half-year later, a number of top admirals and generals were jailed for allegedly plotting to overthrow the government.[15]

The AKP's very success has heightened concerns about the future of Turkish democracy. Like any party that has remained in power for a long time, it has begun to overreach. In recent years, it has been criticized for clamping down on its critics in the media, infringing on human rights, and limiting freedom of expression. It has failed to try to find a political solution to the Kurdish question or to modernize the constitution, as it promised.[16] Critics claim that it has used the EU accession process as a means of sidelining the military.[17] Fear grows that without a strong military in place to uphold Kemalist secularism and civil society still emergent, the AKP will use its dominant position to impose an Islamist agenda. The commitment of Erdogan and his colleagues to democracy is still questioned, even after decades of participation in a parliamentary democracy. Fears were only heightened by Erdogan's brutal crackdown on demonstrators in Taksim Square in June 2013. Erdogan weathered a summer of massive protests throughout Turkey, but in December 2013, his government became embroiled in a extensive corruption scandal that forced four top ministers to resign and threatened Erdogan's own future as prime minister.

Conclusion

The story of Turkish democratization is a long and seemingly success-ful one, although the storyline could change. Much depends on how the AKP chooses to govern going forward. Will it continue to behave as a pragmatic, socially conservative governing party, a model for the rest of the Muslim world of how Islam and democracy can accommodate each other? Or, with the military weakened, will it seize the opportunity to push for a stronger Islamist agenda, forcefully imposing its supporters' religious views on the whole of society and running roughshod over the country's secular constitution? If the latter proves to be the case, how will Turkey's increasingly vibrant civil society respond?

Turkey's armed forces often are singled out as a model of the role that militaries can play in safeguarding democratic transitions. However, the history of the Turkish military's involvement in politics is ambiguous. It seems to have done far more to retard the country's democratic develop-ment than to advance it. What Atatürk sought to do following World

War I was to build a modern, homogenous, secular, and cohesive nation-state out of the remnants of a failed multinational empire. As admirable as that ideal may have been, the reality was that Turkish society was deeply religious and ethnically heterogeneous. The Turkish state never possessed the capacity to impose secularism on a society that was deeply resistant to it or to strip Kurds of their culture and history and make them Turkish. The more that it tried to do so by means of force, the more it undermined its own legitimacy.

Atatürk's policies created two Turkeys: an urban, modern elite that embraced his secularist and modernizing vision and a more rural, traditional, pious, and conservative class that fiercely opposed it and therefore tended to live beyond the reach of the state. As the country moved toward multiparty elections, the latter group overwhelmingly supported parties that were anti-establishment. Fearful that those parties were not acting in the interest of the nation, the military shut them down, one after another. The Democratic Party was first, followed by the Justice Party, the Motherland Party, and, among the Islamist parties, the National Order Party, the National Salvation Party, the Welfare Party, and finally the Virtue Party. But it found, just as it found with the Kurds, that it cannot crush an idea by force. When one party was banned, another would arise to fill the political vacuum. The military's extensive engagement in political life inhibited the development of civil society as an alternative counterweight to the excesses of the party in power, while radicalizing and militarizing marginal groups.

Indonesia

A "latecomer to democracy" during the Third Wave, Indonesia has made important strides toward consolidating democracy over the last dozen years, even as it still faces significant challenges to realizing that goal. Strongman General Suharto ruled Indonesia—which has the world's largest Muslim population—for more than three decades, in effect from 1966 to 1998. Welcomed initially for rescuing Indonesia from the chaos of his predecessor Sukarno's final years in office and for placing the country on a path toward unprecedented economic growth, over time Suharto faced growing challenges to his rule from within society. He deftly parried a number of those challenges until the Asian financial crisis of 1997 sent the economy into a tailspin. In the face of massive public demonstrations, he eventually was forced to resign. His successor organized Indonesia's first free and fair elections, and, to the surprise of many outsiders, power has rotated peacefully among different political parties ever since, although many of the legacies of the Suharto period—a powerful military establishment, patronage politics, and entrenched corruption—continue to haunt the country.[18]

The Suharto Years

In the mid-1990s, few could have foreseen that democracy would be even a remote possibility in this sprawling, ethnically heterogeneous archipelago nation, which includes 17,508 islands. For 32 years, General Suharto had been entrenched as president, gradually consolidating his authoritarian control of the country's politics, society, and economy. He came to power in the mid-1960s following one of the darkest chapters in Indonesia's history. In 1965, a shadowy left-wing group within the military attempted to take power, assassinating six generals and occupying key government facilities. Suharto, the commander of the army, was able to thwart the attempted coup, and he proceeded to purge Indonesia of leftist elements. An estimated half-million Communist Party supporters were killed in the ensuing violence, effectively eliminating the party as a rival to the military. Suharto then instigated a creeping military coup of his own against the country's first post-independence leader, President Sukarno, whose policies had been taking the country in a decidedly leftward direction. Over the course of several years, Suharto gradually eased Sukarno from power, culminating with Suharto's election by acclamation as president in March 1968.[19]

Suharto ruled with a strong hand. Military personnel assumed key posts in the cabinet, parliament, and central and regional governments of his New Order regime, although they often worked alongside civilian technocrats. Suharto transformed Golkar, an umbrella organization of anticommunist groups, into an ostensibly non-ideological, development-focused political party to serve as his electoral vehicle. With branches throughout Indonesian society and significant state resources at its disposal, Golkar routinely delivered the regime 60 to 70 percent of the vote in parliamentary elections. All other political parties were forced to merge into just two: the United Development Party, representing the Islamists, and the Indonesian Democratic Party, representing the nationalists, including remnants of Sukarno's former party.

Other social and economic organizations within society were forced to consolidate in similar fashion into large, government-endorsed corporatist entities. The press was tightly controlled and occasionally banned. Vast patronage networks secured the support of key constituencies throughout society. Government-encouraged corruption greased the skids at both the national and local levels, giving elites a stake in the system. Other potential troublemakers—students, Muslim activists, trade unionists, and dispossessed peasants—were silenced through outright repression. Torture was commonplace. Government repression was especially severe in Aceh, Papua, and East Timor, whose residents had separatist sentiments.[20] As one expert observed, government propaganda made social harmony paramount, stressing that individual and group interests must be subordinated to the national interest: "All forms of division, and political opposition in particular, were labeled inimical to the Indonesian national character."[21]

All the while, Suharto maintained the pretense of abiding by formal constitutional processes. Parliamentary elections, for instance, were dutifully held every five years.[22] However, the playing field was so tilted in favor of Suharto's Golkar Party—through its control of state media, limitations on opposition political parties, generous patronage and opportunities for graft, and outright ballot manipulation—that the results were foreordained. Furthermore, the constitutional rules allotted about a fifth of the seats in the lower house of parliament to the military and to regime-appointed Golkar loyalists, while the upper house, which elected the president, was composed completely of Golkar regional officials, ensuring that the party's continued control was never in jeopardy.

Despite rampant corruption, the Indonesian economy experienced robust growth throughout most of Suharto's reign. With the support of Western donors, Japan, and the World Bank, his regime implemented a series of five-year economic development plans that halted the hyperinflation of Sukarno's time, spurred investment, and developed key productive sectors—first agriculture, then the processing of raw materials, and finally manufacturing. In the first three decades of Suharto's rule, economic growth averaged a hearty 7 percent a year and per capita income surpassed $1,000 a year (more than triple the amount in 1965), vaulting Indonesia into the ranks of the newly industrializing countries (NICs).[23] Fueling that growth in part was a boom in oil prices.

The military and its Indonesian-Chinese business partners were the immediate beneficiaries. The business sector shared with the military "profits in exchange for licenses, special privileges, and protection when illegal activity was involved." Eventually, however, the benefits were felt more widely throughout society, thereby arguably creating the conditions for the regime's eventual downfall. A commercial middle class emerged, albeit one built largely on rent seeking. Expanded educational opportunities helped produce a new generation more interested in entrepreneurship than government sinecures and more critical than their parents of the corruption and repression of the regime.[24]

The Emergence of an Opposition

Signs of dissent first began to appear in the late 1960s. Many intellectuals, journalists, and students who had participated in or at least supported Suharto's ascent to power became concerned by the increasing corruption and unlawful behavior of government officials. Their criticisms were couched as efforts to "save" Suharto and his New Order from the graft and mismanagement that had enveloped the regime. A group of former New Order student activists called for an election boycott following the rigged 1971 elections. In 1974, students protested the visit of the Japanese premier, whose country's exports were seen to be hurting local merchants. The protests quickly transformed into wider riots throughout Jakarta, then into pogroms against the Chinese because of their dominant role in the economy. The government clamped down hard, arresting several hundred people and closing down twelve publications. Further student protests around the 1977 elections led to more crackdowns, including military occupation of university campuses and the banishing of many student-run organizations.[25] In 1980, in a sharply worded statement that became known as the "Petition of Fifty," a group of former government officials and generals criticized Suharto and called for greater political openness and reform. The signatories were promptly ostracized by the regime, stripped of their access to employment, business licenses, bank credit, and travel documents and banned from the media. Nonetheless, many of them gathered for a weekly "working group," unhindered by the government, where they drafted reform proposals that they shared with government ministers.[26]

As authoritarian restrictions increased in the 1980s, many regime opponents retreated into civil society rather than confront the regime directly. They engaged in such seemingly apolitical activities as supporting cultural, educational, and economic development (an approach similar to that taken toward the end of Mubarak's Egypt). By 1996, more than 8,000 nonprofit organizations were operating within the country.[27] The NGO sector was left relatively unfettered to engage in certain kinds of social and community action—for example, assisting less privileged segments of society. Among other things, students and activists ventured into the countryside to help "empower" rural workers and communities. Groups like the Indonesian Legal Aid Institute assisted them in fighting efforts by the Suharto regime and its cronies to seize their lands and despoil the environment.[28] These organizations introduced "new ways of thinking about social, economic, and political change" and enabled new kinds of "political imagining."[29]

The economic boom brought on by the spike in oil prices dampened dissent by raising living standards and expanding the resources that Suharto had at his disposal to distribute as patronage. It brought large numbers of Indonesians into the middle class, but most remained politically quiescent, dependent as they were on government sector jobs or connections for their livelihood. The growth in export-oriented manufacturing in the early 1990s created a new industrial working class. At the same time, agribusiness and state-run development projects in the countryside were pushing peasants off the land, creating a marginalized, dispossessed rural poor that mirrored and shared the grievances of a growing dispossessed urban poor of "marginal traders, unemployed youth, petty criminals, [and] newly arrived villagers." In addition, a new generation of academy-trained military officers was coming of age, one that had not shared with Suharto the experience of fighting in the country's struggle against the Dutch for independence. Those officers were acutely aware that they had neither the perquisites nor the influence accorded their predecessors, which increasingly went to members of Suharto's own family and senior civilian bureaucrats.[30]

As the 1980s closed, a process of political opening was gradually set in motion. The period saw the reemergence of student protests as well as other forms of popular dissent. Some civil society groups shifted from focusing on empowerment to focusing on advocacy—organizing demonstrations on such issues as river pollution, golf course construction, and the regime's treatment of labor activists. At the same time, fissures were appearing within the regime. Suharto, who was now in his 60s, had yet to designate a successor or create a succession plan, and the question inevitably surfaced of what would happen when he was no longer able to serve as president. Various regime factions began jockeying for position.

In June 1989, in a bid to deflect mounting public anger as well as win support for their side, several military representatives within the parliament began speaking openly about succession and the need for political reform. Suharto publicly countered that he would "clobber" anyone who dared to challenge his rule, but in a move calculated to outflank his military critics, he embraced the call for greater openness as his own. The regime announced a loosening of press controls. Soon the media were reporting on subjects that had long been taboo, most notably the collusion, corruption, and nepotism of the Suharto family and the regime in general. "Petition of 50" members were rehabilitated, and their views and reform proposals became prominently featured in the press.

Suharto followed this opening with an effort to court Islamists. It was a strategic about-face that caught even regime insiders by surprise. As the world's most populous Muslim country and home to two of the largest Muslim membership organizations in the world (Nahdlatul Ulama and Muhammidyah), Indonesia had from independence accorded Islam an important role in public life. However, unlike in many other parts of the Muslim world, Islam had come to Indonesia, as late as the thirteenth century, by way of seafaring traders rather than conquest. Consequently, the version of Islam that prevailed in Indonesia was syncretic in character, reflecting a fusion of Muhammad's teachings with indigenous cultural practices. It leaned toward the mystical, as represented by Sufism, instead of the more literal forms practiced by the Deobandis or Wahhabis. In 1945, as a means of uniting the nation's diverse islands, peoples, and cultures through mutual toleration, President Sukarno had proclaimed a founding ideology for the new state, called Pancasila. Its principles included belief in one god, the unity of Indonesia, the dignity of every human being, decisionmaking through consensus, and social justice. In this new state, the traditional *ulama,* or Muslim religious authorities, were accorded due deference, provided funding by the state, and allowed to perform their religious functions, albeit under the watchful eye of state authorities. Political Islamists—those who advocated the creation of an Islamic state or a global Islamic caliphate—received altogether different treatment. Under Sukarno, the Indonesian military had cracked down on Islamist groups as part of a more thorough purge of regime opponents. Suharto had kept a similarly tight lid on Islamist activities, forcing many groups underground. His destruction of the communist and leftist factions in the mid-1960s had left the Islamists, in his view, as the most powerful challengers to his rule.

Facing public unrest and needing allies, he now sought to accommodate the Islamists. A key step was the creation in 1990 of a new Islamic organization, the Indonesian Muslim Intellectuals' Association (ICMI), at whose inaugural event Suharto presided. ICMI quickly drew a mass following of urban, middle-class Muslims, particularly among state employees.[31] Islamist leaders welcomed the dramatic change in policy, which for the first time gave them influence in state decisionmaking and access to state resources. Most abandoned their past opposition to the regime and began to reorient their activities toward working within the system.

Suharto was soon appointing Islamists to key positions within the state bureaucracy and the military. All of this alarmed more nationalist elements within the military, who had long regarded Islamization as one of the main threats to state security.

During this period of openness, Sukarnoputri Megawati emerged as the most important opposition figure. The daughter of Sukarno, Megawati had been elected to the national legislature in 1987. She now campaigned openly for leadership of the Indonesian Democratic Party (PDI), the successor to her father's political party, and was met everywhere she went by large, enthusiastic crowds. The regime sought to disrupt the 1993 party convention at which the leadership vote was held, but its ham-handed efforts to undermine Megawati only boosted her popularity. As party leader, she forged a tacit alliance with Abdurrahman Wahid, the head of Nahdlatul Ulama, a revered traditionalist religious scholar and a frequent regime critic. Her demands on the stump were modest: that the PDI be allowed to be a truly independent political party and that the regime adhere to the constitution. By 1996, her public popularity had grown so great that party members were floating the idea of making Megawati the party's candidate for the presidency.[32]

In response, the regime engineered a leadership coup within the PDI. Regional party leaders were pressured into calling for an extraordinary party congress in 1996, at which Megawati was replaced as party chief. Her supporters took to the streets of Jakarta in protest, then staged a month-long vigil in front of party headquarters. The regime sent in troops to disperse the crowd. About 100 people were injured in the confrontation, and 50 were arrested. A series of nationwide protests ensued, and riots broke out in Eastern Jakarta.[33] Suharto ordered a massive security crackdown. The following days saw protesters engaged in running battles with police in the Jakarta streets. The regime denounced Megawati's supporters on television as communists intent on overthrowing the regime. Security forces raided scores of NGO offices and arrested several hundred activists. Some were tortured; fourteen were tried for subversion and given lengthy prison sentences. Restrictions on the press, which had begun to be reintroduced in 1994, were increased. The regime's experiment with openness was over.[34]

Suharto was successful at the time in tamping down dissent for several reasons. First, the military remained united behind him. He had taken great pains in the early 1990s to remove his more ardent critics from leadership positions and replace them with loyalists, so that while divisions within the military remained, the top brass stood behind him in this crisis. Second, the opposition was divided. The Islamists, heartened by the privileged position that they now enjoyed in the Suharto regime, stood on the sidelines as the protests mushroomed. Third, the opposition proved timid. The regime's strategy of tolerating limited pluralism meant that many of its critics maintained a stake in the existing system. Taking a position of semi-opposition, many were wary of running risks during uncertain times, which could cost them their status and state-provided resources. Also, having bargained and maneuvered within the Suharto system for so long, they were less familiar with how to take on the system itself and perhaps had difficulty imagining a future Indonesia without Suharto at the helm. That was certainly true of the opposition's most prominent leader, Megawati, who throughout the crisis was unwilling to call on her supporters to mobilize against the regime. The influential religious scholar Abdurrahman Wahid was soon reconciling with Suharto's regime, fearful that further opposition risked having Nahdlatul Ulama passed over for state resources in favor of the Islamists.

With his opponents silenced and the PDI split, Suharto's Golkar Party cruised to easy victory in the May 1997 parliamentary elections. Amid widespread vote rigging, the regime claimed that it won almost 75 percent of the vote.[35] Suharto would later appoint B. J. Habibie, one of the founders of ICMI, as his new vice president, further alienating nationalist elements within the military.

The Regime Collapses

Two months after the elections, the Thai baht collapsed, setting in motion the Asian financial crisis. Indonesia's economy, which resembled Thailand's in that a number of large, inefficient, but politically connected firms had taken on large amounts of foreign-denominated debt, was soon under intense financial pressure. As international investors withdrew funds, the exchange rate for the Indonesian rupiah (Rp) plunged from Rp 2,400 to the U.S. dollar in mid-1997 to Rp 17,000 by January 1998. Economic growth fell from a robust 8 percent in 1996 to negative 14 percent in 1998. Prices soared, and more than a million people eventually lost their jobs.[36]

In September 1997, Indonesia was forced to accept International Monetary Fund (IMF) oversight as the price of a rescue package. The pro-market reforms demanded by the IMF targeted many of the regime's patronage networks, shuttering the inefficient, monopolistic banks and enterprises run by Suharto's cronies. Suharto tried to evade the most stringent IMF conditions, but when in January 1998 financial markets hit bottom in response to his proposed annual budget, he had no choice but to relent.[37] As he commenced his seventh presidential term in March 1998, student protests began to gather steam. In late February, two major demonstrations took place on campuses of the University of Indonesia, then quickly spread to universities throughout the country. This time, Islamist student groups also took part. Within a month, the protests had reached beyond university campuses, as members of the middle class—university administrators, opposition leaders, NGOs, and artists—joined the students. In May, when the government raised fuel and electricity prices in accordance with the IMF's demands, more violent protests ensued. In several cities, clashes with police provoked rioting. As the momentum for change built, several prominent leaders—including the heads of the Indonesian Association of Muslim Intellectuals and Muhammadiyah—now called for Suharto to resign.

Then police opened fire on a student demonstration at Jakarta's elite Trisakti University. Two days of bloody rioting in Jakarata ensued, and once again the city's ethnic Chinese community was the principal target. Businesses were looted and set on fire, and nearly 1,200 people lost their lives in the mayhem. The Suharto regime, which had staked its legitimacy on its ability to develop the country and maintain order, was now thoroughly discredited. The country was convulsed by massive demonstrations. Students occupied the parliament building. At that point, the regime leadership itself finally began to crack. Both the speaker of the house and the vice president advised Suharto that it was time to step down.[38]

A Democratic Opening

Suharto finally did so on May 21, 1998, and he was succeeded by vice president B. J. Habibie. The latter wisely recognized that he lacked popular legitimacy and announced that his term would end as soon as elections could be held. With Habibie assuming a caretaker role, calm was finally restored and preparations were made for the country's first competitive elections in half a century, which took place in June 1999.

The voting was split among a number of parties. Megawati's PDI won a plurality of the vote (34 percent), followed by Golkar (22 percent), Abdurrahman Wahid's National Awakening Party (PKB) (nearly 13 percent), the United Development Party (PPP) (11 percent), and Amien Rais's National Mandate Party (PAN) (7 percent). That left Megawati in the strongest position to form a government, but she refused to court other party leaders aggressively. In a series of backroom deals, Wahid ended up cobbling together enough votes to be named Indonesia's first post-Suharto president. Despite his considerable political acumen, Wahid had little management experience or skill. Moreover, he lacked a cohesive base of support from which to govern. During his brief tenure as president, his erratic behavior alienated his coalition partners and the public.[39] In February 2001, the parliament launched impeachment proceedings against him after it was found that he had misused government funds and taken loans from the Sultan of Brunei to buy off religious leaders in the restive province of Aceh. He was dismissed in July 2001, and Megawati, as vice president, succeeded him.[40]

Her own presidency suffered from many of the same weaknesses. Like Wahid, she had little relevant management experience to draw on. Also like Wahid, she created a large cabinet, incorporating all the major political parties, that was so inclusive that it proved difficult to get anything done. She often appeared tentative, even disinterested, and was poor at communicating to the public her administration's objectives and accomplishments.[41] Yet during her tenure, the parliament did pass a number of important constitutional amendments and legislative reforms, including an amendment allowing for the direct election of the president.[42]

Yudhoyono's Election

In 2004, in the country's first direct presidential election, retired General Susilo Bambang Yudhoyono roundly defeated Megawati in a runoff (61 percent to 39 percent). A highly respected professional soldier, Yudhoyono had been a part of the military's nationalist faction and had served as a minister under Wahid and Megawati. Unlike his immediate predecessors, he was a very effective communicator on television and used his popular appeal with voters to catapult himself into the presidency, circumventing the need to build an elaborate party organization. That posed a challenge in governing, however, as his new Democratic Party captured only 7.5 percent of the parliamentary vote. Yudhoyono chose as his vice president the businessman Jusuf Kalla, who won the chairmanship of the Golkar Party in December 2004. Like his predecessors, Yudhoyono found that the need to bring other parties into his governing coalition limited his room for maneuver.

Nonetheless, Yudhoyono did record some important achievements during his first term. He became known not for bold or radical reforms but for cautious, incremental changes that helped move the country forward—although without threatening the entrenched interests of the military or Golkar. He continued to edge the military out of politics. He implemented a new law that allowed for the direct election of regional governors and district heads. Together with his vice president, he secretly negotiated a deal that ended the secessionist revolt in Aceh. And his administration prosecuted a number of corruption cases against senior officials, although rarely the most senior.[43]

Yudhoyona remained highly popular among the Indonesian public and handily won reelection in 2009 (securing 61 percent of the vote to 27 percent for Megawati). His second term has been less impressive than his first. After campaigning on the promise of eliminating corruption, his Democratic Party has been racked by financial scandals. The party's treasurer was sentenced to nearly five years in prison in 2012 on charges of graft. He accused others within the party, including its chairman, of being complicit. The minister of youth resigned after being charged with corruption. With elections looming in 2014, Yudhoyono is increasingly viewed as a weak and irresolute leader.[44]

Conclusion

Indonesia's transition to democracy has been a surprising success, but significant challenges remain. The "corruption, collusion, and nepotism" that protesters condemned during Suharto's rule remain in place today. Governance remains poor and patrimonial forms of political behavior persist. The military, while no longer an active participant in day-to-day politics, continues to be a powerful force and could yet choose to intervene in what is still a fragile democracy. With Wahhabi influence on the rise in the region, Islamization could yet pose a threat. The various secessionist conflicts that erupted at the time of Suharto's fall have been largely resolved. The devolution of many government functions to the regional and local level has diminished secessionist sentiment, but in a nation as heterogeneous as Indonesia, particularist ethnic or regional tensions could yet flare again. In just a dozen years, Indonesia has come a remarkably long way in its transition to democracy, but its democracy remains fragile at best.

The weaknesses of Indonesia's democracy today may be the very reason for its success in making it this far, this fast.[45] Unlike in other countries in transition, Indonesia's post-Suharto leaders chose not to draw a sharp line between its authoritarian past and its democratic present. Because the tentacles of the Suharto regime reached so deeply into every aspect of Indonesian society that everyone was compromised, that was an understandable approach, but it had consequences. Former political and military leaders have not been arraigned for crimes committed during the Suharto regime, and the pervasive corruption of the period has not been investigated. In fact, many of the patrimonial practices adopted by the Suharto regime continue to this day. The military has retained its privileged position within the Indonesian state. Indonesia's transition to democracy "appeared to be the work of a coalition of anyone and everyone."[46] Because of that, Indonesia's new democracy, for all its accomplishments, retains many aspects of the old regime.

Malaysia

Just several hundred miles north of Indonesia, across the South China Sea, Malaysia also faced political challenges to its semi-authoritarian regime during the Asian financial crisis. Unlike in Indonesia, however, the crisis did not upend the existing political order. After more than a half-century of rule, the United Malays National Organization (UMNO) Party continues to dominate the country's political life. However, UMNO faces growing challenges, namely from the opposition leader Anwar Ibrahim and his coalition partners. They failed to unseat UMNO in the most recent general election, but only because electoral gerrymandering that affords greater political weight to rural areas continues to favor the Malay-dominated ruling party. The days of one-party rule in Malaysia seem numbered.

Post-Independence Malaysia

Malaysia remains a curious political hybrid, as it has been since its independence from Great Britain in 1957. On paper, the country is a constitutional monarchy with a parliamentary democracy, and it adopted many aspects of the British political system. The role of monarch, the titular head of state, rotates among the hereditary sultans of the country's peninsular states. The monarch's powers were limited and were scaled back further in the 1980s. The judiciary once enjoyed considerable independence, but its autonomy has been curtailed significantly over the years, including its exercise of the power of judicial review. The parliament, which is elected at least once every five years, appoints the prime minister, who, along with a cabinet, exercises executive authority. Dozens of parties have competed over the years for seats in parliament.

The electoral system, however, greatly favors the United Malays National Organization Party, which in coalition with other parties has ruled the country since independence. Opposition parties regularly win up to a third of the vote but rarely more because the rules of the game are heavily stacked against them. Rural constituencies, in which the Malay—an Austronesian ethnic group prevalent on the Malay peninsula and the adjoining islands of Southeast Asia—predominate, are accorded greater representation than urban constituencies. First-past-the-post election rules also favor the Malay majority. UMNO fully exploits the powers of incumbency, using government jobs, contracts, and projects to reward supporters, and because UMNO and its business supporters own most of the radio and television stations and newspapers, it dominates the media. Licensing rules make it difficult for others to compete. Outdoor public rallies were banned in 1974, although the rules have been relaxed since. Forms of political participation besides voting are generally discouraged. Associations and other nongovernmental organizations are allowed, but they are monitored and restricted. Labor unions are permitted but only on a company basis; they are prohibited from organizing across an industry.[47]

In addition, government controls strictly limit oppositional activities. The government has declared a national state of emergency on two occasions: after ethnic riots in 1964 and 1969. The 1969 emergency ordinance was never rescinded, leaving the government with far-reaching powers that it can exercise at will in the name of maintaining order, including the power to detain suspects indefinitely without trial. The government has also issued state-level emergency decrees on two occasions when opposition parties won control of state governments. The Internal Security Act, which was introduced soon after independence to combat a communist insurgency and remains in force today, allows for detention without trial for reasons of "national security." The Sedition Act and Official Secrets Act limit public criticism and the discussion of sensitive political topics.

Malaysia is an ethnically diverse state in a strategically important but vulnerable location in the South China Sea, which has meant that the country has always placed a premium on stability. Today, just over half the population (50.4 percent) is Malay, about a quarter (23.7 percent) is Chinese, about a tenth is indigenous (11 percent), and slightly less (7.1 percent) is Indian; the remainder (7.8 percent) includes a mix of other ethnicities.[48] The country's racial divisions are reinforced by religious differences: the Malay are required by law to be Muslim; the Chinese are mostly Buddhist, Confucian, and Taoist, although a small proportion are Christian; and the Indians are Hindu. Ethnic and religious divisions are further deepened by differences in language.

Prior to independence in 1957, Malay elites dominated colonial institutions—the bureaucracy, police, and armed forces—while ethnic

Chinese and, to a lesser extent, ethnic Indians dominated the economy. Malay elites struck a deal with their Chinese and Indian counterparts: in return for equal citizenship rights, substantial autonomy for the peninsular states, and protection of the economic interests of minority communities, continuing Malay political dominance would be guaranteed. After independence, Malay elites, as represented by UMNO, joined with the Malaysian Chinese Association (MCA) and the Malaysian Indian Congress (MIC) to form the Alliance Party to compete in national elections. Reconstituted in 1973 as the Barisan Nasional (BN), the UMNO-led coalition, with the addition of other parties, has dominated Malaysian politics since independence.

In 1963, what had been the Federation of Malaya became, with the addition of Singapore, Sabah, and Sarawak, the Federation of Malaysia. The new arrangement did not last long. Singapore's inclusion upset the delicate demographic balance by making the Chinese, with 42 percent of the population, the largest ethnic group at the time. Lee Kuan Yew, the prime minister of Singapore, courted ethnic Chinese on the Malay Peninsula with a campaign for a "Malaysian Malaysia"—a Malaysia in which the Malay were not dominant. Amid heightened intercommunal tension, Singapore was kicked out of the federation in 1965.[49] Intercommunal tension spiked again in 1969. At a time when Malays were feeling economically marginalized and non-Malays were concerned about their political rights within the federation, non-Malay and Islamist opposition parties registered their strongest electoral gains yet, particularly at the state level. In the 1969 general elections, the Barisan Nasional/Alliance share of the nationwide vote fell below 50 percent for the first time. Non-Malays staged exuberant celebrations in the capital, Kuala Lumpur. UMNO held its own counter-rally the following day, which degenerated into anti-Chinese riots that eventually left 196 dead.[50]

UMNO Retrenches

The election proved a watershed moment in Malaysian politics. The government declared a state of emergency and suspended parliament. To address Malay economic grievances, it launched the New Economic Policy (NEP) to reduce poverty and improve economic opportunities for the Malay. The Malay had been disproportionately agrarian; the aim of the new policy was, through education, workplace quotas, and business concessions, to integrate them fully into the modern sectors of the economy. Thereafter the state played a more interventionist role in the economy as well as the political system, which became increasingly authoritarian.[51]

The NEP and subsequent economic policies made Malaysia the quint-essential developmental state. The regime turned its attention to fostering economic growth and staked its legitimacy on its success in doing so. The state invested in export manufacturing and undertook ambitious infrastructure projects. Particularly during the long tenure of Mahathir Mohamad as prime minister, which ran from 1981 to 2003, Malaysia became renowned for its stellar economic performance. Under Mahathir, the economy grew, on average, 6.2 percent a year[52] and the number of Malaysians living in poverty fell from 35 percent to 5 percent.[53] Economic success helped reduce intercommunal tensions and helped ensure that the population remained politically quiescent.

Even as the regime became increasingly authoritarian under Mahathir, it continued to hold regular elections, which had important consequences. First, elections served as a kind of release valve that helped to mitigate radical political tendencies. While the system was heavily stacked against opposition parties, they were able to win seats in parliament and even capture state-level offices, which gave them an incentive to work within rather than outside the system. Second, elections provided a mechanism of accountability in an otherwise top-down system. The fact that the regime regularly had to compete in elections forced it to be more respon-sive to the public. While corruption and patronage politics were rife, they never reached the levels found in many other autocracies. UMNO was at considerable pains not to repeat the 1969 election debacle, which meant it focused on performance.

As in Indonesia, economic growth and expanded educational oppor-tunities brought a rising urban middle class. This middle class, however, was often divided along communal lines, which diminished its weight as a political force. Nonetheless, with the growth of the middle class, a broad range of nongovernmental organizations came into existence, many of which were noncommunal in their orientation and focused on deepening democracy in Malaysia. Also as in Indonesia, Islamism became an important phenomenon, beginning in the 1970s. The largest Islamist party is the Pan-Malaysian Islamic Party (PAS). In 1973, UMNO brought PAS into the new Barisan Nasional governing coalition in an effort to co-opt it, but the party left in 1978. It has been one of the main Malay opposition parties ever since. The regime has consciously adopted a more Islamic face over the years as a way of neutralizing the threat posed by political Islam. Islamic banking practices were introduced, and Islam was integrated more fully into school curricula and state television program-ming.[54] In addition, in 1983 Mahathir brought into his government one of the leading Islamist youth activists, Anwar Ibrahim, who eventually became deputy prime minister—again as a way of co-opting the perceived threat from Islamists.[55]

PAS, as an Islamist party in a mixed religious state, faces challenges that are shared by the other communal opposition parties and have often constrained their ability to unite to win elections. PAS's platform has been religious and communal, attacking UMNO from the right for allying with "infidels" and not doing enough to promote Malay issues.[56] On the other hand, the main Chinese opposition party, the left-leaning Democratic Action Party, traditionally attacks its Chinese counterpart within the governing coalition, the Malaysian Chinese Association, for not doing enough to protect Chinese interests. Similarly, over the years the various Indian opposition parties have accused the Malaysian Indian Congress of not doing enough to protect and promote Indian interests. The sharp divergences in ideologies and interests among these parties have generally made it difficult for them to form a viable opposition movement.

The Asian financial crisis upended politics in Malaysia, as it did in much of the rest of Asia, although it did not ultimately topple the UMNO-led regime. When the Thai baht collapsed in mid-1997, the Malaysian ringgit dropped sharply in value as well, crippling the country's banking system and the economy at large. Unlike his neighbors, Prime Minister Mahathir resisted seeking the support of the International Monetary Fund. Malaysia had greater leeway to do so because it did not have the level of foreign indebtedness that its neighbors did. Instead, Mahathir decried the influence of "Jewish bankers" like George Soros and the role of international financial institutions, who he said were responsible for the region's financial woes. He alluded to the possibility of imposing capital controls. With each speech, the ringgit plunged further. Anwar Ibrahim, who as deputy prime minister and finance minister was increasingly taking responsibility for managing the crisis, was left to "clarify" Mahathir's comments and calm foreign investors.[57]

Anwar introduced a series of measures to address the crisis. He raised interest rates, cut government spending, froze a number of large-scale state investment projects, and sought to restructure or close ailing state-owned firms. The measures threatened the patronage networks on which the regime relied for its support, and Mahathir eventually intervened to save some of the largest projects, including Malaysia Airways, from Anwar's budget knife. He also appointed a special functions minister to oversee economic policy, undoubtedly in an effort to curb Anwar's influence.[58] The economy continued to sputter. For 1998 as a whole, the economy contracted by 8 percent. On September 2, 1998, Mahathir finally sacked Anwar and imposed capital controls. Anwar was later thrown out of UMNO and charged with corruption and sodomy.[59]

Anwar's Challenge

Anwar's removal ignited latent public discontent with the regime. Anwar was regarded by the public as a man of faith and of considerable moral probity, and thousands gathered outside his home in protest following his ouster. Anwar spent the next few weeks traveling around Malaysia, addressing large crowds and calling for Mahathir's resignation and for political reform. On his return to Kuala Lumpur, he addressed a crowd of several hundred thousand from the National Mosque. The police violently dispersed the crowd and then arrested Anwar on September 20, 1998.

Even with Anwar's detention and eventual sentencing, the *reformasi* movement continued, bringing together a diverse group of political parties, advocacy NGOs, religious groups, trade unions, professional associations, artists, students, and ordinary citizens drawn from across all ethnic groups. Disparate as their interests were, they were united in their desire to see an end to Mahathir's rule. Over time, mounting police violence largely forced the movement out of the public squares to the Internet and more private settings. Traveling lectures, or *ceramah*, often held in supporters' homes or offices, became a favored way to educate and recruit others. New pro-democracy organizations also emerged—such as United for Democracy and Humanity, a civic education organization, and People are the Boss, a good governance advocacy group—to channel the new citizen activism.[60]

As imperfect as the electoral system was, the opposition decided that it was open enough to try to challenge the Mahathir regime through elections. In April 1999, Anwar's wife, Wan Azizah, after some difficulty, registered the National Justice Party (KeAdilan) as an official political party by taking over an existing party.[61] KeAdilan and the other major opposition parties—PAS, DAP (Democratic Action Party), and the Socialist Party (PRM)—formed the Barisan Alternatif ([BA] Alternative Front) coalition to compete against Mahathir's Barisan Nasional coalition. Anwar's theme of social justice—which is central to Islam and other religions—helped knit together what had long been a divided opposition. In early November 1999, Mahathir called snap elections for the end of the month.

By the time that elections occurred, however, the opposition had lost a good deal of its momentum. Its most prominent leader had been in jail for more than a year and was unable to campaign. The public demonstrations of the previous year had petered out because of police harassment. And, to Mahathir's further benefit, the economy had recovered somewhat. His government had also had time to enact several generous social programs to win voters to its side. When the ballots were tallied, the BN won 56.5 percent of the vote (10 percent less than in the 1995 election but on a par with prior results) and retained well over two-thirds of the seats in parliament, enough to continue to amend the constitution at will. The opposition, led by PAS, won forty-five seats (a gain of twenty-two over the previous elections). It could have fared even better if the government had not failed to add 680,000 newly registered voters to the electoral rolls in time for them to vote. The BA performed especially well on the peninsula and in urban areas, suggesting that it had made inroads with its reform message in key parts of the country but not yet in the nation as a whole.[62]

Anwar remained in prison for five years. Even after the Federal Court reversed his sodomy conviction, he continued to be banned from holding public office until 2008. In the meantime, Mahathir retired in 2003 after 22 years as prime minister, passing power to his deputy Abdullah Badawi. With a fresh face at the helm, the BN rolled to an easy victory in the 2004 elections, securing nearly 63 percent of the vote and 198 of 220 seats in parliament. Badawi, who presented himself as a reformer, took some important steps to clean up corruption, but ultimately he came to be perceived as an indecisive leader. In 2006, Mahathir publicly criticized his performance as prime minister, suggesting a split within UMNO. In that context, Anwar returned to political life.

In the March 2008 elections, the opposition stunned BN with a surprisingly strong electoral showing, winning 47 percent of the vote to the BN's 50 percent. That translated into 82 of the 222 seats in parliament, depriving BN of a two-thirds majority. Of equal importance, the opposition won control of five of the country's thirteen states. Anwar confidently predicted to the press that he could secure enough defections from the BN in parliament to form a new government by September. When that failed to materialize, Anwar's credibility was hurt.[63]

The discredited Badawi resigned in April 2009 and was replaced as prime minister and UMNO party leader by his deputy Najib Razak. Following a series of religiously motivated attacks on churches and mosques after a court ruling overturned a government ban on the use of the word "Allah" by non-Muslim publications, Razak sought to calm ethnic and religious tensions with the "One Malaysia" campaign. The effort did not gain much traction, but Razak was generally perceived as a more competent leader than his predecessor. In January 2012, the High Court acquitted Anwar Ibrahim on a second set of rape charges.[64] With the Malaysian economy slowing, the opposition seemed poised to make substantial gains in the May 2013 general elections, and expectations for the contest were high. Anwar's Pakatan Rakyat coalition narrowly won the popular vote (51 percent), but because of the gerrymandering of constituencies, it fell short of the majority of seats in parliament that it needed to form a government. Amid charges of fraud, the new People's Tribune was created to investigate election irregularities.[65]

Conclusion

Malaysia's ethnic and geographic differences have long prevented the opposition from coalescing to overturn the one-party rule of UMNO. Malaysia is changing, however, as it becomes more open to the world and its middle class grows. Moreover, the opposition has become more sophisticated and better organized over time, while popular dissatisfaction with UMNO's rule mounts. It seems only a matter of time before UMNO's monopoly over the state is broken.

Pakistan

Pakistan was afflicted from birth with two problems that continue to constrain its democratic development today: borders that make its security precarious and demographics within those borders that make democracy difficult to achieve. Throughout its history, Pakistan has experienced brief periods of democratic rule interrupted by longer periods of military rule. Yet even while extremism continues to plague Pakistan, there are signs that democracy may finally be taking hold. The most recent is that former president Asif Zardari, although weak and ineffectual, became the first democratically elected leader to serve out his entire term and departed peacefully from office.

Pakistan's Founding

The idea of Pakistan, as conceived in the 1930s by Cambridge University student Chaudhary Rahmat Ali, was to give the Muslims of South Asia a country of their own by cobbling together the territories of Punjab, Afghania, Kashmir, Sindh, and Balochistan. (The name Pakistan, which also means "pure" in Persian and Urdu, is an acronym that draws from the name of each territory.)[66] Ali's vision—which sought to unite politically the Muslims in the northwestern provinces of India—left out

Bengal, the most populous Muslim region on the subcontinent. Bengal, which was incorporated by the British into the new state of Pakistan as East Pakistan, was noncontiguous with the rest of Pakistan and, as events later demonstrated, indefensible. Ali believed what Muhammad Ali Jinnah, the anti-colonialist and eventual father of the Pakistani state, belatedly concluded as well: that the interests of Muslims on the subcontinent could be safeguarded only in a separate state of their own. What that reasoning failed to take into account was that an independent Pakistan would be dwarfed on the subcontinent by a much larger and hostile India. On Britain's withdrawal from the subcontinent in 1947, the young Pakistani nation found itself in a very insecure position.

Ali and Jinnah also tended to speak of the subcontinent's Muslims as if they were a unified and homogenous whole. In fact, they comprised a variety of ethnicities, tribes, and sects spread throughout the subcontinent. Those advocating most strenuously for an independent Pakistan were the upper-class elite of Uttar Pradesh, Bihar, and Bombay, who were concerned about retaining their rights and privileges after Britain's departure. However, they were distinct minorities in their parts of the Raj and were well outside the envisioned borders of the Pakistani state. The residents of Muslim-majority Sindh and Western Punjab, which formed the core of the new state, were far less gripped with the issue of independence because they did not feel threatened.

The new state's borders also did not include Kashmir, which was a majority-Muslim area, because its Hindu prince had prevaricated at the time of negotiations, hoping somehow to remain independent. Most of Jammu and Kashmir was made a part of India, provoking irredentist feelings in Pakistan that have been the trigger for repeated wars between India and Pakistan ever since. On the other hand, the Pashtuns east of the Durand Line were incorporated into Pakistan, even though many identified far more strongly with their Pashtun kin on the other side of the line. So too were the Balochs of Balochistan, a distinct tribal group of Iranian descent, a decision that has spawned a series of secessionist movements since independence. The realities on the ground were too complicated to be resolved by simple lines on a map.

The most immediate and tragic consequence of this demographic muddle was the tremendous displacement that occurred at the time of partition. An estimated 13 million Hindus and Muslims were uprooted and up to 1 million killed in the chaos and violence that ensued. A second consequence was that India and Pakistan immediately went to war over Kashmir, as they have done twice since then. A third, longer-term consequence was the impact of Pakistan's convoluted demographics on its governance. It could be argued that at independence, Pakistan's disparate population was united only by religion. Overwhelmingly, the country's leaders were Urdu speakers from parts of the former Raj that were not incorporated into the new Pakistani state. Like them, a significant segment of the population of the new Pakistani state were *muhajirs,* or refugees, who settled either in Punjabi-speaking Punjab or Sindhi-speaking Sindh. (Today a fifth of the country's population is made of up *muhajirs* or their descendants.)[67] However, the majority of the population (56 percent) were Bengalis living in East Pakistan, who were looked down on by the leadership in West Pakistan and were severely underrepresented in the new state and army, whose leadership posts went instead to the *muhajirs.*[68] While most of the population was Sunni, there was a significant Shia population. (Jinnah himself was a member of the Ismailis, a Shia sect.) Most farmland was owned by a small number of feudal lords. All of those factors complicated the task of building a Muslim democracy.[69]

Pakistan's founders were British-educated elites who espoused democracy but were wary of applying its principles in their new homeland. Unlike that in India, Pakistan's independence movement did not do as much to cultivate a popular base. Beginning in 1915, Gandhi's Indian National Congress had engaged in massive peaceful resistance to British rule and grew into a highly effective membership-based political organization, but Jinnah's All-India Muslim League never developed comparable roots or the congress's democratic character. It began to seek mass support only just before World War II, and at one point in 1947, it turned to mob violence.[70] The disjuncture between Pakistan's leaders and its citizens continues to this day.

Pakistan's new leaders set out to build a modern state, but it was a state that gave pride of place to bureaucratic efficiency rather than democratic principles. From the British Raj, the young state inherited a highly trained Punjabi civil and military bureaucracy. The Muslim League political leadership, which had emigrated from India, chose to ally with and work through this civil-military bureaucracy because it lacked the constituency needed to win elections. In colonial times, a small group of prominent landowning families had dominated politics in the Punjab. In addition to controlling most of the country's land and wealth, they could rely on long-standing personal, tribal, and provincial loyalties as well as patronage networks for votes. The Muslim League won the 1946–47 provincial assembly elections, which were in essence a referendum on independence, by securing the support of those landowners.[71] For much of Pakistan's existence, politics has resembled a tug-of-war between the *muhajir*-dominated military and bureaucratic establishment, which is socially progressive but politically conservative (that is, anti-majoritarian), and a landed elite that is socially conservative but politically progressive.[72] Security threats, real and imagined, have often strengthened the position of the establishment at the expense of the landed elite.

Revered as "the father of the nation," Jinnah served as governor-general of the new state (the title of the chief executive was changed to "president" in the 1956 constitution) for only a year before succumbing to tuberculosis. In taking office, he laid out a vision for Pakistan as a democratic state for the subcontinent's diverse Muslim populations—one that would extend equality and tolerance to all. Yet on his first trip to East Pakistan, he insisted that Urdu alone would be the official language of state. A week into his tenure, he exceeded his authority by dismissing the provincial government of the North West Frontier Province; eight months later he sacked the chief minister of Sindh.[73] His deputy, Liaquat Ali Khan, who succeeded him on his death, was assassinated in 1951.

Strong-Willed Generals and Weak Civilian Leaders

A constitution for the new state was formally adopted in 1956, but two years later army chief Major General Ayub Khan staged a coup, partly out of fear that under democracy the balance of political power would shift to East Pakistan. It was Khan who transformed the army's Directorate for Inter-Services Intelligence (ISI) into a powerful internal spy agency. He also launched an unsuccessful clandestine incursion into Kashmir in 1965, thereby triggering the Second Indo-Pakistan War, which ended in a draw. In 1968, amid declining popularity and accusations of corruption, Khan relinquished power to General Yahya Khan.[74]

Yahya tried to address rising Bengali discontent by holding elections in late 1970. The pro-independence Awami Party swept the vote in East Pakistan, giving it a majority in parliament, as had been feared. In response, Yahya suspended parliament, provoking bitter protests in East Pakistan. Yahya sent in troops to quash the unrest, and an estimated 3 million Bengalis were killed in the ensuing slaughter. India then entered the fighting on the side of the Bengalis and dealt the Pakistan Army a resounding defeat. Bangladesh became an independent state, and the disgraced Yahya was forced to hand power back to civilians.[75]

Zulfikar Bhutto, the head of the Pakistan People's Party (PPP), assumed power in 1971 by virtue of his party's strong showing in the previous year's elections. While he dismissed a number of top officers, Bhutto left the military establishment largely intact and enhanced its importance by aggressively pushing forward the country's nuclear weapons program. The left-leaning Bhutto nationalized certain key industries and made modest attempts at implementing land reform. While his term as prime minister represented a long-awaited return to civilian rule, he governed with a heavy—if not sometimes authoritarian—hand, leavened by patronage and graft. It came to an abrupt end in 1977, when opposition protests over the government's rigging of parliamentary elections led the military to intervene.[76]

General Muhammad Zia ul-Haq—who had been handpicked by Bhutto a year earlier as army chief of staff—took over, ostensibly to ensure free and fair elections, but he remained for 11 years. Bhutto was accused by the military of the murder of a political opponent, tried, and hanged. At home, Zia sought to Islamize the country: he banned alcohol; introduced the Hudood ordinances, which stipulated draconian punishments for crimes of morality and theft; built thousands of madrassas; and linked army promotions to officers' moral and religious behavior. Abroad, following the Soviet invasion of Afghanistan in December 1979, he empowered the ISI—with financial support from Saudi Arabia and the United States—to train and equip the *mujahideen*. Zia died in August 1988 in a plane crash, the cause of which remains unexplained.

Zia's death was followed by 11 often tumultuous years of civilian rule. During that period, power passed back and forth between Benazir Bhutto, who inherited her father's leadership of the PPP, and Nawaz Sharif, the leader of the Pakistan Muslim League, who had been recruited into politics by Zia. In November 1988, in Pakistan's first generally free and fair elections, Bhutto and the PPP won the parliamentary elections. Under a constitutional amendment that had been pushed through by Zia that permitted the president to dismiss the government at will, Bhutto was sacked by President Ghulam Ishaq Khan on grounds of corruption in 1990, although the real reason seems to have been that she fired the head of the ISI and was generally at loggerheads with the military. Sharif replaced her, but in 1993 he also was dismissed by the president on charges of corruption, at which point Bhutto was reelected prime minister. Her second term in office lasted three years before she was once again replaced by Sharif in 1997. That time, Sharif had enough votes in parliament to amend the constitution so that the president could no longer dismiss the prime minister at will. However, he and his army chief of staff, General Pervez Musharraf, were soon quarreling over a botched military incursion into the Kargil District of Kashmir, in 1999, that was widely condemned by the rest of the world. Sharif tried to fire Musharraf, giving orders to prevent the plane on which he was returning from an overseas trip from landing in Pakistan, but the general managed to organize a coup against Sharif from the air.

Musharraf ruled for the next nine years, first as "chief executive" and then as self-appointed president. Musharraf initially enjoyed broad popular support. He brought a measure of stability to the country's politics, expanded media and other freedoms, and appeared to be cleaning up the corruption over which his predecessors had presided. He brought in Citibank executive Shaukat Aziz, first as finance minister and later as prime minister, and economic growth picked up, reaching nearly 8 percent in 2005.[77] Early in Musharraf's tenure, al Qaeda launched its 9/11 attacks on the United States. Under heavy U.S. pressure, Musharraf publicly distanced Pakistan from the Taliban leadership in Afghanistan, who were providing al Qaeda with safe haven. He did not, however, sever the ISI's relationship with other Pakistani extremist groups such as Lashkar-e-Tayyiba, Jaish-e-Mohammed, and the Haqqani Network, which were perceived by the military to give Pakistan additional military capabilities vis-à-vis India in Afghanistan and Kashmir. Nor, it is now clear, did he cut off links entirely with the Taliban or al Qaeda. Musharraf's inability or unwillingness to rein in extremist groups within Pakistan would come back to haunt his final years in office.

By 2007, public dissatisfaction had grown with all aspects of Musharraf's rule, which was seen as increasingly dictatorial. That March, Musharraf fired Pakistan's chief justice, Iftikhar Chaudhry. Lawyer groups rallied for his reinstatement, joined eventually by thousands of other professionals and students, and Musharraf was forced to relent in July. The same month, government commandos stormed the Lal Masjid, or Red Mosque, in Islamabad, which had become a hub of extremist activity. Musharraf was widely criticized for his handling of the incident, in which more than a hundred people died. In November, Musharraf declared martial law, once again removed the chief justice and several other justices, and jailed a number of civil society leaders. At the same time, he agreed to let Bhutto and Sharif finally return to Pakistan, resigned his military post, and announced parliamentary elections for the following year. Then, at a campaign rally in Rawalpindi in December, militants gunned down Bhutto.

Democracy Returns

The Pakistan People's Party, with Bhutto's widower Asif Zardari now its de facto leader, cruised to victory in the February 2008 parliamentary elections, claiming 30.5 percent of the vote to 23 percent for Musharraf's Pakistan Muslim League (PML-Q) and 19.6 percent for Sharif's Pakistan Muslim League (Nawaz) (PML-N). The PPP and PML-N formed a coalition government, with Musharraf remaining on as president. After another wave of demonstrations by the Lawyers' Movement calling for the reinstatement of the chief justice, Zardari and Sharif moved to impeach Musharraf. Finally, in August 2008, Musharraf resigned.

Zardari was elected president the following month. However, the country's first democratically elected government in a decade was hamstrung on a number of fronts. The army and the ISI had grown even more powerful, dwarfing the civilian government in terms of their prerogatives and influence. So, too, had the extremist groups that the ISI had covertly been supporting. The Frankenstein of Islamic militancy that the ISI had long nurtured had grown beyond its control, threatening to destabilize not only neighboring countries but Pakistan itself.[78] On the political front, Zardari was a diminished leader. While he had benefited at the ballot box from widespread public sympathy for his wife, he lacked her charm and political savvy. To compound matters, he was widely perceived as corrupt—his business dealings during his wife's tenures as prime minister had earned him the moniker "Mr. Ten Percent," in reference to the commissions that he allegedly demanded in return for government contracts.

His time as president was often marked by chaos and conflict. Just before his maiden speech to parliament, militants bombed the Marriott hotel in Islamabad. Two months later, Lashkar-e-Tayyiba orchestrated a series of ghastly terrorist attacks in Mumbai, which once again brought India and Pakistan to the brink of war. Then the global financial crisis crippled the Pakistani economy, forcing the government to seek a rescue package from the IMF. When some of the worst flooding in Pakistan's history occurred in the summer of 2010, leaving 2,000 people dead and displacing more than 11 million, the government was charged with incompetence in its handling of the relief effort. Those perceptions were only reinforced when U.S. Special Forces captured and killed Osama bin Laden in May 2011 in the bustling military garrison city of Abbottabad, less than a mile from the Pakistan Military Academy.

Bin Laden's death exacerbated the civilian government's strained relations with the Pakistani military establishment and the United States. Both were strained even further by the revelation in October 2011 that an unsigned memo had been sent to the U.S. government requesting assistance in the event that the military attempted a coup d'état. A NATO air strike the following month that hit two Pakistani military outposts on the northwestern border with Afghanistan, claiming the lives of twenty-four soldiers, essentially froze the already chilly diplomatic relationship between the United States and Pakistan.

In the meantime, an increasingly empowered Pakistani judiciary was ratcheting up pressure of its own on the increasingly isolated civilian government. In January 2012, it began hearings into the provenance of the controversial memo. The following month, Prime Minister Yousuf Raza Gilani was called before the high court on contempt charges for failing to request that the Swiss government re-open fraud charges against President Zardari. Gilani was forced from office by the court in mid-2012; his successor, Raja Pervaiz Ashraf, met a similar fate in January 2013, when the court ordered his arrest in a three-year-old corruption case that had been pending against him.

Yet in the midst of all the turmoil, there were some glimmers of positive news. One was that the military has remained on the sidelines—for the time being at least—without intervening in domestic politics as it has so many times before. And in March 2013, Zardari's PPP government, as hobbled as it was, became the first civilian government to serve its full five-year term. Parliamentary elections in May 2013 gave Nawaz Sharif's PML-N a plurality (33 percent) of the vote, and with the help of independents Sharif was able to form a government and become prime minister. In September 2013, Zardari ended his five-year term as president, having diminished significantly the prominence of the office. He was replaced by a relative unknown, Mamnoon Hussain, of Sharif's PML-N.

Conclusion

If Pakistan has been embarked on a transition to democracy, it has been one of epic length. Civilian governments have been elected a half-dozen times since the country's founding in 1947, and four times their terms have been truncated by military intervention. The country's return in 2008 to an elected civilian government was a positive development, as was the peaceful passing of power from Zardari's PPP to Sharif's PML-N. But given the entrenched power of the military establishment, the proliferation of militant extremist groups, and its own internal weaknesses, the ability of Sharif's government to survive and even deepen and consolidate democracy remains open to question.

Two factors among many seem to have made democracy especially problematic in Pakistan. The first is the country's security position. Partition left Pakistan independent but exceedingly vulnerable. Dwarfed by India, divided initially between East and West Pakistan, harboring irredentist designs on Kashmir, and sharing a contested border with what would become an increasingly unstable Afghanistan, the young nation could not help but be preoccupied with security. As a result, a national security establishment has emerged that now vastly overshadows the civilian government in terms of its capabilities and influence. The United States and other international actors have only deepened the asymmetry by often making the military their primary interlocutor and primary recipient of funds and equipment.[79]

The second is the country's demographics. The most successful modern nation-states have been built on populations that have a shared sense of being part of a national community, real or imagined.[80] At partition, Pakistan was a congeries of different ethnic and tribal groups speaking a range of different languages, united only by a common religion. The Pashtun had more in common with their ethnic kin on the other side of the Durand Line in Afghanistan; the Balochs were a distinct people unto themselves; the Bengalis were geographically separate and looked down on as inferior by the rest; and the estimated 8 million refugees who had flooded in from India had no prior attachment to the land at all. Perhaps most critical to the prospects for democracy, the governing elite were almost all refugees from India—a distinct minority with no prospect of ever becoming a majority. That being the case, they had little interest or trust in democracy. A half-century later, democracy has been given yet another chance in Pakistan, largely because the alternative of military rule has been discredited. Whether it will stick this time remains to be seen.

Lessons from Muslim-Majority Asia

There is much that the Arab Spring countries can learn from the experience of the Muslim-majority countries of Asia. A first observation concerns the role of civil society in democratic politics. People power played a decisive role in Indonesia's transition to democracy, helping to unseat President Suharto after 32 years of authoritarian rule. It also emerged as a potent force in Malaysia, challenging the stability of the UMNO-dominated regime following Anwar Ibrahim's imprisonment in 1998 but ultimately failing to topple it. The Lawyers' Movement put a halt to former president Musharraf's efforts to reshape the judiciary in Pakistan. Recently, the Taksim Square protests signaled the emergence of similar civic movements in Turkey. More generally, civil society is growing and becoming increasingly more organized and sophisticated, at least in Pakistan and Turkey. As it does, it is challenging the long dominance of elites over politics and creating demands for greater reforms in governance.

A second observation regards the role of Islamist parties. Islamist parties were important actors in the politics of all four countries discussed. That is not surprising given that all four are deeply religious societies, and it is not unusual for some believers to want their faith to carry over into the political realm. Yet the electoral performance of true Islamist parties—those advocating establishment of an Islamic state—tended to be fairly weak; such parties rarely garnered more than 10 to 20 percent of the vote. A possible exception is Turkey's AKP, which some would brand as Islamist, which won 34 percent of the vote in the first parliamentary elections in which it competed and has won ever larger margins since. However, it has taken great pains to distance itself from the Islamist parties that preceded it by fashioning itself as a "socially conservative" party, along the lines of Germany's Christian Democrats.

Participation in democratic politics seems to have had a moderating effect on Islamist parties. As theory would predict, they have been responsible participants in the democratic process and have behaved pragmatically as they seek to win the public's votes. What remains to be seen is whether Turkey's AKP will maintain that pragmatism and continue to behave responsibly now that it is in its third term in office—or whether hubris will lead it to exceed its authority, as so many secular incumbent governments in nascent democracies have before. The recent events in Taksim Square demonstrate that while the AKP (or at least Erdogan) has become overconfident as its tenure in office grows, Turkish civil society has grown strong enough to challenge the government when it oversteps its mandate.

A third observation regards the role of the military. Militaries, many have reasoned, can play a caretaker role in young democracies by serving as a kind of referee between contending factions and institutions, ensuring that the democratic process stays on track until it is consolidated. On close scrutiny, the role that the military has played in Pakistan, Indonesia, and even Turkey (which many point to as a model) has been far less productive. In Pakistan and Turkey, the military has repeatedly halted the country's experiment with democracy by taking the reins of power.

Military leaders may have intervened because they believed that democracy was not functioning properly—and they may even have been correct in that belief—but their intervention neither advanced the cause of democracy nor offered a better form of governance. All four countries face the challenge of getting the "deep state" under civilian control and shrinking its size so that democracy, as messy as it initially may be, has a chance to function. Despite what was done (or not done) in Indonesia, dealing with past crimes committed by the military is integral to that process.

CHAPTER FIVE

LATIN AMERICA

The modern history of Latin America, like that of the Arab world, was shaped first by colonialism and then by authoritarianism. Like the Arab world, Latin America has suffered from significant economic inequality and the legacy of state-dominated economies, factors that have made the challenges of democratization all the greater. Also like the Arab world, Latin America has struggled with the problem of getting powerful militaries to return to the barracks so that civilians could rule.

Democracy has a long but very troubled history in Latin America. The Spanish-speaking world has enriched the English political lexicon with such colorful terms as "caudillo" (strong-man rule), "junta" (military rule), and "autogolpe" (a "self-coup" by an established ruler to overthrow the constitutional order), all of which suggest in different ways the intermingling of force of arms and governance, which historically was a far too common occurrence in Latin America. The European colonial powers that settled Latin America—Spain, Portugal, and France in particular—brought with them their own political traditions, including both democracy and the bureaucratic authoritarianism still seen in some countries today.

The Development of Democracy in Latin America

By the late 1820s, almost all of Latin America was independent, the notable exceptions being Cuba and Puerto Rico. The end of colonialism, however, often meant the end of exclusive trade arrangements with the mother country. Latin American countries found that they could compete most effectively in the international marketplace as suppliers of a range of natural resources, from rubber and agricultural products to, eventually, petroleum and natural gas. Those resources tended to be tightly controlled by a small coterie of major landholders who derived all the benefits from their exploitation. The economic dominance of the landholders enabled them to establish political dominance by putting in place political systems that allowed them to protect their economic spoils. While such political systems often were democratic in name, the real power generally lay with the large landholders. Extensive patronage networks were created to buy the political support of broad segments of the population. When trouble surfaced and the system was threatened, the military was brought in to stifle dissent and restore order. Consequently, at the end of the nineteenth century, at best Uruguay could be said to be democratic, although Argentina, Chile, Costa Rica, and Colombia each had some democratic features.[1]

Latin America's political development in the first half of the twentieth century is often characterized as an endless cycle of change between the extremes of *caudillismo* on one hand and populism on the other. In truth, the history is a bit more complicated, but periods of democratic rule were repeatedly interrupted by military interventions whenever political elites thought that their vital interests were being threatened. Experiments with democratic rule were often brief and often followed by strong-man rule.

Castro's takeover of Cuba in 1959 heightened further the polarization between the elites and populist political movements. Like the Arab world, Latin America became a pawn in the cold war struggle between the United States and the Soviet Union, with each side providing political, economic, and military support to its favored clients in the region. Over time, the region's militaries grew frustrated by the ineffectualness of successive democratic governments and alarmed at the possibility of further left-wing revolutions. No longer content to serve solely as referees of the political process, militaries now proceeded to impose direct military rule. A period of bureaucratic authoritarianism ensued in most of the region, with militaries putting in place technocratic governments that had generals installed firmly at the helm. Amid the optimism of the times, they promised their populations that they would deliver the economic modernization that had long eluded civilian governments. Only Colombia, Costa Rica, and Venezuela avoided dictatorship in the 1960s and 1970s.[2]

The Third Wave Hits

As the cold war was drawing to a close, the Third Wave of democratization reached the shores of Latin America. In 1973, politics in Latin

America took a decisive turn, beginning with Ecuador's transition to democracy. The same year Juan Perón returned from exile and won the presidential election in Argentina. Remarkably, during this period Latin American militaries began to retreat to the barracks. The end of the cold war brought a sea change in behavior, in that generally "Latin American militaries no longer mix[ed] openly in politics."[3] No government has reverted to military rule since Haiti in 1991. There have been only a dozen attempted coups since then, and none of them have been successful, with the notable exception of the controversial 2009 coup in Honduras.[4]

This time around, democracy seems to have stuck. The notion that power should rotate on the basis of decisions made by voters at the ballot box has become a prevailing norm within the region. Military rule seems to have become a relic of the region's dark past. Political leaders rotate in and out of office according to the results of elections, which are in most cases free and fair. Voting has become an ingrained habit among the region's citizens, who in public opinion surveys express a preference for democracy over dictatorship by a margin of 4 to 1.[5]

There appear to be several reasons for Latin America's decisive turn toward democracy. First, the military dictatorships of the 1960s and 1970s performed quite poorly, politically and economically, although the Chilean economy under General Augusto Pinochet was a notable exception. Despite the economic promises of the generals, national economies tended to stagnate during their rule, while corruption and state brutality proliferated. Import substitution and other state-led economic policies only exacerbated the region's foreign debt problems. Poor economic performance undermined the perceived legitimacy of—and the most compelling rationale for—military rule.

Second, the end of the cold war removed the national security rationale for coups, and the United States became more comfortable accepting leftist parties as legitimate players in democratic politics as the prospect of left-wing revolutions dimmed and posed less of a threat to American interests. U.S. policymakers also came to recognize that authoritarianism in the region was impeding both economic and political development—a recognition that U.S. policymakers are only haltingly coming to now with regard to the Arab Middle East.[6] The close of the cold war era allowed for an end in Latin America to what one expert termed "democradura"—"an assemblage of democratic procedures and structures constrained by the fear of individuals or groups deemed 'sufficiently dangerous' that their citizenship rights should be restricted"[7]— that is, an illiberal democracy in which elections are held but political choices and political liberties are restricted. As U.S. interests evolved, the impediments to free and full political competition were removed.

Third, a consensus seemed to emerge within countries and across the region regarding the political and economic rules of the game. As democracy swept across the region, it quickly acquired the status of a regional norm. By 1992, the Organization of American States had ratified the "Washington Protocol," which allowed for the suspension of a member state should its democratically elected government be replaced through a military coup. Politicians on the left and right came to recognize that markets had an important role to play as engines of growth, and state-led economic policies such as import substitution soon joined military dictatorships in the dustbin of Latin American history.

Since 1973, democracy in the region has proved remarkably durable. Despite the Latin American debt crisis of 1982, severe recessions in 1990 and 1995, and the impact of the global recession of 2008, democracy has remained, for the most part, the only game in town. Democratic elections continue to be regarded as the only legitimate way of selecting political leaders. Given the region's history, that is a remarkable change.

Democracy's Challenges

However, democracy in the region is not without its challenges. While there is still broad public support within the region for democracy, there is growing dissatisfaction with the actual performance of democratic governments.[8] Although elections have become enshrined as an enduring feature of political life throughout the region, political leaders have succeeded in whittling away at the power of many of the other key institutions of democracy—from constitutions, parliaments, and courts to an independent media and a vibrant civil society. Many countries in the region have become *electoral* democracies, in that they hold regular elections to choose their leaders, but far fewer have become *liberal* democracies, which safeguard the individual rights of citizens and are governed by the rule of law.

While military coups have largely become a thing of the past, the incidence of "interrupted presidencies" has risen dramatically since the 1970s. Many a presidency has been cut short, not by military intervention but by "street coups"—popular unrest in the streets.[9] From 1980 to 1990, only seven of thirty-seven changes in government were the result of military intervention, and only two of the seven had a nondemocratic intent. In the 1980s, successful coups were confined to Bolivia, Guatemala, Paraguay, Haiti (twice), and Suriname (twice); since 1990, only Haiti, Peru (in an autogolpe by Fujimori), Honduras, and Paraguay (in what some have called a "parliamentary coup") have seen a constitutional government replaced by force. However, from 1985 to 2004, thirteen presidents left office early in response to public pressure.[10]

Recent years have also witnessed the rise of the "charismatic" or "plebiscitary" presidency. Successive Latin American political leaders have used the prerogatives of the presidency and the new powers afforded by modern communications technology to appeal directly to voters, often circumventing not only traditional political parties but also political institutions more generally. They have used their popular support to flout the constitutional rules of the game, thereby hollowing out democratic institutions. Venezuela's Hugo Chávez, who died in 2013, was only the most extreme example of the threat that charismatic presidencies pose to democracy in Latin America today.

Structural Impediments to Democratic Development

There are several structural factors that have always made democratic development in Latin America difficult. The first is deep-rooted economic inequality. Income distribution in Latin America is the most unequal in the world, with a Gini coefficient of 5.0. However, thanks to vigorous economic growth and conditional cash transfers that target the poorest of the poor, inequality in the region has fallen slightly over the last decade.[11]

Persistent economic inequality presents profound challenges for democracy. How can a democratic system, which is based on the will of the majority, exist where a small minority owns everything and the large majority has next to nothing? The answer is that it is quite difficult. In politics, the primary interest of the rich is to protect their privileged position within the economy, while the primary interest of the poor is to in some way redress the gross misallocation of wealth and property. In Latin American history, the rich have been willing to tolerate democracy only up to the point that it begins to impinge on their vital interests. When past democratic experiments devolved into populism and assaults on private property, the military was brought in and dictatorship ensued. When military rule became too oppressive, the country experimented with democracy once more and the cycle began again.

The second structural problem complicating democratic development in Latin America has been one of constitutional design. The countries of

Latin America inherited from their colonial masters presidential rather than parliamentary systems of governance. The region's constitutions provide for presidents to be elected directly by the people, independent of a parliament, and accorded a broad range of executive powers. As others have observed, because presidentialism concentrates so much power in the hands of a single individual, it gives political leaders strong incentives to forgo all constraints in the interest of securing the prize of the presidency, thereby encouraging a winner-take-all mentality.[12] In societies already polarized by large disparities in wealth, such an all-or-nothing political system only heightens the intensity of political contestation. Moreover, the structure of presidentialism means that crises of government become systemic crises.

At the same time, Latin American presidents are often said to "reign" rather than "rule." The winning candidate may claim the very large prize of the presidency, but to govern effectively, he or she requires the consent of parliament, which is elected separately and, because seats are typically distributed according to proportional representation, is often highly fragmented. Other political parties have few incentives to go along with the president; in fact, the incentives are far stronger to foil the president at every turn. Few Latin American presidents in recent years have enjoyed commanding majorities in parliament. From 1978 to 2000, only one in four enjoyed a parliamentary majority.[13] Often efforts to address these design defects with constitutional revisions have themselves fallen prey to politics. As others have observed, constitutional tinkering has more often than not exacerbated the problem rather than lessened it.[14] Constitutional reform has tended to be used as a pretense by the party in control to gut all constitutional restraints on presidential power.

Latin America's presidential system has given presidents strong incentives to circumvent parliament and other political institutions in order to avoid constitutional gridlock and get things done. The possibilities that new communications technologies provide to reach out directly to the public have only heightened the temptation for presidents to go around political parties, often including their own. That has led to the rise of what some have termed the "plebiscitary president"—one whose legitimacy is derived more from public opinion than from the constitution. Presidents have sought a governing mandate directly from the people, and often they have then used that mandate to run roughshod over existing political institutions. Thus, a president's ability to get anything done in a weak presidential system has come at the price of hollowing out democratic institutions.

Deinstitutionalization

The problem of Latin American democracy has often been portrayed as one of weak political institutions. Social mobilization, it is argued, has outstripped the degree of political institutionalization within society—institutions are not prepared to cope with the diverse social demands placed on them as a result of the enlargement of the franchise.[15] That characterization, however, is not fully accurate. Latin America does not lack for political institutions, nor are there insurmountable problems regarding their design, including the aforementioned problem of constitutions that provide for a presidential rather than a parliamentary system. The problem is that these institutions lack legitimacy because political leaders—in the interest of getting their way or of getting things done—have chosen to ignore rather than strengthen them and the public has allowed leaders to get away with it. That has weakened institutions like parliament and the courts and hampered their ability to exercise horizontal accountability and check the aggrandizement of presidential power.[16]

The deinstitutionalization of government systems has extended to political parties. In a number of Latin American countries, stable party systems once promoted political stability. Parties help connect voters to the political process by offering a set of political candidates and policy ideas that reflect a particular ideology or world view. By giving voters a range of ideological choices—whether conservatism, liberalism, or social democracy—party systems help coalesce citizens' preferences into clear policy positions, while by their very inclusiveness parties limit the appeal of extremists who might otherwise challenge the democratic order.

In many countries of the region, long-standing, stable party systems have broken down. Often viewed as unrepresentative, feckless, and even corrupt by voters, the traditional political parties have lost much of their support and legitimacy. A new crop of political leaders—from Hugo Chávez to Evo Morales, Eduardo Correa, and Ollanta Humala—mounted successful bids for the presidency using political parties of their own creation. They introduced "plebiscitarian forms of representation in which populist presidents displace parties as the primary vehicles for expressing the popular will."[17] These new, populist parties often lack traditional grass-roots organization skills, but they are savvy in their use of mass media technologies to get their message out to the poor, rural, and indigenous constituencies often ignored by the traditional parties.

The Reemergence of the Left

One reason for the weakness of traditional parties is that the socioeconomic consensus that helped usher the Third Wave of democratization into the region appears to have broken down. Democratic transitions were possible in the 1980s because military governments were discredited, along with their economic model of state-led growth through import substitution and the championing of national industries. The political right was willing to countenance democracy as long as it did not impinge on the vital interests—the economic privileges—of its members. The left, recognizing the new economic reality of capital mobility, was willing to work within the constraints of international market forces as long as growth was shared.

In the years since then, Latin America has suffered through a series of external economic shocks that have had the cumulative effect of discrediting neo-orthodox economics. The region's debt problems brought a round of economic austerity measures imposed by the International Monetary Fund (IMF) that the region's leaders often had little choice but to adopt. The draconian nature of the cuts in public sector salaries, services, and subsidies proved highly unpopular and prompted widespread, large-scale public protests. The bitter economic medicine eventually worked, in that it set the region on the path to more sustainable and robust growth. Since 1990, annual economic growth in Latin America has averaged just under 4 percent; during the 1980s, it was only about 2 percent.[18] But the gains from that phenomenal growth have not always been broadly shared. As a result, the International Monetary Fund and the neo orthodox economic policies that it has prescribed have been wildly unpopular throughout the region, along with the politicians who have become associated with them.

Economic discontent has led to the reemergence of the left as a political force in Latin America. Whereas the 1990s saw a marked rightward shift in Latin American politics and an effort to get the state out of the market, the first decade of the twenty-first century witnessed a turn away from market-oriented candidates and parties in Venezuela, Peru, Brazil, Ecuador, Argentina, Uruguay, Bolivia, and Nicaragua. The notable exceptions were Chile, Colombia, Mexico, and parts of Central America.[19] The most extreme manifestation of anti-market sentiment, of course, was embodied in the rise of Hugo Chávez in Venezuela. "Chavism" was heralded as a socialist alternative to the neoliberal economic policies promoted by the

United States. If "the left is back," as one observer phrased it, its return was in many respects inevitable.[20] Moderate or centrist figures tended to be entrusted with guiding countries' transition toward democracy. When those figures fell out of favor for their mismanagement of state affairs and the economy, voters naturally looked leftward, and the region's continued severe economic inequality has given the left a large support base from which to draw. At the same time, the right's earlier fear and distrust of the left dissipated as countries' democratic transitions progressed.[21] In addition, the fact that capital moves across borders rendered earlier schemes for radical redistribution of wealth infeasible, making the prospect of the left in power less threatening.[22]

However, the left now manifests itself in two distinct variants. On one hand, there is the "renewed left" (or the "right left," to use another formulation) of politicians like Lula in Brazil and the Kirchners in Argentina; on the other is the "new left" (or the "wrong left") of Chávez and Correa. The renewed left is now strongly committed to electoral politics and is predominantly moderate when in power. The new left has a more radical agenda, and its commitment to the democratic process is less certain.

The reemergence of the left, particularly the new left, reflects the crisis of representation in Latin America—the failure of traditional political parties to retain the loyalty of voters. The resurgence of left-wing populism appears to be connected to the large number of workers now operating in the informal sector, which is estimated to be as high as 50 percent among urban workers.[23] Economic conditions are pushing more and more workers into the shadow economy—with its lower wages, fewer legal protections, and more uncertain tenure—and beyond the reach of unions, whose membership has therefore declined precipitously. When individuals are economically marginalized, they tend to be politically volatile—and the economic dislocation brought about by globalization has created a pool of marginalized workers who are highly susceptible to radical appeals. The new populism and the threat that it poses to democratic institutions has less to do with political exclusion and new actors coming onto the political scene—the poor and the indigenous have already found their voice in Latin American politics—than it has to do with new economic circumstances that have created a disjuncture between traditional political parties and an easily mobilized segment of the voting population.

The North Andean countries of Venezuela, Colombia, Ecuador, Peru, and Bolivia in particular have experienced high electoral volatility.[24] Because of poor government performance in the economic and social spheres along with the deterioration of public security, citizen dissatisfaction with democracy is high across all levels of income and education in the Andean region.[25] In Peru and Venezuela, the traditional political parties have collapsed. As in the rest of Latin America, because shifting economic interests have proven to be an insufficient bond, political parties there have turned to clientelism to keep the allegiance of voters.

Civil Society's Role

Across Latin America, anti-establishment candidates are making political inroads. Taking a page from Hugo Chávez, they are currying support by inveighing against the inefficacy and corruption of established political leaders and condemning U.S. policy toward the region. In some cases, like that of the Kirchners in Argentina, they have risen to power within traditional party structures, but more often they have created their own political parties as a vehicle for their ambitions.

Once anti-establishment figures are in power, the extent to which they employ extraconstitutional means to achieve their political objectives appears to depend in part on the strength of civil society. At key moments, civic groups in some countries have mounted vigorous opposition when they believed that political leaders were diverging from the constitutional path. The "no" vote in Chile's 1988 national referendum that prevented General Augusto Pinochet from serving another eight-year term and the public pressure in Argentina to prevent Néstor Kirchner from extending his own term are but two examples. Civil society has helped defend democratic processes at a time when other political institutions—courts, parliaments, political parties—have been weak or ineffectual. In other countries, such a check on excessive executive power has been weak or nonexistent. Yet even in Venezuela, where civil society was relatively quiescent in the face of Chávez's rise, civic groups were able to quash a 2007 referendum that would have changed the constitution to allow him to run for reelection.

Historically, associational life has been rather rich in Latin America. However, it has been a largely urban—and largely elite—phenomenon. Latin America has notoriously poor public education systems, and the low level of educational attainment has limited the depth of civic life in the region. Access to primary education has expanded markedly in recent years, but the region's youth still average only 8.3 years of schooling; in contrast, those in advanced industrial countries average 11 years.[26] Moreover, the quality of schooling remains remarkably poor. That limits the reach and vibrancy of civil society. Civil society, of course, cannot be a panacea. As one observer noted: "Civil society continues to play a vital role in strengthening democratic governance throughout the region. Yet, though they can often articulate interests, defend causes, and deliver services, such organizations cannot possibly supplant political parties."[27] Nor, it should be added, can they govern.

Another factor influencing the ability of the new political actors to employ extraconstitutional means of achieving their objectives has been natural resource wealth. Chávez was better able to pursue an independent course because of his country's abundant oil reserves and the revenues that those reserves generate. Bolivia and Ecuador have had budget surpluses rather than budget constraints. As others have noted, such surpluses seem to have facilitated the undermining of democracy more often than its enrichment.[28] Since the Third Wave of democratization hit Latin America, several countries have fared better than others in their transition toward democracy. Here we highlight two of the more successful (Chile and Argentina), as well as two where democracy appears endangered (Venezuela and Bolivia).

Chile

Chile is often held up as a model of a successful Latin American transition to democracy. Among Latin American countries, it has been exceptional in its level of economic growth and degree of political stability for well over two decades. However, it certainly did not start out that way.

Pinochet and After

The 1960s and 1970s were a period of profound political polarization and crisis in Chile. The nadir was a 1973 military coup against the democratically elected president, Salvador Allende, a committed socialist who had moved to nationalize key parts of the economy. A military dictatorship soon ensued, with the coup leader, General Augusto Pinochet, as president. His tenure in office was marked by both political killings and human rights abuses and significant reforms to restore Chile's battered economy.

Pinochet called for a referendum in 1988 to revise the constitution in order to allow him to remain in office another eight years. Civic groups mobilized in opposition to the referendum under the umbrella of Concertación, a coalition of various political parties, and the "no" votes, to everyone's surprise, carried the day, with 56 percent of the vote. Chile returned to democracy in 1990 with the election of moderate Patricio

Aylwin, the Christian Democratic leader of Concertación, as president. General Pinochet and the military remained ever present in the background, which posed continual challenges for the country's democratic transition. Their presence had the benefit, however, of reassuring the right that the left could not go too far, while giving the parties within Concertación strong incentives to stick together. Experts emphasize that Chile's was not a pacted transition, in that no formal agreement was struck between democratic forces and the military. However, elites did come to a common understanding at the time on the future socioeconomic structure of the country: this "estado de compromiso" provided for a market economy with a significant role for the state.[29]

Democracy Undergirded by Consensus

Consensus building, which has continued for the past two decades, is viewed as integral to Chile's successful transition. Concertación has practiced democracy by agreement, negotiating with its right-wing opponents over major legislation. "Constant negotiations among the president, cabinet officials, legislators and party leaders [have been] the norm."[30] In this way, Chile's democratic leaders have been able to overcome the defects of a weak constitution, introduced by the military in 1980, and the fragmentation generally associated with presidential systems. The role of the two major parties has been reinforced by a binomial voting system—which essentially divides representation between the two parties garnering the largest share of the vote—that gives them an advantage over smaller parties.

The results have been impressive. As a result of wise public investment and robust economic growth, Chile's poverty rate was cut from 40 percent to 18 percent between 1990 and 2006. Together with Costa Rica and Uruguay, Chile enjoys high rankings from Freedom House with regard to political rights and civil liberties, while Transparency International ranks it just below the United States but above Italy and France for transparency.[31] Experts single out Chile as an example of how "third-generation reforms"—strengthening state institutions and the rule of law—can enhance democratic development.[32]

However, many of the same factors that contributed to its early success are the source of new challenges today. The binomial voting system has helped ensure political stability, but it has also excluded smaller parties at the expense of the two largest. A gulf has emerged between the rulers and the ruled. Citizens have been dissatisfied with what they perceive to be collusion among the political elite and the absence of avenues of representation for new political views and interests.[33] Until 2010, when Sebastian Piñera, the conservative National Renewal Party candidate, won the runoff for president, Concertación had been in power continuously for two decades. Also, the close consultation among key political elites has come at the cost of a weakened parliament. Accordingly, frustration with the political establishment has bubbled over in recent years. In 2011, trade unions demonstrated in Valparaíso against the government's environmental, education, and labor policies. Shortly thereafter, thousands of high school and university students took to the streets to demand improvements in the educational system. Copper miners then went on strike to protest government plans to restructure the industry.[34]

Conclusion

A challenge for Chilean democracy going forward will be how to respond to citizens' new political demands. The successful 1988 "no" campaign by civic groups prevented General Pinochet from extending his term, beginning a process that saw the military retreat from politics and the country return to democracy. The major political parties forged an "estado de compromiso," creating a socioeconomic consensus that allowed for dramatic economic growth (building upon Pinochet's economic reforms) coupled with state investments to address poverty. Nonetheless, as is evident in the other Latin American cases that follow, those gains could be threatened if the political system does not become more inclusive. A political system tightly controlled by the elite will be vulnerable to challenges from more radical elements outside the system.

Argentina

Argentina also has been a relative success in its transition to democracy. Since the end of military rule in 1983, democracy has endured and deepened, although corruption remains endemic and the government continues to limit freedom of the press.[35] Argentina's democratic development has been abetted by the fact that it is one of the least unequal countries in a region plagued by profound inequality. [36] Instrumental to its success has been the presence of a strong civil society.

The Military and Its Legacy

Beginning with its independence from Spain in 1816, Argentina experienced periods of democratic rule that were repeatedly interrupted by military interventions. In 1955, the post–World War II populist regime of Juan Perón finally ended in a military coup, followed by a succession of short-lived military governments and civilian governments that relied on the military for their support. In the 1970s, military leaders initiated a secret "Dirty War" against their left-wing opponents that left thousands dead or missing. Those atrocities and the poor economic performance of successive military governments between 1976 and 1983 discredited military rule and laid the groundwork for the return of democracy in 1983.

One inadvertent consequence of the Dirty War was the development of a vibrant human rights movement within Argentina, which introduced into the country's political culture a strong rights-oriented politics. It also led to the creation of a number of civic institutions, such as the Permanent Associative Network for the Supervision of State Authorities, that have demanded "social accountability" of the government. As one expert phrased it, Argentina has benefited from having strong "civic and social antibodies" in place; on a number of occasions, "state abuse [has been] met with vigorous civic mobilization."[37] A strong civil society helped Argentine democracy weather two very difficult economic crises, in 1989 and 2001. It also has helped to compensate for the lack of horizontal accountability within the government, a result of a weak parliament and court system and the dominance of the Peronist political party over all others.

The Peronists

The Peronist Judicialist Party has a large share of the responsibility for democracy's perseverance in Argentina as well as for many of its continued flaws. The Peronists returned to power in 1989 after Raúl Alfonsín (1983–89) retired early from the presidency in the face of widespread social protests and rioting as a result of skyrocketing food prices and more general hyperinflation. His successor, Carlos Menem, had campaigned on a platform that included wage increases and the nationalization of major industries, but he moderated his stance considerably once in office and eventually managed to stabilize the economy by implementing a series of market reforms and pegging the peso to the dollar. It is a formula that has worked well for Peronist leaders: to decry rhetorically the injustices of a globalized economy while governing much more pragmatically, with market-conforming policies—in other words, to look left while governing closer to the center.

Menem's neoliberal economic reforms imposed significant hardship, but this time, unlike during Alfonsín's presidency, the Peronist-leaning working class did not take to the streets. The party operated emergency soup kitchens and provided other social services to address the needs of poor neighborhoods. Whereas Alfonsín faced thirteen general strikes, only one occurred during Menem's first term.[38] The economy soon rebounded and recorded some of the highest growth rates in the region. His popularity buoyed by a soaring economy, Menem pressed the opposition to agree to amendments to the constitution that allowed him to run for a second term. During his decade-long tenure, Menem often ran roughshod over democratic institutions. Like his predecessor, he packed the supreme court with his own justices. He bypassed the parliament by issuing emergency decrees, which were not provided for in the constitution until 1994. The courts thwarted his bid for a third term by ruling it unconstitutional.

Financial Crisis

Menem's successor, opposition leader Fernando de la Rúa, took office in December 1999, just as the Asian financial crisis was turning the country's peg to the dollar into a troublesome liability. The dollar had appreciated by 70 percent over the course of the year, while Brazil, Argentina's largest trading partner, had devalued its own currency, making Argentine exports increasingly uncompetitive. At the same time, Rúa's administration was rocked by allegations that it had bribed senators to pass labor legislation. Rúa responded to the economic crisis by introducing an IMF-sponsored austerity package and currency controls, prompting wide-scale protests and rioting. When Rúa called a state of emergency and ordered a crackdown on protesters that resulted in two dozen deaths, the public reaction was so overwhelmingly negative that Rúa had to resign.

Adolfo Rodríguez Saá, the interim president who succeeded Rúa, was forced to declare a default on part of the country's sovereign debt. After further rioting, he too was compelled to resign. Amid a "Throw Everyone Out" campaign by the public, the congress selected the Peronist Eduardo Duhalde as president. Duhalde ended the peso's peg to the dollar, sending the peso plummeting in value by 70 percent in the span of a year. Public demonstrations mushroomed, with protesters pioneering new forms of civil unrest: poor and unemployed *piqueteros* barricaded streets and highways; others, called *cacerolazos*, protested by pounding pots and pans.[39] Newly formed neighborhood assemblies demanded that all the politicians resign and a new constitutional assembly be convened. However, the crisis eventually abated, and democracy endured. It likely helped that the Peronists were able to use their patronage network to assist many poor neighborhoods and help defuse popular anger.[40]

The Kirchners

In 2003, Néstor Kirchner became president after his fellow Peronist Carlos Menem withdrew from the second round of balloting. By then, the other major opposition parties, FREPASO (Front for a Country in Solidarity) and UCR (Radical Civic Union), had all but collapsed. Kirchner was tough in negotiations with the IMF to restructure the country's bad debt and implemented a series of heterodox economic measures. The economy, which had begun to recover at the end of 2002, soon began to surge, and Kirchner's popularity surged with it. Kirchner fired a number of Dirty War–era generals and widened the scope for human rights investigations into that era. Like his predecessors, Kirchner purged the court by threatening sitting justices with criminal charges. He aggressively centralized power in other ways as well, making frequent use of emergency decrees and broadening significantly his discretion over the budget. Nonetheless, an effort by Kirchner allies to permit unlimited reelection of government officials at the provincial level was blocked by a concerted civic campaign led by the Catholic Church. That rebuff appeared to convince Kirchner not to seek a second term, but instead to put his wife, then a member of the senate, forward as a candidate for president.[41]

In 2007, Cristina Fernández de Kirchner won the presidency, with 45 percent of the vote. Her husband died of a heart attack in 2010, eliminating the possibility that power would again be passed from one spouse to the other. Helped by strong economic growth, Kirchner easily won reelection to a second term in October 2011, with 54 percent of the vote. During her tenure in office, several prominent military officers have been given life sentences for crimes against humanity committed during the Dirty War era.[42] In mid-term elections in October 2013, the political opposition, led by Sergio Massa and his Renewal Front, performed strongly, suggesting that the Peronists' long domination of the Argentine political scene may be coming to an end.

Conclusion

Ironically, it was the excesses of the Dirty War that paved the way for Argentina's return to democracy in 1983, by discrediting the military and heightening the political engagement of civil society groups. The Peronist party has been the dominant Argentine political party since then because of its history as a workers' party coupled with its pragmatic social and economic policies, which recognize the realities of global markets. The party has at times taken advantage of its popular support to roll back the curtain on some of the worst atrocities committed during the generals' rule.[43] The Peronists themselves have often ignored the constitutional limits on their power, only to be rebuffed at times by civic groups, including the Catholic Church.

Venezuela

If Chile and Argentina are examples of Latin American countries whose transition toward democracy has gone more or less well, then Venezuela and Ecuador are examples of countries in which democracy appears to be headed off the rails. In the case of Venezuela, many argued that Hugo Chávez was moving his country not toward but away from liberal democracy, in the direction of a "quasi-tyranny of the majority"; many even question whether Venezuela is a democracy anymore.[44] A strong and credible left-wing party and an active civil society served to anchor Argentina firmly within democratic procedures, even as it was hit by a series of international economic shocks; however, Venezuela's strong but less representative party system meant that as hard economic times buffeted the country, disgruntled members of the working class gravitated toward a new, more populist party to articulate their grievances, one not as grounded in democratic traditions.

Guided Democracy

Historically, the military, church, and landed elite dominated Venezuelan politics. But in 1958, General Marcos Pérez Jiménez, who had ruled as a military dictator for six years, was overthrown, and nationwide strikes forced the military to allow civilian rule. The major political parties forged the so-called Pact of Punto Fijo, which guided Venezuela's transition toward democracy for decades.

Rómulo Betancourt was elected president of Venezuela in the 1958 general elections. He and his Democratic Action (AD) Party were despised by the military, but during his presidency, Betancourt and the military fought a successful counterinsurgency against Castroite leftist guerrillas, which ended up creating a lasting bond between political parties and the military. Because of its experience with being politically marginalized in the 1940s and 1950s, the AD Party decided to open up political space for all but the most intransigent of its rivals.

In the 1961 constitution, the leaders of the major political parties agreed to share power and oil wealth, effectively giving the state the right to determine how oil resources were to be used and the rents distributed. In the words of one expert, AD "agreed to representative institutions and veto points that limited its own ability to implement its militantly leftist agenda, which greatly reassured the military."[45] That respect for political differences is regarded as an important factor in Venezuela's ability to avoid succumbing to bureaucratic authoritarianism, as its neighbors did at the time.

The country's democratic regime was seen to benefit the middle class, unionized labor, business interests, and politicians, the latter of which became increasingly arrogant, insulated, and corrupt. In 1978, per capita income, which had been rising steadily for some time—in part because of oil wealth—began to fall as oil prices fell. By the time that Carlos Andrés Pérez, who had served as president from 1974 to 1979, was inaugurated for the second time in 1989, the country's foreign exchange reserves had been depleted. After only three weeks in office, Pérez was forced to turn to the IMF for help. The ensuing IMF-imposed austerity measures precipitated two days of rioting in ten of the country's cities. Pérez had to call in the army to restore order, which generated a tremendous amount of resentment within the military, particularly among junior officers who were seeing many of their perquisites taken away as part of the government's cost-cutting measures.[46]

The IMF's harsh medicine brought economic recovery in 1990 and 1991, but the ruling class was perceived to be appropriating most of the wealth that was generated. Junior officers staged two unsuccessful coups against Pérez's government in 1992; the following year, the attorney general introduced charges that the president had misused funds, which eventually led to his suspension from office.

Chávez Emerges

In 1993 former president Rafael Caldera, running this time as an independent candidate, was elected to succeed Pérez, although Caldera received just 30 percent of the vote. Caldera went after the banks, precipitating the collapse of the entire financial system. Out of the shadows of this economic catastrophe, Hugo Chávez, a former military officer who had orchestrated a failed coup in 1992 and consequently landed in prison, began to emerge as a national political figure. His appeal sprang from a popular urge to dismantle "savage capitalism" and to replace "an oligarchy that had masqueraded as a democracy for over 40 years."[47] The crisis destroyed any agreement that may have existed across Venezuelan society regarding the economic rules of the game.

In the lead-up to the 1998 presidential election, Chávez, running as a candidate of the Fifth Republic Movement, the social democratic party that he had founded, began to overtake the rest of the field. In a desperate bid to stop Chávez, the traditional parties abandoned their nominees and—only a month prior to the voting—collectively threw their support behind the governor of Carabobo, Henrique Salas Römer. It proved futile, as Chávez won with 56 percent of the vote.

In his inaugural address in February 1999, Chávez announced that he would replace the 1961 constitution. He organized a referendum in which 85 percent of those voting endorsed the creation of a new constituent assembly, and he skillfully engineered the delegate selection process so that he ended up controlling 93 percent of the seats in the assembly even though his candidates received only 53 percent of the vote.[48] His new constitution created five branches, adding to the traditional three branches the "Electoral Power" and "Citizen Power" branches. The electoral power oversees all elections within Venezuelan society; the citizen power, which includes the ombudsman and chief prosecutor, ensures that all citizens and elected officials abide by the law. His election and subsequent actions provoked wide-scale capital flight, and the economy shrank that year by 6 percent.[49] In 2000, in the new elections stipulated by the new constitution, chavistas swept into power at every level of government. Chávez announced his Plan Bolívar, which was to provide greater social services and infrastructure to poor areas, and funneled the funds through the military rather than the bureaucracy, which he distrusted. Bolivarian Circles—workers' councils named after Simon Bolívar—were created in the slums to organize Chávez supporters politically and provide social assistance.

Despite determined efforts by Chávez to convince foreign investors that he would be a responsible economic steward, the Venezuelan economy remained in the doldrums. Consequently, the opposition seemed to hold the upper hand during 2001–03, but ended up overplaying it. In April 2002, members of the political and business elite and the military orchestrated a coup against Chávez. Demonstrators protesting against his regime diverted from their approved marching path, and shots were fired. The ensuing mayhem was used by the military as a pretext to arrest Chávez and ferry him into exile on an island. However, suspicion spread that the United States was behind the coup, and the new interim authority behaved so ineptly and dictatorially that public sympathy quickly gravitated toward Chávez. After only two days, the military was forced to bring him back as president. The opposition then organized a recall referendum against Chávez in 2004, but by then world oil prices were trending steadily upward and the Venezuelan economy was on the rebound. The referendum failed, 59 percent to 41 percent.

With the economy buoyed by an influx of petrodollars, Chávez handily won reelection in December 2006, this time running as the head of the new United Socialist Party of Venezuela (PSUV), which was intended to subsume all leftist parties. His opponent, Governor Manuel Rosales of Zulia, received 37 percent of the vote to Chávez's 63 percent. The only silver lining for the opposition, which had long been quite divided, was that Rosales's New Era party demonstrated that it was "an opposition party capable of challenging the chavistas on a nationwide scale."[50] In his inaugural address, Chávez requested that the National Assembly grant him special power to rule by decree for eighteen months (Ley Habilante), which it did. He also announced that he would nationalize key industries and promised changes to the country's constitution. In December 2007, voters narrowly rejected his constitutional reform proposal, which drew inspiration from Castro's Cuba and included a provision that abolished any term limits on the president. He tried again in February 2009 with a second referendum, which included only the abolition of term limits, and this time he prevailed, with 54 percent voting in favor. In 2010, the opposition, now united as the Unity Roundtable, garnered 47 percent of the parliamentary vote, but because of jerry-rigged election rules that gave greater weight to rural votes, it secured only 65 of the 165 assembly seats.

Chávez won reelection convincingly in October 2012 (55 percent to 44 percent), but by then his health was failing. In June 2011, he flew to Cuba to have a cancerous tumor removed and returned there for treatment after complications emerged. On March 5, 2013, his vice president, Nicolás Maduro, announced that he had passed away. Maduro assumed the presidency and has continued Chávez's unique brand of charismatic, anti-American populism.

Conclusion

Like Chile's compromiso de estado, for a time Venezuela's Pact of Punto Fijo provided a consensus among elites that allowed democracy to emerge. Over time, however, the poor and marginalized began to sense that the elites were dividing up the spoils and that the existing political system was not addressing their needs. Hugo Chávez emerged as their political voice and capitalized on their support to rewrite the constitutional rules of the game in a way that consolidated his hold on power. It remains to be seen whether his successor, Maduro, can maintain the same iron grip on power as the challenges to the regime from within society grow.

Bolivia

Bolivia under Evo Morales has followed a path very similar to that of Venezuela under Hugo Chávez. Like Venezuela, Bolivia today looks more like a plebiscitary or delegative democracy than either a constitutional or representative one. The country holds regular elections, but Morales has been as unrestrained in flouting democratic institutions as Chávez was. Like Chávez's United Socialist Party, Morales's Movement toward Socialism (MAS) has endeavored to be first among equals, working to eliminate or control all other political parties.

From Coups to Concertation

Bolivia's transition toward democracy began in 1983. In 157 years, from its independence from Spain in 1825 until 1983, the country experienced a remarkable 180 military coups.[51] One reason is that Bolivia, which has the largest proportion of indigenous people on the continent, is also the poorest country in South America. Moreover, its smaller Spanish settler population has tightly controlled the country's natural gas and mineral wealth, and that has led to recurring conflict over the distribution of resources. The transition to democracy began with a modest agreement among the dominant political parties to address the country's raging hyperinflation, which stemmed from the collapse of the country's tin market. Cooperation soon led to a broader pact that paved the way for elections and a move toward democratic politics. The agreement in essence divided up the spoils of government among the leading parties, becoming an invitation for all kinds of petty patronage.

By the time that Gonzalo Sánchez de Lozado became president for the second time in 2002, the pillaging of the state by the major political parties was so acute that the country faced a fiscal crisis. Sánchez de Lozado found himself hemmed in by the patronage demands of the major parties on one side; the increasingly assertive demands of other societal actors, like the labor unions, on the other; and growing government deficits on the third. He introduced a tax reform plan to boost revenues, which led to a bloody revolt by members of the police force. Then, when word leaked that his government had struck a deal to sell natural gas to the United States via a pipeline through Chile, Sánchez de Lozado had to send in the military to put down rioting in La Paz. The military crackdown turned bloody—more than 120 people were killed in what has become known as the Bolivian Gas War—and Sánchez de Lozado was forced to resign and flee the country.[52]

Morales's Rise

A key figure in both protests was the cocoa grower and union organizer Evo Morales. An Aymara Indian, Morales had come to prominence for his active opposition to U.S.-led efforts to eradicate coca in Bolivia. He helped found a series of political parties, the last of which took the name of Movement for Socialism (MAS), to represent the interests of coca growers, indigenous people, and the poor. Morales had finished second to Sánchez de Lozado in 2003 (inadvertently aided by comments of the U.S. ambassador in the final weeks of the campaign suggesting that Bolivians should think twice before electing someone who advocates exporting cocaine). With Sánchez de Lozado's resignation, his vice president, Carlos Mesa, became interim president, but it was Morales who was driving events. His supporters continued to put pressure on Mesa to rescind the gas deal with the United States. After they took to the streets once more in 2005, Mesa eventually was forced to resign.

With 54 percent of the vote, Evo Morales handily won the ensuing presidential elections in late 2005, becoming Latin America's first indigenous president. By then the Bolivian economy had recovered, which only added to Morales's public popularity. The same pattern of patronage politics has continued under Morales, but with gas prices on the rise, he has not faced the same fiscal constraints as Sánchez de Lozado. Morales nationalized the oil and gas industries on taking office but allowed the big multinational producers to stay under renegotiated terms. High world prices for the country's gas and mineral exports, combined with pragmatic economic policies, have fueled unprecedented economic growth in Bolivia.

Opposition from the Regions

Morales has not enjoyed power as unconstrained as Chávez's largely because of the power of the regional prefects, or regional governors. In 2005, a civic movement emerged pushing for direct election of the prefects, and its members, who mounted a million-person rally in Santa Cruz and smaller rallies elsewhere, eventually prevailed. The elected regional governors of the four major departments to the east of La Paz—which have been called the Media Luna (half-moon) because they form a rough semi-circle around La Paz —represent the chief opposition to Morales.

In 2007, Morales convened a constituent assembly in Sucre, where he sought to ram through a new constitution over the heads of the opposition. It would, among other things, curtail the power of the prefects in Bolivia's richer eastern lowlands and shift it toward the poorer highland provinces. MAS supporters were bused into La Paz, where they surrounded congress and prevented opposition politicians from blocking a change in rules to the constituent assembly. MAS supporters then met in Oruro, without opposition members in attendance, and passed a new constitution. In response, the "half-moon" departments approved their own "autonomic statutes," which rejected the new constitution's stipulations limiting the autonomy of the prefects. Controversy over the new constitution flared repeatedly between 2006 and 2009. Morales easily survived a recall referendum in August 2008, winning 67 percent of the vote. The following month, a clash between pro-Morales peasants and antigovernment opponents in Pando resulted in the death of fourteen peasants and triggered a criminal indictment against the regional prefect. Facing continued resistance from the departments of Tarija, Santa Cruz, Beni, and Pando, the government and its opponents turned to the Organization of American States (OAS) to help mediate the conflict. A compromise draft was agreed to that maintained many of the government's proposed changes but removed several provisions restricting the media; it also made future constitutional revisions more difficult and limited presidents to two consecutive terms. More than 61 percent of voters approved the new constitution in January 2009.

The same year, Morales won reelection, with 64 percent of the vote, against Cochabamba mayor Manfred Reyes Villa of the Progressive Plan for Bolivia party. Despite complaints about Morales's abuse of state resources and selective prosecution of political opponents to tilt the playing field, the European Union judged the results to be generally free and fair. In the face of corruption charges, Reyes Villa fled the country.

Surprisingly, in his second term Morales has confronted challenges from the left more than the right. In late December 2010, while he was traveling abroad, government officials declared a sudden end to the domestic subsidy on gasoline, effectively raising its price by 73 percent. Mass protests and rioting in the streets, including by coca growers, a key base of Morales's support, followed the announcement. The subsidies were quickly reinstated.[53] In 2011, the inhabitants of the Indigenous Territory and National Park of Isibore Sécure (TIPNIS), together with civic organizations, opposed the government's plan to build, with Brazilian financing, a $415 million highway through their region to facilitate trade between Bolivia and Brazil. TIPNIS residents began the long 325-mile march to La Paz to make their case. At one point, the police threw tear gas and clubbed the marchers, injuring seventy people, but the marchers continued on to the capital, where others joined their protest. Confronted with another challenge from his base, Morales relented, sacking his defense and interior ministers and passing legislation to ban highway construction in TIPNIS.[54]

In 2011, Bolivia also held the first elections in Latin American history for judges. The measure was conceived as a way to address the large number of vacancies in the courts because of resignations and charges of malfeasance. Because Morales's MAS party controlled large majorities in both houses of parliament, he was able to handpick the candidates for judgeships. However, the voters delivered what appears to have been a stunning rebuke by casting more blank ballots in protest than valid ones.

Conclusion

Morales has styled himself as a politician in the mold of Hugo Chávez. Like Chávez, he rode to the presidency on a wave of disillusionment among indigenous peoples and other marginalized groups with elite-dominated politics. Like Chávez, he has built his charismatic presidency on pro-poor rhetoric and anti-American taunts. Like Chávez, he has sought to tinker with Bolivia's constitution to cement his grip on power. And like Chávez, he has benefited from high oil prices, which allow him to reward key constituents. However, he too faces growing public opposition to his heavy-handed rule, spearheaded in this case by opposition regional governors.

Lessons from Latin America

Latin America has made impressive strides in moving toward democracy. During the 1960s and 1970s, all but Colombia, Costa Rica, and Venezuela fell under the sway of military dictatorships. Today, although demagogic leaders in Venezuela, Ecuador, and Bolivia threaten to return their countries to authoritarianism and Cuba remains a closed and repressive state, the rest of Latin America has embraced democracy. Democracy has been enshrined in the charter of the Organization of American States as a regional norm. Freedom House rates twenty-two of the thirty-three countries of the region as "free." The military, once such a dominant figure in political life, has largely been consigned to the barracks. Elections have become deeply ingrained in the region's culture as a regular and expected feature of each country's political life.

Yet for all this progress, democratic institutions remain weak and continually subject to challenge. Despite the existence of governing institutions that in some cases have been in place for over a century—brought over by the region's former European colonial overlords—and many long-established and highly institutionalized political parties, democracy in Latin America remains remarkably driven by the personality of elected leaders and therefore inherently unstable. In political systems that are almost exclusively presidential rather than parliamentary in design, the region's elected presidents hold broad political sway. They have often run roughshod over other democratic institutions, whether parliament, the courts, or the free press. The advent of television and other mass media has only enabled them to circumvent further political parties and elected representatives, the traditional intermediaries between the state and citizens.

The sharp divisions of wealth within Latin America have created fertile ground for political leaders to resort to populist appeals in their bid for power. Leftist populist movements have torn apart the once cozy political arrangements among elites under which the spoils of government were divided up. All in all, the integration of the left into democratic politics after the end of the cold war has been one of Latin America's greatest political achievements. For the most part, the left—or at least what has been termed the "right left"—has become a responsible player in the democratic process. Pacts between left and right in many countries have created a new consensus on economic issues that respects the power and possibilities of global market forces to raise living standards while recognizing the need for social investments that target the poorest strata within society. Where that has not been the case—where the poor have instead been ignored or marginalized—they have tended to turn to more nondemocratic alternatives to make their voice heard, namely to the "wrong left" of Chávez, Morales, and the like.

While the old elite political structures have been cast aside, in most cases they have not yet been replaced by strong institutional alternatives. The region's elected presidents continue to dominate the political landscape. They follow the constitutional rules of the game and respect existing political institutions to the extent that it suits their interests. When it does not, they may try to tinker with the constitutional rules or simply ignore them entirely. Constituent assemblies have become a tool for the party in power to try to rewrite the constitutional rules to their permanent advantage. Parliaments and the courts remain weak. In places like Chile and Argentina, an increasingly flourishing and politically engaged civil society is emerging as a possible counterweight, albeit a still underdeveloped one, to executive overreach.

The Latin American example is rich with lessons for the Arab world. First, it shows that democracy is possible even in countries with vast disparities in wealth and education. Inequality certainly heightens the divisions within a democratic polity, often pitting a rich oligarchy against the more numerous, poorer masses. But while those divisions may make democracy more problematic, the experience of Latin America demonstrates that they are not insurmountable. Pacts in particular have become an effective way of bridging the divide on economic policy issues.

Second, the Latin American example suggests that strong militaries may be more of an impediment to than an enabler of democratization. As was seen during the early stages of Egypt's transition, militaries are sometimes looked to as a possible arbiter of the democratization process—a powerful national institution that can stand above the fray and referee among competing interests as democracy first takes root. In Latin America, the military ended up being a key obstacle to democratization. During the 1950s and 1960s, the military halted fragile experiments with democracy and took over the task of governance itself. Only after it failed miserably at that task—committing numerous human rights abuses and running economies into the ground—was it thoroughly discredited in the eyes of citizens and forced to retreat from politics. Only then did democracy really begin to take hold in the region.

Finally, the Latin American example shows the benefits of inclusion— of bringing nondemocratic actors or actors with an ambiguous commitment to democracy into the political system. During the cold war, the left was carefully excluded from democratic politics. Consequently, many leftist groups pursued their aims outside the formal political system— through militant revolutionary movements. As the cold war came to an end, many political restrictions were lifted, and the left has for the most part played a responsible (and leading) role in governance since then. Arguably, an important exception has been chavism, which has flouted the constitutional rules of the game and based its legitimacy instead on a kind of plebiscitary democracy, drawing on the economically and politically marginalized for its core support. Despite Chávez's death, his form of populism continues to pose the greatest threat to the future of democracy in Latin America. Democracy's greatest promise lies in the increasingly vibrant and engaged civic sector that has emerged in many countries to serve as an effective counterweight to populism's excesses.

CHAPTER SIX

SUB-SAHARAN AFRICA

Like Latin America, Sub-Saharan Africa has had more than its share of strong men dominating national politics. Yet a continent that often has been written off as a lost cause—one mired in poverty, kleptocracy, ethnic and tribal tensions, civil wars, and state failures—has in fact had its share of stunning successes. What the grim statistics about Africa hide is that while viewed in the aggregate the continent continues to be extremely impoverished and to experience high rates of conflict and instability, a number of countries within Africa are in fact performing remarkably well, both politically and economically.[1] The story of Sub-Saharan Africa over the last two decades is really a tale of two continents: one in which democratic and market reforms have laid the foundation for more effective governance and robust economic growth and another that continues to be plagued by the same maladies—authoritarianism, state-dominated economies, conflict, disease, and poverty—that have afflicted Africa since independence. Understanding the dynamics behind African countries' divergent trajectories can provide valuable insights on the prospects for democratization in the Arab world.

The Third Wave's Impact

The Third Wave of democratization had a transformative effect on large parts of Africa, much as it did on Latin America and the former Eastern bloc. The Third Wave began in Africa in November 1989, just as the Berlin Wall was coming down in Germany, when voters in Namibia elected representatives to a constituent assembly to write a new democratic constitution for their country. In 1990, a national conference gave civil society leaders in Benin an opening to call for a multiparty democracy, leading to the end of the 19-year reign of strongman Mathieu Kérékou. In February 1990, South African opposition leader and anti-apartheid crusader Nelson Mandela was released from prison, setting in motion South Africa's eventual transition to democracy.

Those developments ended up having dramatic ripple effects across the continent. At the time, much as in Latin America, dictators reigned in almost every country of Sub-Saharan Africa; the lonely democratic exceptions were Botswana, the Gambia, and Mauritius. The great hopes fostered by the independence movements of the 1950s and 1960s had dimmed as Africa's new leaders consolidated their control, rigging elections and ignoring any constitutional constraints on their power. The term "rule of the big man" aptly captured the nature of politics in most of Africa. Towering post-independence figures like Mobuto Sese Seko, Kenneth Kuanda, Kwame Nkrumah, and Julius Nyere dominated the state and the economy.

The Third Wave brought dramatic changes to many parts of the continent. The first was a profound change in norms throughout the region that led to free and fair elections being regarded as the sine qua non of political legitimacy. In response to public pressure, a number of governments announced plans for elections and expanded the rights of citizens in the early 1990s. Between 1990 and 1994, thirty-eight Sub-Saharan African countries held competitive elections, twenty-nine of which were considered to be "founding" elections. Whereas Africa had seen no more than two competitive elections a year in the 1980s, there were fourteen in 1993 alone. During this period, eleven incumbent presidents were voted out of office, while another three chose not to run again.[2]

The second change was the rapid withdrawal of the military from political life in many Sub-Saharan African countries. However, the change was not nearly as complete in Africa, where the military has remained a very prominent and powerful political actor in a number of countries, as it was in Latin America. But in other countries, the military rather abruptly ceased to play a domineering role in political life. In many parts of the continent, military-run governments are no longer regarded as a legitimate form of government, just as military coups are no longer regarded as a legitimate means of effecting regime change.

The speed with which political expectations changed was fairly breathtaking. In very short order, the norm of elections as the only legitimate basis for political authority was adopted fairly widely in the region, which had been dominated since independence by authoritarian dictators and their militaries. There were many reasons for the change. The end of the cold war eliminated the competition between the United States and the Soviet Union for influence in Africa, so authoritarian leaders could no longer count on the unqualified military and financial support of Moscow or Washington to prolong their tenure. That change coincided with an end to international bank lending to Africa and other countries. The global oil shocks of the 1970s had adversely affected most African economies, stunting growth, throwing budgets into deficit, creating trade imbalances, and drying up foreign investment. To compensate, African leaders borrowed heavily from foreign banks, running up significant foreign debt; however, when Mexico defaulted on its bank debt in 1982, such international lending all but dried up. Many governments were then left with little choice but to turn to the International Monetary Fund (IMF) to finance their debt. The IMF placed heavy conditions on its lending, requiring countries to undertake painful macroeconomic reforms as part of their debt restructuring programs. Such strong economic medicine was to pave the way for eventual renewed economic growth in many countries, but over the short term the required austerity measures brought only pain and provoked large-scale protests and popular unrest, which peaked in the late 1980s and early 1990s. At the same time, citizens were growing weary of the broken promises of their leaders, pervasive corruption, and suppression of basic individual freedoms as well as stagnant, state-dominated economies. The late 1980s and early 1990s saw a marked increase in political protests throughout Africa. Many Africans watched the political events unfolding in Eastern Europe and wondered whether democracy was possible in their own countries too.[3]

A number of African countries—Benin, Cape Verde, Comoros, Lesotho, Madagascar, Malawi, Mozambique, São Tomé and Príncipe, South Africa, and Zambia, among others—experienced political openings and held founding elections in the early 1990s. Then, in the latter half of the decade, the wave seemed to subside, sparking concern that democracy's moment in Africa had come and gone. Between 1994 and 1999, Ghana was the only new country to adopt democracy, while Comoros, the Republic of Congo (Brazzaville), the Gambia, Niger, and Zambia experienced backsliding as the result of coups and stolen or canceled elections. Then, in Nigeria, dictator Sani Abacha died suddenly in 1998, paving the way for multiparty elections there. In 2000, elections brought a peaceful transition of power to the opposition in Ghana when John Kufour defeated Jerry Rawlings's hand-picked successor, John Atta Mills. Kenya, Senegal, and Zambia all moved into the ranks of democracies shortly thereafter, while the end of Sierra Leone's and Liberia's bloody civil wars led to multiparty elections and peaceful transfers of power in those countries.[4]

While today Freedom House categorizes seventeen of the fifty countries of Sub-Saharan Africa, or about one-third, as electoral democracies, there were just three when the Third Wave of democratization first touched the shores of Africa in late 1989.[5] Those democratic changes took place in some of the poorest countries in the world. The prevailing assumption within the social science literature had long been that democracy required a middle class—that a country needed to attain a certain level of economic development, in terms of the per capita income of ordinary citizens, for democratization to succeed. Yet ten of the region's seventeen electoral democracies have an annual per capita income today of below $6,000 (and below that of Egypt, which is estimated at $6,600).[6] Some of the poorest countries on earth—Liberia, Malawi, Mali, Comoros, Sierra Leone, Zambia, Benin—have been among the ranks of Africa's new democracies.

As remarkable as these changes are, it is important not to overstate what has been achieved. There are two major caveats. First, the democratizing countries represent only half of the story of Sub-Saharan Africa since 1990; the other half is much more tragic. The same forces that with the end of the cold war precipitated a turn to democracy in some parts of the continent—the end of the U.S.-Soviet rivalry in Africa, the subsequent drying up of foreign subsidies and loans, and the collapse of state-dominated economies—triggered in others a mad scramble for resources and power and a sharp upsurge in violence. Rather than giving way to democracy, autocracy was replaced by civil war and anarchy. Countries like Somalia and the Democratic Republic of the Congo (DRC) became engulfed in violence and degenerated into failed states.

In short, some countries in Sub-Saharan Africa have fared remarkably well politically and economically since the 1990s. They have opened up their political systems and become electoral democracies and reformed their once state-dominated economies. As a result, their citizens enjoy greater freedoms than in the past, governance is improving, and their economies are growing at a rapid clip.[7] However, many others are still plagued by the same pathologies that have long dogged the continent: autocracy, corruption, state-dominated economies, ethnic conflict, hunger, and disease. In those countries, "big-man rule" has yet to give way to more rule-based politics. Poor governance has resulted in diminished economic performance, which in turn has only increased the predatory behavior of political leaders. Some resource-rich countries, like Nigeria and Angola, have fallen somewhere in between. They have fared better economically than many because of their natural resource wealth, but precisely because they have not faced the same resource constraints as others, their leaders have successfully resisted pressure to move toward real democracy.[8]

Second, caution is in order because Africa's new democracies remain works in progress. Many are categorized as electoral democracies because they hold regular, multiparty elections, but they are democracies only in a narrow sense. They are not "consolidated democracies," either in the technical sense—in that power has rotated back and forth at least twice between opposing political parties on the basis of elections—or in the broader sense of being countries where democratic norms have been internalized sufficiently by all political actors that they are unlikely ever to revert to authoritarianism. Nor are they "liberal democracies," in the sense that the power that elected political leaders exercise is circumscribed both by the individual rights of citizens and by a set of rules embodied in a constitution and a code of laws.

The Contours of African Democracy

With a handful of exceptions, Africa's new democracies might be accurately labeled nascent or fragile democracies. They have had a political opening and, as a result of that opening, a founding election. However, what has come after has varied widely. After their initial political opening, many countries experienced setbacks. In some cases, civil war interrupted the transition to democracy (DRC, Sierra Leone, Liberia). In others, a military coup halted democratic progress, sometimes even in long-standing democracies (Mali, Mauritius, Cape Verde, Nigeria). Those setbacks were not always permanent, and the democratic experiment often resumed after a lengthy pause. Over time, sometimes following a series of democratic reversals, elections have become a regular and increasingly ingrained feature of African politics.

Africa's new democracies remain fragile because personal rule has yet to be replaced fully by the rule of law. The "big men" continue to shape African politics, even if they must now stand for election. In the early 1990s, African leaders acceded to the demands of their citizens and the international community for elections, but they were far less willing to cede power through them. At the very start of the Third Wave, a number of long-standing African leaders were caught flat-footed by the sudden public demand for democratic change and ended up losing power in initial founding elections. Other African political leaders watched their neighbors going down in defeat and learned quickly how to convene elections without jeopardizing their hold on power. In a phenomenon that close observers of the Arab world would find all too familiar, African political leaders in the mid-1990s talked of democracy and introduced political reforms such as elections, but they maintained an iron grip on power. They introduced some of the characteristics of democracy—the most notable being elections, but also some greater freedoms for their citizens—while adopting little of its real substance. Political leaders struck a careful balance, offering the people just enough democracy to garner international approval and maintaining just enough repression to keep opposition forces at bay.[9] Most of the changes introduced were more cosmetic than real. The key criterion became "presentability"—being able to appear to the international community to be democratic.[10]

While bowing to the public's demand that they hold elections, the "big men" ensured that the elections were heavily skewed in their favor. Incumbents tilted the electoral playing field to their advantage by dominating state media election coverage, financing their campaigns from public coffers, dispensing state patronage to loyal supporters, physically intimidating the opposition, and harassing any independent media and civil society groups. By one calculation, incumbent presidents have won 86 percent of the elections that they contested.[11] For that reason, only in a few instances (for example, Ghana and Zambia) has power shifted at least twice from one political party to another, thereby meeting what many regard as the technical definition of consolidated democracies. Even where elections are relatively free and fair, presidents continue to "reign rather than rule."[12] Their presidencies are "imperial presidencies" because once they are installed in office, their power remains largely unchecked. Between elections, the region's leaders tend to do as they please, ignoring legal and institutional constraints on their power. Often they rely on personal decrees rather than legislation to get things done. The parliament and judiciary tend to be too weak to serve as a countervailing check on executive power.

Yet important democratic progress has been achieved in many African countries since the 1990s. First, as imperfect as elections have been in many instances, the very fact that there have been elections has created the presumption that there will be more. Elections have become deeply ingrained in African political life. Multiparty elections have become "both contagious and resilient."[13] Citizens now expect to be able to choose their leaders. Second, the quality of elections has improved over time. The mechanics of how elections are conducted have received much greater scrutiny as both the international community and local citizen groups have become much more sophisticated in their monitoring of elections. Independent election commissions and domestic monitoring organizations have made it much more difficult for incumbents to simply steal elections. Third, leaders have been forced to recognize that there are limits on their power. What now compels political leaders to exit from office are no longer coups, but elections and term limits. The formal rules of politics now matter.[14] The rule that has the most force is the rule limiting the number of consecutive terms that a president can serve. By one recent estimate, thirty-three African countries now have term limits, and the tenures of fourteen presidents have been ended by those limits since 1990.[15]

Fourth, other centers of political power are gradually emerging to challenge the dominance of the executive. In many countries, legislatures, which historically have been relatively powerless, are becoming more professional and enhancing their institutional capacity. While their formal authority remains limited, they are challenging many of the prerogatives once reserved for presidents, including their budget-making authority. Legislatures are now calling presidents to task when they exceed their constitutional and legal authority. Judiciaries also are becoming more professional and independent. Limits are being placed on the ability of executives to pack courts with their own people. Brave judges are on occasion taking cases involving corruption and abuses of power by the executive branch.

In addition, independent media are growing exponentially and becoming a force in their own right. New communications technologies are making it more and more difficult for political leaders to completely control the narrative. In some countries, intrepid journalists are daring to investigate previously untouchable topics such as government graft, human rights abuses, and political campaign financing. Civil society groups also are proliferating. Africa has a long tradition of associational life, from tribal organizations to churches, unions, associations, and clubs. They have been joined by newer groups such as human rights organizations, public interest groups, election monitoring organizations, public policy institutes, and the like, often funded by international donors. In general, however, Africa's nascent civil society has been no match for the power of the state. Africa's "big men" have been very effective at marginalizing civil society opponents through payoffs, intimidation, imprisonment, and extrajudicial killing. Nonetheless, at pivotal moments in some African states, civic groups have intervened in dramatic ways to nudge the cause of democracy forward.

At the very beginning of the Third Wave, it was the takeover of a national conference in Benin by civic leaders that created one of the first democratic political openings in Africa and led to multiparty elections there. The anti-apartheid movement—which drew in not only blacks and colored people of diverse ethnicities and classes from all across South Africa but also liberal whites—was decisive in ushering in a new, democratic South Africa. More recently, civic groups have been instrumental in mounting public demonstrations in opposition to political leaders who rig elections, attempt to stay beyond their legal term of office, or otherwise violate the constitutional rules of the game. And where they have faced overwhelming public opposition, leaders have generally found it in their interest to back down. Notable examples include the push in Zambia by citizens to end Kenneth Kuanda's one-party rule and the efforts of Ghanaian civil society groups to prevent Jerry Rawlings from pushing through a new constitution outlawing political parties; the same groups subsequently worked to improve the country's election procedures.

Such growing civic activism has been accompanied by a change in public attitudes toward political authority. As the Afrobarometer surveys have documented, at the start of the Third Wave Africans were willing to accord significant deference to their political leaders. The traditional "big-man" culture of African politics was deeply ingrained, and citizens looked to their new political leaders to bring their countries the modernization and democratization that they had been promised. Over time, citizens' frustration with their leaders grew and their trust in them declined because leaders did not fulfill their promises. In many countries, political learning seems to have occurred, whereby citizens have come to understand that democracy is not something that is going to be handed to them by their political leaders but something that they must claim through their own active engagement in politics. They recognize that a government of the people rests on their participation as much as it does on well-crafted institutions and periodic public balloting. This evolution in thinking seems to be most pronounced in countries that have had the longest experience with democracy.[16] The remainder of the chapter examines four case studies of democratization in Sub-Saharan Africa. Two of the cases—Ghana and Zambia—are relative successes when it comes to democratization; the other two—Nigeria and Uganda—have been far less successful. After a rocky start in the early 1990s, Ghana is once again a leader in Africa in terms of its political development and an exemplar of progress. Zambia remains a democracy with many blemishes, but a democracy nonetheless, one that has weathered many storms over the past two decades and has now seen power rotate from the long-time incumbent party to the opposition. Nigeria and Uganda seem to be moving very slowly in the right direction, toward becoming at least competitive electoral democracies, but they have demonstrated far less progress than Ghana and Zambia. Strong militaries and, in the case of Nigeria, ethnic tensions have repeatedly intervened to stymie democratic progress.

Ghana

After serving as a champion of the African independence movement, Ghana foundered politically for many years, buffeted by repeated military interventions in its politics. Nonetheless, a well-educated and engaged citizenry has worked hard to realize the promise of democracy in Ghana. As a result of those efforts, the country has become an encouraging example of the possibilities of democracy in Sub-Saharan Africa.

Nkrumah and Beyond

Ghana was one of the first Sub-Saharan African countries to achieve its independence, breaking free from the United Kingdom in 1957. Kwame Nkrumah was the leader of its independence movement, its first prime minister, and following elections in 1960, its first president. He was esteemed throughout the continent as a champion of African self-government, as a leading philosopher of pan-Africanism, and as a driving force behind the creation of the Organization of African Unity. However, after about a decade in office, he also became increasingly authoritarian, and he was overthrown by a military coup in 1966 while traveling outside the country. Over the next 25 years, political power in Ghana oscillated between civilian and military governments. The military would rule for a time, call for elections, allow the elected civilian leadership to rule briefly, and then intervene again as the cycle repeated itself. Following the coup against Nkrumah, the military ruled for about three years, then organized elections for 1969, which resulted in Kofi Busia being named prime minister after his Progress Party captured most of the seats in parliament. Three years later, Busia was deposed by the military. A junior officers' putsch followed in 1979, led by Jerry Rawlings, and the military again allowed elections to take place. President Hilla Limann served for three years, only to be unseated in another coup led by Rawlings at the end of 1981.

During that period, Ghana lost its leadership role on the continent; at the same time, it began to founder economically. Nkrumah had championed a policy of industrialization at all costs, combining grandiose national investment projects with damaging import-substitution trade policies. By the time of Rawlings's second coup, the economy had contracted substantially and the country's exports of cocoa, its principal crop, had fallen precipitously. Rawlings, a self-styled populist revolutionary, tried for a time to fix the crisis through administrative controls, but when that failed, he reluctantly adopted a structural adjustment program developed by the World Bank and the IMF. The bitter medicine worked, and between 1984 and 1988, Ghana registered 6 to 7 percent growth and emerged as a model of economic reform for the continent.[17]

Rawlings and the Third Wave

When the Third Wave hit Africa, Rawlings sought to capitalize on his economic success to legitimize his continued rule through elections. In preparation for both presidential and parliamentary elections, he initially tried to push through a new constitution that banned all political parties, but Ghanaian human rights groups vehemently opposed the ban and Rawlings eventually relented. In the 1992 presidential elections, Rawlings and his new National Democratic Congress (NDC) party faced a number of opponents, foremost among them Adu Boahen of the New Patriotic Party (NPP), a successor to Kofi Busia's Progress Party. The elections, which were marred by a host of irregularities, were overseen by an electoral commission appointed wholly by Rawlings, and there were just 200 election observers—all of them international. The commission hastily compiled a voter registration list that was plagued with inconsistencies. Rawlings used the prerogatives of his office fully to further his candidacy, unveiling new infrastructure projects for key regions, giving government employees 60 percent raises, and dominating the state-run media's coverage of the campaign.[18] On election day, the opposition cried foul, citing a long list of flaws in the election process, and announced a boycott of the following month's parliamentary elections. The electoral commission, without dissent from international observer groups, nonetheless declared Rawlings the winner, with 58 percent of the vote to 30 percent for Boahen.[19]

Despite the controversy surrounding the 1992 elections and the seating of a new parliament dominated almost wholly by Rawlings's NDC, during the following years important progress was made toward achieving democracy. Individual rights were expanded, the independent media grew, and civic groups proliferated and assumed a much larger role in Ghanaian political life. The electoral commission took a number of measures—including the re-registration of voters—to prevent the election-related problems cited by the opposition from recurring. The Inter-Party Advisory Committee (IPAC) brought representatives from all the major parties together regularly to discuss preparations for the 1996 elections. A number of prominent nonprofit organizations, such as the Christian Council, the Conference of Catholic Bishops, and the Ghana Legal Literacy and Resource Foundation, conducted voter education campaigns. Local civic groups also established a nonpartisan umbrella organization, the Network of Domestic Election Observers, which trained and deployed about 4,100 domestic election observers. Most important, on election day, party representatives—some 60,000 in total—were posted at every polling precinct in the country to help tally and sign the vote count in each.[20]

The extensive preparations for the elections by political parties and civic groups altered dramatically the environment in which the 1996 elections took place. Rawlings was forced to take the elections seriously and actively campaign across the country. For the first time in his 15-year rule, he deigned to give an interview to the media. Also, in response to accusations of insider deals, the government for the first time published the details regarding all recent transactions in which state enterprises had been privatized.[21] John Kufour, a former Rawlings minister, was the candidate of the Great Alliance, a new coalition that brought together the NPP and Nkrumah's former political party. Rawlings prevailed again, amassing 57 percent of the vote to Kufour's 40 percent, but the opposition managed to secure a third of parliament's seats, a victory that gave it, finally, a voice in parliament. Rawlings still benefited immensely from the advantages of incumbency, but the actual voting on election day, while not without significant flaws, proceeded much more smoothly than it had four years earlier.

The constitution prevented Rawlings from running for a third term in 2000. That did not stop him from trying to amend the rules, but he encountered strenuous opposition, both at home and from abroad, and he was forced to back down. Kufour, running under the banner of the NPP, defeated Rawlings's handpicked successor, John Atta Mills, receiving 57 percent of the vote to Atta Mills's 43 percent in the second round of voting. With Kufour's inauguration, power was passed peacefully from one elected civilian leader to another of a different political party for the first time in Ghana's history.

Kufour's Presidency

Kufour, who was elected to a second term in 2004 by again defeating Atta Mills, racked up significant accomplishments during his eight-year tenure. He and his NPP, which commanded a majority in parliament, generally received high marks for good governance, sound economic management, innovative poverty reduction and social welfare programs, and prudent investment in public infrastructure. During Kufour's presidency, Ghana regained its standing as one of the most progressive countries in Sub-Saharan Africa.

However, in many respects Kufour's presidency continued to be an "imperial presidency," one that had only limited regard for the legal and constitutional constraints on presidential power or for broader public opinion. Kufour's administration continued to be perceived as corrupt, and several top government officials were implicated in a cocaine scandal. Ghanaians were angered by the extravagance often displayed by Kufour and his family, who built a palatial presidential office complex using state funds. His administration never adequately accounted for its lavish spending on the country's 50th anniversary celebration. The Kufour government was also perceived to be giving preferential treatment to the Akan-Ashanti group of tribes, the major base of its political support.

Like Rawlings, Kufour ran up against the two-term constitutional limit, which set up a closely contested election battle in 2008 to succeed him. Kufour's chosen successor, Nana Addo Dankwa Akufo-Addo, the attorney general and then foreign minister under Kufour and a long-time human rights campaigner, narrowly lost to John Evans Atta Mills of Rawlings's NDC in the second round. (Atta Mills received 49.9 percent of the vote, giving him just a 40,586 vote margin out of 9 million votes cast.) The country was tense during the week leading up to the electoral commission's final announcement of the election results, and sporadic rioting broke out across the country, but the NPP ultimately accepted the election result.

That such a razor-thin election result did not provoke civil breakdown is a testimony to the professionalism of the electoral commission and the sophistication of the Ghanaian public.[22] The near parity of votes received by the two leading parties suggests just how competitive the country's party system has become. (The 2012 elections also were a tight contest, with Nana Akufo-Addo and his NPP again being narrowly defeated,

50.7 percent to 47.7 percent, by the NDC's John Dramani Mahama, who became a candidate for president following Atta Mills's death.) President Kufour's 2008 handover of power to John Evans Atta Mills was the second peaceful transition of power from one civilian government to another; it also represented the fifth successful set of elections in Ghana over the previous twenty years. Beginning with the 1992 elections, each set of elections has been freer and fairer than those that preceded it.

Conclusion

Ghana has once more become the poster child for democracy in Sub-Saharan Africa. The growing success of elections as a mechanism for periodically refreshing the country's political leadership has strengthened the public's faith in their political system. In recent surveys, 79 percent preferred democracy to any other form of government.[23] Better governance has also helped narrow the gap between rich and poor. Whereas half the country once lived below the poverty line, today just a quarter does. Ghana now ranks eighth among the forty-six Sub-Saharan African countries in terms of human development.[24]

Yet profound challenges remain. The recent elections saw strong ethnic bloc voting in key parts of the country. The NPP drew a disproportionate share of its vote from the Ashanti region in the south-central part of the country (where the Akan-Ashanti tribes live) and from more affluent voters, while the NDC dominated in the northern Volta Region, where the members of the Ewe form a majority. A large share of the electorate remains politically passive and civically unengaged. According to Afrobarometer, for example, 43 percent have never attended a community meeting.[25] If democracy is to sink deeper roots in Ghana—to represent more than just periodic elections—those deficiencies must be overcome.

Zambia

In the early 1990s, when elections ended Kenneth Kuanda's 26-year reign, Zambia got off to a much more promising start than Ghana had. However, the country's democratic prospects dimmed significantly as the opposition party that had ousted Kuanda, the Movement for Multiparty Democracy (MMD), adopted many of his authoritarian ways and won election after election for the next twenty years. Only recently, with the election of a president from the long-time opposition party, have prospects for democracy brightened considerably.

Kuanda and the UNIP

Zambia achieved its independence from Britain in 1964, and independence leader Kenneth Kuanda was elected president the same year. He was reelected in 1968 in elections that were relatively free and fair, although he and his United National Independence Party (UNIP) lacked any viable opposition. When a real opposition began to emerge, Kuanda eliminated the threat by declaring Zambia a one-party state in 1973. For the next 18 years, all candidates for office had to be UNIP members.[26]

The Third Wave swept Africa just as Zambia was feeling the effects of years of economic mismanagement by Kuanda's government and falling copper prices. In 1990, there were bread riots in the streets and the military launched an abortive coup. In the midst of a profound political and economic crisis, civic and opposition groups banded together to push for a multiparty democracy, and their protests eventually forced Kuanda to agree to competitive elections. The opposition then formed the MMD as an umbrella political party that included labor unions and business groups to compete against Kuanda in the 1991 elections. The MMD's presidential candidate, labor leader Frederick Chiluba, defeated Kuanda handily, 76 to 24 percent.

Chiluba Takes Over

Over time, Chiluba proved as capable of strong-man tactics as his predecessor. Moreover, his Movement for Multiparty Democracy ironically came to dominate Zambian politics nearly as thoroughly as Kuanda's UNIP had. In the run-up to the 1996 elections, for example, Chiluba reworked the constitution to require presidential candidates to demonstrate Zambian parentage in order to prevent Kuanda from running against him. Accusations of great extravagance and corruption dogged Chiluba throughout his presidency, and later he was formally charged with corruption and embezzlement (he was eventually acquitted of all charges).

As Chiluba's second term drew to an end, several supporters campaigned to amend the constitution to allow him to serve a third term. However, opposition politicians and civic groups intervened to prevent Chiluba from extending his stay in office. Opposition politicians circulated a petition opposing any change in presidential term limits, which was followed by calls from members of parliament for Chiluba's impeachment for corruption and abuse of power.[27] Civic groups staged demonstrations in a number of cities, and citizens donned green ribbons to protest any change in term limits. In the end, Chiluba was forced to drop the idea of pursuing a third term. His designated successor, Levy Mwanawasa, narrowly won election in 2006, eking out a victory by just 33,997 votes and with a mere 30 percent of the popular vote. The election campaign was managed by Chiluba himself, who liberally deployed the resources of the state at his disposal on the mistaken assumption that under Mwanawasa he could continue to manipulate Zambian politics. In fact, Mwanawasa's administration was later to investigate him on charges of corruption.[28]

In 2008, Mwanawasa died suddenly. His vice president, Rupiah Banda, also of the MMD, called for snap elections. The early election date prevented the electoral commission from updating the voter rolls, which meant that some 500,000 Zambian youth—who polls showed favored the opposition 2 to 1—were prevented from voting. In an extremely tight race, Banda beat out the Patriotic Front's Michael Sata by 35,209 votes of the 1,791,806 cast. Sata demanded a recount, but the supreme court denied his legal challenge.[29] The election marked something of a landmark in Sub-Saharan Africa, in that it was the first time that a new leader was elected peacefully following the death of a president.[30]

The MMD Is Defeated

After five election victories, the MMD's impressive run finally came to an end in September 2011. Michael Sata defeated President Rupiah Banda, 43 percent to 36 percent. For the first time since 1991, power in Zambia passed peacefully from the civilian leader of one party to that of another. During the election campaign, Sata played heavily on anti-Chinese sentiment to mobilize voters. The Chinese have made substantial investments in Zambia, particularly in its natural resource sector, which has engendered significant resentment among the local population.[31] The previous year Chinese managers had responded to labor unrest at a copper mine by gunning down protesters, and to the anger of Zambians, the government eventually dropped all charges against the managers. Sata capitalized on that anger in winning the election.

As president, Sata has shown no greater willingness to respect the rights of the political opposition than his predecessors did. He jailed Nevers Mumba, the current leader of the MMD, for two nights for unlawful assembly and sought to have his party deregistered for not paying its statutory fees, a move that the supreme court blocked.[32] More recently, he called for the public prosecutor to investigate the wealth of his other main political rival, Hakainde Hichilema, the president of the United Party for National Development.[33]

Conclusion

While Zambia's political leaders often still behave like the "big men" of African lore, the country has witnessed important changes since Kenneth Kuanda was unseated in the country's first multiparty elections in 1991. It was civic groups that pressed Kuanda to hold multiparty elections and civic groups that 15 years later dissuaded his successor, Frederick Chiluba, from trying to amend the constitution to run for a third term. Those are small steps forward—the country's elected leaders continue to see themselves as above the law and corruption continues unabated—but gradually society is placing limits on the prerogatives of its political leaders.

Nigeria

Strategically located along the Niger River, where west and central Africa meet, Nigeria is the most populous country in Africa and one of its most abundant in terms of natural resource wealth. Because of its size and strategic location, it has been looked to as a leader on the continent. It was a long-time supporter of African anticolonial movements, a founding member of the Organization for African Unity and the Economic Community of West African States, and the leader of a number of regional peacekeeping missions. Yet its own experience with democracy has been checkered at best. Since gaining independence from the British in 1960, the country has endured a series of military coups and often brutal military-led governments. Civilians have governed for only 25 of the 53 years since independence. Elections have been few and far between; when they have occurred, they have been plagued by widespread irregularities, fraud, intimidation, and corruption. Nigeria's leaders, military and civilian, have badly mismanaged the country, using the country's vast oil resources as their personal patrimony to reward political friends and punish enemies. By and large, they have ignored the writ of law, ruling as they see fit, without regard to constitutional niceties or the will of the people or of parliament. Through their conduct, they have tended to undermine rather than support the development of democratic institutions. They have also damaged severely the country's economy. Despite Nigeria's significant oil wealth, 70 percent of the population lives below the poverty line.[34] As one expert observed, "dishonest elites have systematically mismanaged this oil-rich . . . country."[35]

Post-Colonial Struggles

Like many other African states, Nigeria was cobbled together by its colonial masters through administrative fiat. Today the country comprises more than 250 ethnic and linguistic groups, the most important being the dominant Hausa-Fulani group in the northwest, the Yoruba in the southwest, and the Igbo in the southeast. Roughly half the population is Christian and half is Muslim. Under any circumstances, ruling a country as ethnically diverse and as far-flung as Nigeria (its landmass is double the size of California) would be a challenging task, but the country's leaders have hardly risen to the challenge. More often than not, rather than helping bridge the country's ethnic and religious divides, they have exacerbated them for short-term political gain.

Upon independence, the country was ruled for six years by a parliamentary government, which was overthrown in 1966 by a military coup. Military-led governments ruled for 28 of the next 32 years; the one exception, the short-lived Second Republic, was in power from 1979 to 1983. In 1985, General Ibrahim Babangida ousted General Muhammadu Buhari from power. Babangida portrayed himself as a reformer, and for a time he liberalized political life and proposed a gradual transition toward elections and democratic rule. The timetable for such changes, however, became repeatedly prolonged and Babangida's rule became increasingly repressive. Finally, elections were set for mid-1993. Early returns leaked to the news media showed Moshood K. O. Abiola, a Yoruba Muslim businessman, with a commanding lead over Alhaji Bashir Tofa, a Kano-based businessman who represented the northern Muslim heartland, which had long dominated politics. However, a civic group of questionable origins and backing that purported to support continued military rule mounted a series of lawsuits challenging the election process and succeeded in blocking the release of the final results. Several days after the election, the military annulled the elections entirely, even though they were widely viewed as relatively free and fair.[36]

Protests and riots ensued, with more than 100 people killed as the military cracked down. Under pressure from human rights groups, unions, professional organizations, some of the political parties, and the international community, Babangida stepped down two months later, transferring power to an interim national government headed by Ernest Shonekan with Babangida's ally General Sani Abacha as defense minister.

Without a popular mandate, Shonekan's civilian government lasted all of three months before Abacha, using a strike over fuel prices as a pretext, took over.[37]

Military Rule under Abacha

General Abacha's rule marked a low point in Nigeria's short history. Abacha's military government was notable for the sheer magnitude of its repression, human rights violations, corruption, and siphoning of state resources. Like Babangida, Abacha held out the promise of an eventual transition back to democracy but repeatedly postponed delivering on his promise. Abacha abrogated the constitution written under Babangida and convened a constitutional conference to write a new one. The eventual recommendations of the conference were largely ignored, although the government repeatedly referenced but never published a 1995 constitution that was purportedly based on its work.

A divided opposition and Abacha's dissolution of all political parties hampered resistance to his rule. Because support for Abiola, the presumed election winner, was concentrated among the Yoruba and most democracy activists were Lagos-based professionals, regime opponents had a hard time attracting broader-based support. A year after the disputed elections, Abiola announced that he was the legitimate president, with the backing of the newly formed, multiethnic National Democratic Coalition, which was made up of opposition politicians. He was promptly thrown in jail for treason. His arrest provoked more riots and protests, concentrated primarily in the country's Yoruba-dominated southwest. For nine weeks, a strike by both Pengassan (the union of oil company administrators and executives) and Nupeng (the union of oil workers) crippled the country, but the country's largest trade union federation stood aside. Abacha and his military cracked down hard—shooting protesters, arresting union leaders and democracy activists, and shuttering opposition media—and ultimately prevailed.[38]

The crackdown was followed in 1995 by the hanging of the renowned journalist and activist Ken Saro-Wiwa and eight others, who had campaigned against the environmental and economic damage wrought by Royal Dutch Shell on the Ogoni people in the country's southeast. In 1996, unidentified gunmen shot and killed Abiola's wife, in what was believed to be part of an orchestrated set of attacks by the government on regime opponents. At the same time, economic conditions deteriorated significantly. Whereas per capita GNP had been $1,000 in 1980, it had declined to $250 by 1996. Abacha appeared to be engineering the conditions that would allow him to succeed himself through presidential elections when he unexpectedly passed away in 1998.

General Obasanjo

General Abdulsalami Abubakar, Abacha's successor, pressed forward with plans for elections, which were complicated by the sudden death of Abiola, the presumed frontrunner, while meeting with U.S. officials in Washington. In 1999, in elections marked by significant fraud and irregularities, General Olusegun Obasanjo, the candidate of the People's Democratic Party, prevailed over Olu Falae of Abiola's successor party, the Alliance for Democracy, 62 percent to 38 percent. A Christian of Yoruban descent who had been jailed by Abacha, Obasanjo had led the 1976–79 military government that paved the way for the short-lived civilian government of the Second Republic.[39]

Obasanjo's two terms were remarkable mostly for their turbulence. Despite his pledges to clean up government, high-level corruption continued largely unabated. At the same time, ethnic and religious violence skyrocketed. More than 10,000 people are estimated to have died during his presidency as a result of sectarian strife. On the positive side of the ledger, Obasanjo is credited with implementing far-reaching economic reforms that improved macroeconomic conditions in Nigeria and created the foundation for more sustainable growth.

In 2006, Obasanjo sought to amend the constitution to enable himself to run for a third term, but he was rebuffed by the senate.[40] Undeterred, he blocked his rival, Vice President Abubaker Atiku, from winning his People's Democratic Party (PDP) nomination, throwing his support behind Umaru Yar'Adua, the rather obscure and sickly governor of a northern state. Obasanjo then worked feverishly behind the scenes, employing the powers of incumbency and the state resources at his disposal to ensure Yar'Adua's election. The 2007 elections were, in the words of one expert, "blatantly fraudulent," representing a low-water mark even for Nigeria.[41] The process was marred by widespread fraud, intimidation, vote tampering, and corruption. The government-appointed Independent Election Commission (INEC), which was charged with overseeing the integrity of the election process, tilted decidedly in favor of the incumbent PDP party. Yar'Adua officially won with 70 percent of the vote, but the elections were so flawed that many outside observers questioned the credibility of the entire process. The only silver lining in the vote was that the country did not descend once again into ethnic violence.

Amid a flurry of legal challenges, Yar'Adua was inaugurated in May 2007. His term was brief. In 2009, he flew to Saudi Arabia for medical treatment. His vice president, Goodluck Jonathan, took over his duties on a temporary basis during his illness, then permanently upon his death in 2010. Jonathan stood for election in 2011 and won with 78 percent of the vote, in elections that were riddled once more with fraud and violent clashes.

Conclusion

Nigeria is now in its fourteenth year of elected civilian governments, the longest such period in its history. Power has now been passed to three civilian leaders—Obasanjo, Yar'Adua, and Jonathan—through elections, as messy as each of them was. The PDP, however, has controlled the presidency throughout. It has often ruled with as much of an iron fist as its military predecessors and has continued many of the same corrupt practices and patronage politics. Under Jonathan, Boko Haram, a militant Islamist group based in the country's Muslim north, has committed increasingly wanton acts of terrorist violence against Nigerian Christians, churches, and foreigners, threatening the country's delicate political stability.

However, the macroeconomic reforms implemented by Obasanjo have helped revive the economy. The PDP's practice of rotating presidential candidates from the north and south has tamped down ethno-regional conflict. The judiciary has become more independent, and civil society is becoming a more powerful actor. Whether Nigeria can overcome its stark ethnic and religious differences and long history of brutal military government to become again a leader of Africa remains to be seen.

Uganda

Once the poster child of international aid donors—a rare model on the continent of citizen participation and efficiency—the regime of Uganda's president, Yoweri Museveni, is looking more and more like the failed "strong man" regimes that long defined politics in the rest of Africa. The regime deserves ample credit for returning stability to a country ripped apart by the murderous Idi Amin and for implementing far-sighted measures to restore economic growth, but in political terms it has proved as despotic as many of its most retrograde neighbors. Museveni's espousal of "movement democracy" (which eschewed political parties but sought to unite the nation into a single movement) as a kind of "third way" between Western democracy and African despotism has proven as empty of substance as the high-minded political philosophies articulated by earlier African independence leaders like Kwame Nkruma and Julius Neyere—noble words to legitimize their continued tenure in power.

From Independence to Despotism to Civil War

Uganda achieved its independence from Great Britain in 1962. After founding elections, Milton Obote, a Protestant politician from the north of the country, became the country's first prime minister. His solution for addressing the complex ethnic, religious, and regional politics of Uganda, in which the southern kingdom of Buganda had long predominated, was to try to centralize by force political decisionmaking that had long been accomplished through negotiation. He abandoned his coalition with the Kabaka Yekka, the main ethnic Bagandan party; abrogated the constitution, doing away with its federalist provisions; and declared himself president, consolidating power within that office. However, his despotic and corrupt rule left him politically isolated and vulnerable.[42]

In 1971, General Idi Amin seized power in a military coup. Despite his initial promises to serve as a transitional leader until democratic elections could be held, he soon transformed the Ugandan state into his own personal fiefdom, building his increasingly arbitrary and brutal rule on a cult of personality. His murderous regime was responsible for extrajudicial killings that likely numbered into the hundreds of thousands, incitement of ethnic violence, wide-scale torture, mass expulsion of the country's sizable Indian population, and countless other human rights abuses. Following an ill-conceived invasion of northwestern Tanzania, he was overthrown in 1979 by the Tanzanian army and two rival Ugandan exile groups, one led by Obote and the other by Yoweri Museveni.

In subsequent elections in 1980, Obote claimed victory and again assumed the presidency. Museveni declared the elections rigged, and he and his National Resistance Army (NRA) launched a guerrilla war against the Obote regime that was to last five years and claim several hundred thousand more lives. In 1985, Obote was overthrown by a group of military officers who, six months later, were themselves overpowered by NRA forces.

Museveni and the NRM

Upon taking office in early 1986 after prevailing in an armed struggle between the two factions, Museveni declared that he and his newly

renamed National Resistance Movement (NRM) would bring fundamental change to Uganda and return sovereignty to the people. He
would later outline plans for a "movement democracy," which would
combine elements of participatory (direct) and parliamentary (representative) democracy. Uganda would build its own democracy: rather
than slavishly imitating Western democratic models, it would craft its
own forms in conformity with African traditions and culture. Local citizens in each village would directly elect the members of new "revolutionary councils" that would help administer community affairs. The
councils would elect representatives to a higher body, which in turn
would elect representatives to sub-county councils. From the sub-county
councils, members of parliament would be elected, although the government retained the right to appoint three-eighths of those members. In
the interest of preventing the ethnic and regional divisions of the past,
political parties would be banned temporarily from putting forward
candidates for election.[43]

The new government quickly garnered international support. Museveni and the NRM impressed the West with their ability to bring security and stability to a country that had been ravaged by the predations
of both the Obote and Amin regimes and a bloody civil war. With the
exception of an insurgency in the north by a murderous and idiosyn-
cratic militia now known as the Lord's Revolutionary Army, Museveni
succeeded in ending the killings. His government expanded individual
rights and press freedoms. With the help of the IMF and World Bank, it
implemented a structural adjustment program that significantly liberalized the economy. Together with other international donors, the government launched an innovative public education campaign to counter the
spread of HIV/AIDS. At one point, international donor contributions
represented 40 percent of the government's budget.

While the former rebel force was largely successful in bringing domestic peace and significantly improving the quality of governance and the
state of the economy, it had a harder time sharing power and allowing
other actors into the political process. A lengthy constitution-writing
effort produced a new basic law in 1995 that broadened political rights
but maintained what was supposed to have been a temporary ban on
political party activity and failed to strike from the books many of the
more draconian provisions from the Amin period. In 1996, Museveni
roundly defeated Paul Ssemogerere and Mohamed Mayanja, securing
75 percent of the vote, in a "no party" presidential election that international observers judged to be generally free and fair.[44]

Museveni and the NRM also never fully shed their militarism. They supported the Rwandese Patriotic Front, many of whose officers came from the ranks of the NRM, during the Rwandan civil war. In addition to continuing to battle the Lord's Resistance Army in the north, the NRM-controlled army made military incursions into Sudan in 1997 and the Democratic Republic of the Congo in 1998 in support of the People's Liberation Army insurgency in the south of Sudan and the incursions into Congo of Rwanda's Tutsi-led government.

Besigye's Challenge

In the 2001 presidential elections, Museveni's main challenger was Kizza Besigye, a former military officer who had become an outspoken critic of the regime. According to the official results, Museveni beat Besigye handily, 69 percent to 28 percent, but Besigye challenged the case in court, citing widespread vote rigging and election-related violence. The high court unanimously decided that fraud had occurred but then narrowly ruled against overturning the election results. Bisegye was arrested for treason, but he managed to flee the country.

In 2004, the Museveni government put forward proposed constitutional changes that included provisions to allow a president to serve more than two terms and to dilute the power of both the judiciary and the parliament. To allay critics and get the amendments passed, Museveni was forced to agree to end the ban on political party activity. Then, in the run-up to the 2006 election, Besigye returned unexpectedly from exile and began campaigning vigorously for the presidency, drawing large crowds throughout the country. Within weeks of his return, he was arrested on charges of rape and treason. When the high court granted him bail, the military took him into custody on terrorism charges. By the time that Besigye was released, the campaign period was nearly over. On election day, when the early returns broadcast by an independent media outlet showed Museveni receiving less than a majority of the vote—meaning that he would be forced into a runoff election—the government swiftly shut the vote-count operation down, jammed its radio frequency, and blocked its website. The final official results had Museveni with 59 percent of the vote to Besigye's 37 percent.[45]

In 2011, Besigye once more ran against Museveni and once more was soundly defeated, in an election that was marred by administrative errors that left many voters disenfranchised and by lavish spending by the government to benefit the incumbent.[46] Following recent revelations that

$13 million had been siphoned from the prime minister's office budget, the European Union and other international donors suspended all budgetary support to the government, a move that has had a significant impact on the country's economy.[47] GDP growth slipped from a vibrant 6.6 percent in 2011 to just over 3 percent in 2012.[48]

Conclusion

Uganda remains an electoral autocracy. Museveni and his National Resistance Movement tightly control the country's economy and politics. To date, their ability to provide stability and economic growth in a country where both were lacking for a long time has kept the population relatively quiescent. Whether the Museveni government can continue to provide its citizens with economic growth while staving off opposition challenges to its rule will become evident only over time.

Lessons from Africa

The case studies presented here show how far some countries in Africa have progressed in terms of their democratic development and how very far the continent has to go. Ghana and Zambia are shining, if imperfect, examples of democracy's great promise in Africa, but across much of the continent the trials and tribulations experienced by Nigeria and Uganda are more the norm.

Two especially striking observations can be made about the case studies. The first is the extent to which elections, however imperfect, have over a relatively short period of time become the focal point for political life. Even in Uganda, which remains a one-party state, elections have become a regular feature of politics. They remain far from free and fair, but the fact that they are happening at all, in Uganda and so many other places on the continent, represents important progress. As flawed as the elections may be, they provide a mechanism for the beginning of competitive politics and open up the possibility for even more profound changes over time. Ghana serves as an example of how, through the determined efforts of citizens and citizen groups to improve election procedures and monitor their implementation, elections can eventually be transformed from mere political pageantry—a show that regimes put on to boost their legitimacy at home and abroad—into a genuine contest for political power.

The second observation is how little the introduction of elections has actually changed the behavior of political leaders. Africa's newly elected democratic leaders generally proved to be no more virtuous than their predecessors. Once in power, they employed many of the same authoritarian practices that they had decried when they were in opposition. In Ghana, John Kufour was often as heavy-handed a president as Jerry Rawlings had been before him. In Zambia, Frederick Chiluba used many of the same strongman tactics as his predecessor Kenneth Kuanda, and his Movement for Multiparty Democracy began to behave as dictatorially as Kuanda's United National Independence Party had done before. Their presidencies have been "imperial presidencies"—after their election, their power has been largely unconstrained by institutions or law. The same could be said of many presidencies in Latin America. The notable difference is that in Latin America, political institutions and laws—though often ignored—have long been in place, whereas in Africa they are underdeveloped or nonexistent.

Yet politics in Africa is slowly changing, not because political leaders have become more virtuous or fundamentally altered their calculations of their own self-interest but because the norms and behavior of African citizens are changing. In many countries, ordinary Africans are taking a much more active role in their nation's politics. Change is occurring from the bottom up as citizens place new constraints on the power of their elected leaders through active political engagement. They are rebuffing politicians who try to overstay their tenure, abuse their public position for private gain, or encroach on the individual liberties of their citizens. They are creating new norms regarding the rights of citizens and the limits of government, and they are demonstrating their willingness to defend them if necessary by manning the barricades. In so doing, they are slowly beginning, in some countries, to bring the realities of African politics more in line with the lofty proclamations of their putatively democratic constitutions.

Africa's fledgling democracies have made clear progress over the last 20 years, but they remain vulnerable. Their democratic gains can easily be reversed—by a political leader who decides to overstay his welcome, by a disputed election that ignites intercommunal violence, by a military commander who stages a coup, or, as seen in Mali, by the intervention of militant extremist groups. Africa's political institutions remain weak, its democratic political culture shallow, and governments' capacity to meet the rising expectations of their citizens limited. These new democracies also remain susceptible to exogenous shocks—both positive ones like the Arab Spring, which has had ripple effects throughout Africa, and negative ones like the global financial crisis or al Qaeda-linked terrorist groups.[49]

But Africans have spoken. They have determined that they want democracy, and they are becoming more actively engaged in politics to try to secure it. Over the long term, much as in Latin America, their engagement is likely to be the best guarantor of democracy on the continent.

CHAPTER SEVEN

THE NATURE OF DEMOCRATIC TRANSITIONS

As the transition to democracy has bogged down in Egypt amid political polarization, as Libya and Yemen continue to be dogged by instability, and as Syria's civil war spirals further out of control, it is tempting to dismiss the uprisings in the Arab world as a false spring and yearn for a return to the region's old autocratic order. For all its faults, it did provide a modicum of stability. However, the preceding chapters show that at least during the Third Wave, democratization was always a difficult and messy process, so it would be premature to give up on the prospects for Arab democratization just yet. Democratization will be a more long-term, complex, and perilous process than initially envisioned; however, for many Arab countries, though likely not all, with time it will be an attainable goal.

During the Third Wave, about ninety countries attempted a transition to democracy, some on multiple occasions. Most eventually succeeded in becoming at least electoral democracies, and as many as a half became liberal democracies.[1] What the cases featured in earlier chapters make plain is that there is no single path to democratic transition, and often the differences in democratization experiences are striking. Each country's story is as unique as the country itself. The context in which democratization occurred—each country's history, culture, economic structure, level of wealth and its distribution, social composition, and so on—was different in each case, dramatically so in many instances. Each followed a very different path from its initial political breakthrough to what was often a quite extended transition toward democracy, and many of those transitions remain ongoing. Democratization, as these cases demonstrate, is a highly contingent historical process.[2] Despite the great variety of contexts in which democratization took place and the differences in the countries' experiences, some commonalities can be discerned that are rich with implications for today's Arab world. This chapter discusses some of the most important ones, in particular the critical role that citizens can play in promoting democratic transitions and the importance of the development of a political constituency for democracy to the long-term success of such a transition.

Democratic Breakthroughs

The early democratization literature, which drew heavily on the Iberian and early Latin American experiences, stressed the negotiated nature of countries' initial moves away from authoritarianism toward democracy. Such "democratic breakthroughs" were assumed to be the product of negotiations among political elites—often the result of compromises struck between more reformist elements within an autocratic regime and more moderate forces within the opposition. In many Third Wave countries and during the Arab Spring, however, the push for democratization has come not from elites at the top but from below—from citizens demanding a greater say in governance. Often, in fact—particularly in the case of Eastern Europe and the countries of the Arab Spring—elites were caught flatfooted as citizens suddenly massed in the streets demanding change. The "people power" phenomenon that first manifested itself in the Philippines in 1986 has become global.

The success of these movements in creating a political opening has depended on their ability to mobilize broad segments of society. Citizens' chief weapon against the coercive apparatus of the modern state is the sheer force of numbers. A government can jail a hundred people protesting its actions, and it can jail a thousand, but when broad sections of society rise up against it, even the most authoritarian government must take heed. As seen in chapter 3, repressive regimes were finally brought to their knees in Poland, the former Czechoslovakia, and Serbia only when all groups—intellectuals, students, workers, inhabitants of the countryside as well as the cities—united. The same has been true during the Arab Spring. Tunisia's Ben Ali and Egypt's Mubarak felt compelled to resign because they faced the determined opposition of most segments of their respective societies, people who were fed up with the corrupt nature of their rule and their inability to address citizens' socioeconomic needs. In Bahrain and Syria, by contrast, the discontent was no less palpable, but fissures emerged along largely sectarian lines among the regimes' critics. The Bahraini monarchy has endured in part because members of the Sunni minority elite supported its crackdown against Shite protesters. Similarly, in Syria, Bashar al-Assad has been able to cling to power because of the continued support of his fellow minority Alawites and elements of the military and business establishment.

Success was often contagious. The preceding chapters show that one of the most striking aspects of the Third Wave of democratization is the speed with which it spread within each continent. In the 1970s, almost all Latin American regimes were military dictatorships. Then, suddenly, the public became disillusioned with military rule and no longer regarded it as a legitimate form of government. The military was forced to retreat to the barracks, where it has largely remained ever since. In Eastern Europe, the year 1989 brought breathtaking changes: the fall of the Berlin Wall cemented the dramatic political changes that were already under way in Poland and Hungary while encouraging citizens in Czechoslovakia, Romania, Bulgaria, and beyond to take to the streets to challenge their own regimes. By year's end, almost all the region's communist dictatorships had collapsed like a house of cards; two years later, the Soviet Union itself was dissolving. In Africa, where there had been no more than two competitive elections a year in the 1980s, there were fourteen in 1993 alone and thirty-eight in total between 1990 and 1994. By 1997 almost all African states had held some kind of multiparty elections, and the number of democracies had grown to well over a dozen. Globally, the Third Wave had by then crested and stabilized at about 120 countries that could be characterized as electoral democracies.[3]

That contagion effect was witnessed in the Middle East and North Africa as well. The January 2011 protests in Tunisia emboldened democracy activists in Egypt. As images of the Egyptian protests in Tahrir Square were transmitted across the Arab world, youth throughout the region were galvanized into action. Protests soon followed in Yemen, Bahrain, Libya, Syria, Morocco, Jordan, and Oman and then in most other Arab countries. The Middle East and North Africa are witnessing today the same kind of revolutionary enthusiasm that swept other parts of the world in the 1980s and 1990s. No matter how much some may yearn for the stability of the old order, there is no turning back the clock. That does not mean that all of the twenty-two countries of the Arab world will become democratic in the near future; even under the best of circumstances—and the current polarization and political violence in the region make for circumstances that are less than ideal—democratization takes time. What it does mean is that societal norms are changing rapidly.

Arab citizens have found their voice, and they are not going to surrender it anytime soon. The memory of Tahrir will not be easily erased. They are going to demand a greater role in governance and an end to the insider dealing, corruption, and misrule that has long characterized regimes in the region. While the changes that swept Latin America in the 1970s did not lead immediately to democracy, for the most part they did put an end to the military's interference in politics; while those that swept Africa in the 1990s generally did not bring liberal democracy, they did create an expectation of multiparty elections that continues to this day. The same is likely to be true in the Arab world. An Egypt in which as many as 22 million citizens reportedly signed a petition calling for the removal of a president—a petition that also required them to give their national identity number and place of residence—is an Egypt that is profoundly different from the one that existed under Mubarak. Liberal democracy may be a long way off, but there is unlikely to be a return to the kind of authoritarianism embodied by Ben Ali and Mubarak.

From Breakthrough to Consolidation

The early literature on democratization also assumed that once a democratic breakthrough occurred—once elites agreed to move toward democracy—transitioning from breakthrough to democratic consolidation was largely a straightforward, technical task, a matter of organizing elections that were free and fair and putting the proper democratic political institutions in place. Once power had passed back and forth twice between opposing political parties through elections, democracy was considered to be consolidated and the democratization process complete.[4] In fact, as the preceding chapters show, among Third Wave democratizers the path from democratic breakthrough to consolidation has often been full of twists and turns—a much more uncertain and contingent undertaking than once imagined.

Tunisia, Egypt, Libya, and Yemen have begun to transition away from authoritarianism, but it is far less certain that all of them will end up as democracies. A small group, under the right conditions, can orchestrate the overthrow of a dictator, but it takes far more than that to establish an enduring democracy. As mentioned in chapter 2, the conditions that make for a successful popular revolt and those required for successful democratization have some similarities, but they are far from identical. Democratization needs to be understood as a long-term process whose fate will not be decided by a single event or decision—such as how a constitution gets written—but instead will emerge out of a broader struggle between citizens and their political leaders over the rights and prerogatives of citizen and state. Democratization rarely follows a linear path. Along the way, there are likely to be stunning advances and heartbreaking reversals. Success will ultimately be determined by longer-term attitudinal changes and political struggles over where power lies in the new state. Even in liberal democracies, the task of democratization is never wholly complete. The pursuit of what the American founders termed "a more perfect union" is a struggle without end, an invitation to seek ceaselessly to defend and expand liberty in the face of continual encroachments. "The price of freedom," Jefferson is reputed to have said, "is eternal vigilance."[5]

The Role of Power

Like all of politics, democratization is about power. It is about a shift in the locus of power from the state toward society, from the grip of an autocrat and his circle of cronies to the citizen, where sovereignty in a democracy is supposed ultimately to lie. Those who wield power, however, whether it has been obtained by force or granted by the people, never part with it easily. As Lord Acton famously observed: "Power tends to corrupt and absolute power [to] corrupt absolutely."[6] The challenge of democratization is to impose limits on the power of political leaders, to make politicians accountable to the people for their actions. To circumscribe the power that political leaders wield, citizens may seek to force them to submit periodically to the public for approval by competing for election, to divide power among different branches of government and different jurisdictions, and to enact laws that limit their discretion.

But particularly in emerging democracies, none of those safeguards alone is sufficient to counteract the corrupting influence of power. As Madison said, "The essence of Government is power; and power, lodged as it must be in human hands, will ever be liable to abuse."[7] Once centralized, power can prove exceedingly difficult to decentralize. Countries that have embarked on a transition to democracy have discovered that to separate, limit, and delegate power is extremely problematic.[8] Left to their own devices, political leaders are unlikely to cede powers that they could otherwise exercise themselves. New rules can be put in place, new institutions created, and "independent authorities" and "ombudsmen" established in an effort to circumscribe the discretion of political officials, but that effort will come to naught if those measures are not perceived to be backed up by the popular will. It is only natural, not to mention far too tempting, for those wielding power to seek to maximize their discretion, to place their own private interests above the public interest, and even to ignore any restraints on their authority—if they think that they can get away with it.

What is striking in the country case studies in the preceding chapters is how often incumbents appeared to be the greatest obstacle to further democratization. During the Third Wave, democratic breakthroughs were generally followed by founding elections that produced an elected political leader, whether president or prime minister, who took the reins of power. Once in office, however, leaders often found the trappings of office too alluring to give up willingly. Given their own political history, Americans often regard the winners of founding elections as visionaries—legendary figures charting a new democratic future for their country—and many such winners certainly viewed themselves that way. During the Third Wave, however, there were far more Musevenis and Mugabes than Mandelas and Washingtons. Some sought to extend their terms. Others did away with elections. Still others employed the full powers of their office to ensure that any subsequent elections were tilted heavily in their favor. Self-interest trumped ideology. No matter what pledges to adhere to democratic values and processes political leaders may have made prior to their election—no matter whether they were liberals, nationalists, socialists, populists, or conservatives—once in power, they proved extremely unwilling to relinquish it. As O'Brien observes to Winston in George Orwell's *1984*, "We know that no one ever seizes power with the intention of relinquishing it."[9] The perquisites of office turned out to be more powerful than any ideology. And with the incumbent firmly entrenched, democratic transitions got stuck. The problem was most pronounced in Africa, where the culture of "big man" politics remains strong, but it was prevalent across all regions. The problem of getting incumbents to govern within their mandate and step aside when their term is complete is a key challenge confronting transitions around the world.

It is still early in the Arab Spring—the first founding elections were less than two years ago—but this phenomenon is already at work. In Egypt, the Supreme Council of the Armed Forces announced after Mubarak's resignation that it would play only a temporary caretaker role until democratic elections could be held; it ended up being the dominant force in Egyptian politics until President Morsi sacked General Tantawi in August 2012. For its part, the Muslim Brotherhood–linked Freedom and

Justice Party (FJP), seeking to allay domestic and international concerns about its role in politics, announced initially that it would limit itself to a third of the seats in parliament and not put forward a candidate for president. The FJP ended up capturing almost half the seats in parliament, in part by making deals with its favored candidates for the third of seats reserved for independents. And it ended up naming its own candidate for president, first deputy supreme leader Khairat el-Shater—and then, following his disqualification, Mohamed Morsi. In many ways an accidental president, Morsi did not take long to grow into and even exceed the authority of his office. Now the military is back in power, put there by secular protesters angered by Morsi's performance as president, who naively saw the military as the only means to remove him. Despite its promise of a rapid return to democratic government, the military shows no signs of removing itself from politics anytime soon.

The Role of Citizens

How does a country deal with the incumbent who is determined to overstay his or her mandate? How does it check the authority of the "big men" who too often dominate politics? Horizontal mechanisms of accountability, such as a strong court system, dynamic parliaments, independent oversight agencies, and effective auditing and control mechanisms, can all help check attempts at executive overreach. In the United States, citizens venerate the separation of powers between the executive, legislative, and judicial branches for that reason; each branch serves as a check on the authority of the other. However, in nascent democracies, the ruling elites often find it easy to collude to ensure that parliaments and judiciaries remain subservient to the executive, that "independent authorities" are corralled back under the control of the executive, and that elections are stacked to the advantage of incumbents. Parliamentarians do not want to risk being removed from party lists or denied the political patronage that executives can distribute. Justices may bend to political pressure from executives because they fear having their salaries cut or terms shortened. Generally, horizontal accountability works only if it is reinforced by vertical accountability—only if ordinary citizens, civil society organizations, and the media demand that the mechanisms of democratic government function as intended.[10]

The penultimate lesson to be drawn from democratization experiences around the globe is that over the long term successful democratization requires the emergence of a political constituency for democracy: a critical mass of citizens who, regardless of their personal political ideology or party affiliation, value democracy as an important end in its own right and are willing and able to advocate for it. It is a group, however loosely defined, whose members are united by a shared set of values—above all, a belief in democracy as the proper ordering principle for their country's political affairs—and organized politically to achieve that end.

Many complex factors go into making a successful democracy. The way that a constitution is structured, the caliber of the political leadership, the care with which political institutions are crafted, the quality of election procedures, the dynamism of political parties, the structure and health of the economy, the sophistication and independence of the media, and the pressures applied and the inducements offered by the international community all are important. But if democracy is to take root and endure, citizens must be willing to defend their nascent democratic institutions. Without public insistence that political leaders respect the limits on their power imposed by those institutions, the entire edifice of democracy is vulnerable. In the case studies presented in this book, the emergence of a political constituency for democracy appeared to be the surest guarantee that democracy would take root—that political leaders would come to respect the rule of law and abide by the new political rules of the game.

Following the citizen revolutions that swept Eastern Europe in 1989, there was a renewed appreciation for, even a reification of, civil society as the bedrock of any healthy democracy. However, just what "civil society" meant and what its value was to democratic development were rarely fully or carefully explored. Did the term refer to all associational activity between the state, on one side, and citizens, on the other, within a society? Or simply to that part of political society that exists outside the realm of political parties? Or was it something altogether different? Was the term synonymous with nonprofit and nongovernmental organizations or something much broader? Was its function educational (to impart civic values or the habits of reciprocity and association), political (to serve as a bulwark against encroachment by the state on the freedom of citizens), or cultural (to provide a creative space outside the reach of politics and the state)?[11] Like "motherhood and apple pie" in the United States, "civil society" became a hackneyed buzzword for all good things that the demos—the people—could do to enrich democracy.[12]

What stands out clearly in the diverse array of democratization experiences described in this book is the decisive role played by citizens. The country case studies elucidate the important contribution that citizens, civic groups, and civil society writ large can make to the process of democratization. Among the countries profiled in the case studies, some did eventually succeed in making democratic political institutions "stick" by getting political leaders to recognize that there are limits on their power, limits imposed by the new rules of the game. Other countries may rewrite their constitution and create or reform their political institutions but never manage to alter fundamentally the nature of the political system; political leaders continue to exercise unlimited and often arbitrary authority despite the efforts to rewrite the rules of politics. The crucial difference between the successful cases and the failures seems to be the actions undertaken (or not undertaken) by citizens in order to advance the cause of democracy. Democratization emerges out of a prolonged struggle between political leaders intent on maintaining their perquisites and citizens determined to circumscribe the power of those leaders in the name of creating more transparent, accountable, and participatory governance and protecting personal and political freedoms. In the successful cases, citizens demonstrate to political leaders, through repeated collective action, that they stand ready to defend the new democratic constitutions and political institutions and that politicians violate them at their peril. By standing up to political leaders, citizens can prevent them from overstepping their mandates. Over time, repeated citizen action can have a deterrent effect, making political leaders far less likely to trespass on the constitutional rules of the game because they know that doing so will only ignite public opposition. In nascent democracies, when constitutions are still being written and political institutions developed, such countervailing pressure from below—from within society—can be critical to keeping the democratic process on track. Over time, democratic institutions take firmer root and democracy tends to endure, although citizens nevertheless need to be ever vigilant against encroachments on their liberty.

In the Arab world, it will take sustained engagement on the part of the people if they are to wrest control of government from the small circle of elites that have long dominated it and dismantle the "deep state" that successive authoritarian leaders have erected. Civil society has a crucial role to play not just in bringing down dictators but also in the messy and unending business of ensuring that even the most well-intentioned democratic political system does not become dictatorial.

As the case studies show, the democratization process often resembles the process by which a climbing team ascends a steep peak. As with a mountaineering expedition, everyone involved has a role to play depending on his or her expertise and the conditions. At one moment, a heroic journalist may take the lead, daring to delve into government insider dealings that have never before been scrutinized. At the next, an advocacy group may be in front, pressuring state officials to publish government accounts. Only the clear and unequivocal support of the public can prevent both of them from being knocked aside. At still another moment, the public itself may be at the forefront of change rather than in the background—by, for example, participating in protests to call for an end to corruption and demand greater transparency in governance. With such displays of people power, they make the work of the journalist and the public advocate easier by helping to clear a path. Through the actions of all of them, the cause of democracy is incrementally advanced. In the quest for greater democracy, progress may be slow and halting; it may also be perilous and reversible. But with time and effort, progress is possible.

This does not mean that citizens must be continually engaged in the day-to-day affairs of state. Even in the most advanced democracies, citizens' interest and engagement in politics waxes and wanes. The whole purpose of representative government is to delegate the responsibility of governing to elected officials so that citizens can attend to their own affairs. A well-governed polity provides conditions under which citizens can go about their own business, confident that the collective needs on which their enterprise and that of others depend— such as the common defense, public order, roads and other infrastructure, schools, and social services—are taken care of. But unless citizens exercise some oversight of the actions of their elected officials, beyond the blunt instrument of elections, those officials cease to be representatives of the people and instead begin to act solely in their own interests. Without citizen engagement at key "constitutional moments" of crisis, a representative democracy can cease to be both representative and democratic.

That is a lesson that citizens seem to have slowly learned in many Third Wave democracies. Gradually they have come to understand the importance of civic engagement to a healthy democracy. The path from subject to voter to active citizen can be a long one, but with time and political learning such transformations do take place. A recent study of public opinion in Africa, for instance, found that in relatively young democracies (for example, South Africa and Namibia), citizens tended to trust and defer to their elected political leaders. However, those polled in countries with more experience with independence and democracy were no longer willing to accord such deference because they had learned that their political leaders could not be counted on to hold themselves accountable—only engaged citizens can ensure such accountability.[13]

Not just in Africa but in emerging democracies around the world, citizens are learning tactics to use to hold their governments more accountable. Collective action is never easy because individuals are always tempted to let others act on their behalf. But citizens are discovering new ways to overcome the problems inherent in collective action and engage successfully with their political leaders. By bringing together diverse networks of like-minded individuals, they are creating a political constituency for democracy.

Toward Collective Action

Several of the case studies—the most notable being Slovakia, Serbia, and Ukraine—demonstrate in depth how a political constituency for democracy can emerge. Often the first step is a change in values. Not a change in all values, but specifically a change in political attitudes with respect to how the individual sees his or her place in the polity. In authoritarian societies, relations are organized vertically: the ruler sits at the apex of society and his or her subjects below are expected simply to obey the ruler's commands in exchange for security and material welfare. Relationships among all members of society tend to mimic the vertical, hierarchical relationship that governs society at large, from how shopkeepers treat their customers, bosses relate to their employees, and teachers address their students to how parents behave toward their children.

As noted in chapter 2, political attitudes can change over time as societies evolve and citizens become more affluent, educated, and exposed to other societies. In several of the case studies, technological advances in communications and transportation, along with increased international trade—what has come to be described as "globalization"—have made societies more permeable and brought the countries of the world closer together. As a result, authoritarian and totalitarian regimes have slowly lost their monopoly on the flow of information and no longer are able to control the national narrative completely. Through travel, international education, satellite television, and the Internet, individuals are exposed to other societies and can compare more easily than ever their own way of life with that in other societies. As a result, values are changing—the first step in the emergence of a political constituency for democracy. Culture is not going away—it continues to shape profoundly how individuals see the world—but one important aspect of culture, how individuals view their relationship to political authority, is evolving. Individuals once emphasized security, material well-being, order, and tradition above all else, but with increased security, wealth, education, and knowledge of the outside world, they are according greater priority than before to higher-order concerns like individual choice and self-expression.

This change in values—the shift from an emphasis on survival values to self-expression values—leads individuals to behave differently in their personal and public lives. At home, they may seek a greater role and say within the family, just as in the wider world they may seek a greater role and say in their community and nation. Rather than accepting the world as it is, they may now seek to shape it through their own actions. No longer content simply to obey authority, they may challenge it, thereby beginning their transition from subject to citizen. As a result, vertical patterns of behavior based on hierarchy may gradually give way to more horizontal patterns based on reciprocity.

A second step in the emergence of a political constituency for democracy is collective action. Often the individual can be effective at making changes in the broader world only if he or she bands together with other like-minded individuals in common cause. However, the difficulties associated with collective action are not trivial. The greater the number of people involved, the greater the temptation of any one individual not to take part and let others bear the burden instead. In authoritarian societies, there are the added difficulties of both fear and lack of experience. Individuals do not know how to confront authority because they have never attempted to do so. They have spent their lives obeying or circumventing authority, but they have never engaged with it directly. Learning is required to develop more horizontal modes of interacting with political leaders.

As seen in several of the case studies, collective action therefore often starts at the local level, where the numbers required to effect change are lower—so the free-rider problem is less significant—and often the element of fear is lower. It may start, for example, with a small group of citizens protesting the construction of a local dam or petitioning to have a clinic remain open. From such small acts of defiance, citizens learn methods of effective collective action, gain confidence, and develop networks of like-minded individuals. By tackling local problems, citizens often become empowered to turn to larger challenges.

A third step in the emergence of a political constituency for democracy is the coming together of diverse networks of change-oriented citizens to engage with national governments. Like a snowball, the local civic actions described above often grow over time into broader movements for national change. Local activists find common cause with activists elsewhere in the country and combine their efforts and their networks to address national problems. With time, they learn to engage and challenge national authorities in much the same way that they learned to challenge local authorities.

Civic movements have attracted attention for the role that they have played in toppling authoritarian leaders, beginning with the people power movement in the Philippines. However, as seen, the civic sector can play an equally valuable role in helping keep democracy on track long after a dictator has fallen. It can prod, petition, protest, and persuade newly elected leaders to respect new democratic institutions and procedures. When new constitutions are still being written, political institutions are just emerging or have yet to be formed, and political parties are weak and fragmented, the presence of a political constituency for democracy, pushing from below to enforce the new democratic rules of the game, can be critical.

CHAPTER EIGHT

THE STRATEGIC CHALLENGES OF THE ARAB SPRING

The experiences of Third Wave democratizers hold further lessons, at the strategic level, for Arab democracy activists. As noted earlier, these activists have been a key driver of the events of the Arab Spring. They have sought to leverage the power of crowds, modern technology, and the support of the international community to create a better future for their countries. Having felled dictators, they now face a number of equally daunting challenges as they seek to move toward democracy, including how to structure a transition process that all will regard as legitimate; how to overcome the deep-seated polarization within many Arab societies; whether to include nondemocratic actors in the democratization process; what role the military should play in politics; and how to make the shift from protest to politics. This chapter offers Arab democracy activists some lessons learned from countries elsewhere in the world that have grappled with those challenges.

Developing a Transitional Roadmap

After the collapse of an authoritarian regime, there inevitably follows the question of what comes next: What kind of transitional authority should be established in its place? Who should be responsible for writing (or rewriting) a constitution? Who should organize founding elections? Of course, countries do not always have the luxury of choosing the ideal transition process. What comes after the dictator departs is often the result of intense negotiation among contending political forces, constraining what is and is not possible. This chapter discusses only the ideal.

The Arab Spring countries have much to learn from transition experiences elsewhere in the world. To date, their own transitions have often been riddled with strategic errors. Egypt, in particular, has foundered repeatedly in its efforts to create a broad-based and inclusive transition process to launch the country on a path toward democracy. It was a mistake following Mubarak's resignation to entrust the military to lead a caretaker government because it was neither up to the task nor devoid of interests of its own. Rather than serving as the desired honest broker, it only added to the uncertainty and instability surrounding the country's transition. It was also a mistake to expect an elected constituent assembly to take on the task of constitution writing in addition to its ordinary legislative functions. Furthermore, it was a mistake to turn to the military again for help in ousting Mohamed Morsi's government.

The challenge in any transition is to create a new national decision-making process that enjoys broad legitimacy. An equitable, transparent, and inclusive process can enable a country to overcome deep-seated mistrust within society and decisively break with its authoritarian past. Democratic transitions generally begin with a political breakthrough that includes an agreement to hold multiparty elections and write a new constitution, but who oversees the process and how events are sequenced matters greatly.

Several lessons are worth sharing. First, a caretaker government that is broadly representative, in that it includes all major political forces within society, should be established to manage the transition. Because such a government has the virtue not only of inclusivity but also of impartiality, it is likely to be viewed as fair by all and therefore to enjoy the trust of the citizenry. In an ideal world, it should supervise the writing of a new constitution and the convening of the first multiparty elections. One successful example of such a caretaker government is the Czechoslovak national unity government that followed the Velvet Revolution, which included representatives of the former communist regime, Civic Forum, and other political forces within society. Because of its representativeness, inclusivity, and limited mandate, it enjoyed broad popular trust and its actions were deemed to be legitimate.

In far more cases, the former regime ends up retaining responsibility for managing the transition to democracy, as is now the case in Myanmar. On occasion, that approach has worked. In Indonesia, for example, Suharto's successor, B. J. Habibie, knew that his legitimacy hinged on establishing a credible election process; because of that, he ended up playing an effective caretaker role. Generally, though, such an approach—the political equivalent of putting the foxes in charge of the hen house—is fraught with problems. In many Third Wave transitions, an autocratic regime agreed to elections merely as a tactical ploy—a way of defusing public discontent and legitimizing its continuation in office (Romania and Bulgaria are but two examples). The regime had no intention of allowing for real political competition and used its powers of incumbency to ensure that any constitutional revisions that took place worked to its advantage and that any elections held were tilted in its favor.

Second, constitution writing should ideally take place before the partisan makeup of any future government is known. There is a far better chance that the decisions taken will be impartial when those deciding the new rules of society do not yet know what their long-term interests will be—a condition that the philosopher John Rawls has referred to as "the veil of ignorance."[1] Ideally, then, constitution writing should precede the start of normal politics. When elections are held before a consensus is reached on the constitutional rules of the game, constitution writing tends to get entangled with partisan political calculations. Different political factions know their relative strength at the voting booth and may be tempted to write the rules to their own advantage. The particular political faction that commands a majority today may try to institutionalize its advantage so that it continues to control the political process well into the future. In several of the Latin American cases (for example, Venezuela and Bolivia) "constitutional tinkering"—convening a new constituent assembly to make changes to the constitution—became a tactic for the party in power to rewrite the formal rules of politics in its favor.

Third, when elections cannot be deferred until a constitution is adopted, the tasks of writing the constitution and conducting normal legislative business should be kept separate. It takes time to draft a constitution, forge a consensus on the final version, and adopt it. Often a country cannot afford to maintain a political vacuum until the constitution writing process is complete. In such instances, a constituent assembly or committee of experts should be tasked with preparing a constitution while the parliament or other legislative body is left with the responsibility for handling legislation. Tunisia gave its constituent assembly both legislative and constitution-writing authority; however, the mixing of constitutional and normal politics politicized the former while complicating the latter.

Overcoming Societal Polarization

One of the more troubling aspects of the Arab Spring has been the degree of polarization that has emerged within society once a dictator has been cast aside. Tensions have surfaced between Muslims and Christians, Sunnis and Shias, Islamists and secularists, and rich and poor; they also have appeared between different regions. Such divisions within society often have threatened to tear societies apart. Syria is riven at the moment by a civil war that pits Bashar Assad and his mostly Alawite supporters against opponents of his regime, who are predominantly Sunni. The protests in Bahrain divide Sunnis and Shias. Yemen faces divisions between northerners and southerners, not to mention armed challenges by Houthi rebels and militant Islamic extremists. Libya continued to struggle with divisions between Benghazi in the east and Tripoli to the west throughout 2013, until a deal was brokered between the country's two leading politicians. Egypt is highly polarized between supporters of the Muslim Brotherhood and its more secular opponents, a polarization that became so acute in the summer of 2013 that the military intervened, at least ostensibly to preserve civil harmony. The government officially labeled the Brotherhood a terrorist organization and banned it in December 2013. In 2013, Tunisia was similarly polarized between Islamists and secularists before political leaders reached a compromise on the new constitution and a political roadmap for the future.

Polarization often is blamed on democracy. The democratic process, it is claimed, has brought to the surface age-old antagonisms, pitting different groups within society against one another. In fact, as others have argued, often those antagonisms are themselves a legacy of authoritarianism.[2] In an effort to divide and rule, the region's former dictators set different groups within society against one another, accentuating societal differences in order to remain in power. Hosni Mubarak, for example, used the Muslim Brotherhood as the bogeyman for many of the problems of his regime. He argued to both foreign and domestic audiences that he alone stood as a bulwark against a Muslim Brotherhood takeover of the country. Animosity, stirred up by the old regime but previously kept within bounds by armed force, now sets groups apart from one another and bedevils the democratization process.

Polarization can be highly problematic for democracy. As James Madison keenly understood, democracy functions best when no single faction dominates political life. It helps when citizens have diverse and constantly evolving identities and interests. When cleavages are enduring and mutually reinforcing rather than cross-cutting—when one group is permanently a majority and another a minority—democracy becomes significantly harder to maintain. Absent other protections for the minority group, democracy can come to look like nothing more than a system to legitimize the majority's control of political life.

Identities are complex. An individual often carries many—as a child, parent, resident of a particular neighborhood, member of a particular ethnic group, adherent of a particular faith, fan of a particular football club, and proud citizen of a particular state or nation. Some aspects of identity are fundamental—human beings are born with particular genetic traits (skin color, facial characteristics, physique) into families and societies that have histories and customs that may link them to one group of people while setting them apart from others. Another part is clearly instrumental: in an effort to build in-group solidarity or secure political gain, certain fundamental characteristics may be emphasized and others overlooked while new characteristics are invented from whole cloth.[3]

Particular identities may wax or wane in importance depending on circumstances. Individuals may choose to emphasize or give preference to one identity over others, particularly when individuals perceive an important aspect of their identity to be under threat. In recent decades in the Arab world, the sense that Islam is under siege has heightened religiosity and led many to return to wearing more traditional forms of dress as a symbol of their beliefs. More recently, feelings of insecurity have exacerbated long-latent tensions—for instance, between Sunnis, Shias, and Kurds in Iraq and Sunnis, Alawites, and Christians in Syria. The resurgence of ethnic identities complicates the prospects for democracy, as it turns politics into a zero-sum game and limits the possibilities for compromise. When a particular ethnic group feels threatened because of violence—when security becomes its paramount concern—fundamental identities may predominate, leading the group to give preference to its own interests over the interests of the state.

The prospects for democracy—and even a functioning state—become even dimmer when different groups within a society do not have a common vision of the state or its geographic borders. Nations are "imagined communities," conjured from the identities and aspirations of the people who compose them.[4] When there is a disjunction between nation and state—when citizens do not share a common understanding, when one group within society does not recognize the legitimacy of the state's borders or even seeks to confederate with another state—democracy can be severely imperiled. Political wrangling over whose state it is and what its contours are may obscure all else.[5] Those issues do not necessarily preclude democratization; they may just make it far harder to achieve.

The same is true for sharp divisions in wealth. When the gap between haves and have-nots, rich and poor, is significant, politics tends to become a zero-sum game. The rich seek to protect their wealth and property, while the poor are keen to have resources shared more broadly within society. Those divisions can become especially problematic in resource-based economies in which resources are tightly controlled by one family or group because such a monopoly ensures that the existing inequities in wealth remain permanent. Like ethnic divisions, divisions over wealth can create enduring cleavages that make achieving democracy difficult.

These problems are not unique to the Arab world. Latin America has experienced extreme polarization between rich and poor, which often has coincided with differences between settlers on one hand and indigenous and migrant communities on the other. Africa has even more severe income inequality as well as ethnic and linguistic divisions. The Balkans were torn asunder by ethnic conflict in the 1990s, while ethno-national tensions during the same period threatened political stability in other East European countries like Romania, Hungary, and Slovakia.

Several lessons emerge from the experience of countries that embarked on a transition to democracy during the Third Wave. First, once countries become polarized on issues of identity politics, it can take a long time to ratchet down tensions and return to more issue- or interest-based politics. When people feel that their identity or even personal security is threatened, they tend to view politics only through the prism of group identity. It will be a long time, for instance, before Syria's embattled Alawite community or Iraq's Sunnis look at politics in anything but sectarian terms. Politicians may face strong incentives to play the ethnic, racial, or religious card in order to garner votes, but when they do, it can have long-lasting consequences. Arab democracy activists, as well as the United States and the rest of the international community, must endeavor to tamp down divisive (and violent) politics before, not after, it spirals out of control.

Second, societal polarization may make democratization more difficult, but it does not make it impossible. Countries that experience heightened polarization, whether it is based on race, religion, ethnicity, or class, do not have to experience it forever; it is not an immutable condition. Many Latin American societies were highly polarized between rich and poor, right and left, from independence onward. Some of that polarization persists, but most countries have managed to move beyond it and build stable democratic societies. Serbia was a highly polarized society in the 1990s and into the early part of this century, but it has become significantly less so in recent years. In Africa, countries like Sierra Leone and Ivory Coast endured brutal, highly polarizing civil wars, but they have relatively rapidly moved back toward a democratic path.

Third, one key to overcoming polarization is somehow to reassure minority groups that their rights will be protected within a democratic system. Thus, when the left returned to democratic politics in Latin America, it sent an important signal to the right, letting it know that the left was no longer interested in the nationalization of wealth. Conversely, the failure of anti-Assad protesters to reassure Syria's minority Alawite community that it would have a place and rights in the country's political future helped transform their anti-Assad protests into a sectarian civil war.

Fourth, elite bargains also can be a helpful mechanism for overcoming societal polarization, by establishing an understanding of how otherwise antagonistic groups can structure political decisionmaking in ways that redound to everyone's benefit. As mentioned previously, the early literature on democratization, based largely on the Iberian and Latin American experiences, emphasized the role of elite bargains in the process. Such bargains were believed to be essential in creating the political opening that enables a democratic transition to begin, and the nature of a bargain was believed to shape significantly how a transition subsequently unfolded. In fact, most Third Wave transitions were driven much more from the bottom up—from citizens taking to the streets to demand change. Elite bargaining did at times occur but often in response to pressure from below. However, even if elite bargains were rarely the driver behind most Third Wave transitions, such bargains can nonetheless play an important role in overcoming some of the hurdles to democratization described above. They can help diminish the uncertainty that transitions introduce by clarifying the new rules of the game. They can create a shared vision—or at least a shared understanding—of the future when one is lacking. And in so doing, they can remove certain highly combustible issues from routine politics.

In societies with gross disparities in wealth, social compacts like those forged in many Latin American countries have helped ameliorate political tensions between rich and poor by ensuring that the state invests in the human development of its poorest inhabitants. Brazil's Bolsa Familia program—through which direct cash payments are made to help support poor families in return for a commitment to keep their children in school—is but one example. This is a social investment that both rich and poor, right and left, have felt comfortable supporting in Latin America.

In ethnically divided societies, various consociational arrangements have ensured that minority groups are provided some representation in political life.⁶ The challenge is to ensure that such bargains do not ensconce certain elites even more firmly in power (as in Lebanon), making the possibilities for real democracy ever more remote. They should instead be designed to help open up greater opportunities for citizen engagement and to make government more accountable to all of its citizens.

Fifth, civic movements that cut across ethnic, racial, religious, or ideological lines can be another way of helping to overcome political polarization. Groups that work across the fault lines within society to address shared challenges can whittle away at the divisions driving people apart. They can demonstrate that far larger challenges exist than those based on race, ethnicity, or religion and that those challenges can be tackled successfully only if all members of society work together. Widow and survivor groups played a powerful role in this respect in Serbia; environmental groups have fulfilled this function in other contexts.

Sixth, to overcome the divisions within society, a way must be found to address the crimes committed in the past. In post-authoritarian or post-totalitarian societies, the legacies of the past often weigh heavily on the politics of the present. New political leaders often face intense political pressure from the public to remedy the wrongs committed by their predecessors. They may be confronted by an array of issues related to crimes perpetrated in the past, from whether former political leaders should be prosecuted for their transgressions to whether particular individuals or groups should be banned from political life and whether ill-gotten assets (property, businesses, or other wealth) acquired under the old regime should be confiscated.

A society must confront these issues if it is to learn from its past and move on from it. As George Santayana observed, "Those who cannot remember the past are condemned to repeat it."⁷ It is important that past wrongs be exposed so that citizens understand the full depths of the injustices that were committed and try forever after to ensure that they are not repeated. A clear line needs to be drawn between what happened in the past and what is permissible in the new order of things.

The case of Indonesia illustrates the dangers inherent in not dealing adequately with the past. Following the ouster of Suharto, the political leaders of Indonesia's still-nascent democracy feared delving into his regime's crimes because they did not want to alienate the country's powerful military. Sweeping past crimes under the carpet has allowed Indonesia to move forward: democratization in Indonesia has enjoyed "the backing of anyone and everyone." But this political amnesia has come at a cost. Democratization in Indonesia has simply meant the transfer of power from one group of elites to another; democracy has not sunk deep roots among the people. The same patronage politics perfected by Suharto persists to this day; the military continues to exert outsized influence over political life; crony capitalism continues unabated. And now retired generals Prabowo Subianto (Suharto's son-in-law, who was accused of numerous human rights violations) and Wiranto (who is believed to have ordered government troops to fire on student protesters during Suharto's last days in office and to have been complicit in atrocities committed by the Indonesian military in East Timor) are among the country's most popular politicians and leading contenders in the upcoming 2014 presidential elections. Indonesia's unwillingness to confront its past may yet end up severely undermining democracy there.

At the same time, a society that is too vindictive in dealing with past crimes risks alienating or even disenfranchising large segments of the population. In Iraq, Paul Bremer's decision as administrator of the Coalition Provisional Authority to abolish the Iraqi army and ban all Baath Party members from public sector jobs was one factor fueling the Sunni insurgency of 2004–07 that followed the U.S. invasion. Clearly, a careful balance needs to be struck between bringing to light the most heinous crimes from the past and not alienating entire swaths of the population from the democratic process. In a number of countries, including Argentina, Chile, South Africa, and Ghana, truth commissions have provided a mechanism for achieving such a balance. They have focused on unearthing as much as possible about the crimes committed during previous regimes so that citizens can understand fully what happened and learn from it, while prosecuting only the most egregious cases. In this way, a measure of justice has been achieved, without ripping apart the social fabric of society through witch hunts against all who participated, wittingly or unwittingly, in a past regime's transgressions.[8]

Dealing with Nondemocratic Actors

One of the most vexing challenges that societies face in moving toward democracy is deciding what to do with political parties and movements whose commitment to democracy is at best ambiguous. Should nondemocratic actors or actors with an uncertain commitment to democratic principles be allowed to participate in elections and other democratic processes? This issue has gained prominence following the Arab Spring as Islamist groups that enjoyed significant popular support for their long-standing opposition to old secular dictatorships and their perceived commitment to Islamic values now seek to compete for political power.

The dilemma of whether to allow them to participate is not unique to the Arab world. Latin America's nascent democracies faced similar challenges with leftist political parties that espoused revolutionary doctrines as well as with ultra-right-wing parties associated with paramilitary violence. Eastern Europe's new democracies grappled with what to do about the participation of unreconstructed communist parties as well as historically ultra-right-wing, racist parties such as those in Romania and Hungary, not to mention neo-Nazi and skinhead parties in East Germany. Various Muslim-majority countries in Asia have wrestled with the place of Islamist parties in their political systems.

Several lessons on how to grapple with this strategic challenge can be gleaned from the experience of Third Wave democratizers. First, generally it is better to bring nondemocratic elements into the democratic process than to cut them out. The concern in including such actors in electoral politics is that if elected they will use their newfound power to subvert the democratic process to their own advantage. Democracy, it is feared, will amount to a one-person, one-vote, one-time event. That is a valid concern, but the historical evidence suggests that in most instances the benefits of inclusion outweigh those of exclusion. Excluding a popular political group at the outset, simply on the grounds that it might not follow the democratic rules of the game if it won election, risks alienating a large swath of the population altogether. The legitimacy of the political system may then be threatened and the task of building a political constituency for democracy made all the more difficult. Exclusion may produce external challenges to the political system that may be more damaging than those that arise from within. A democratic Egypt, for instance, is harder to fathom without the participation of the Muslim Brotherhood and its supporters, who probably represent at least one-fifth of the electorate.

Historically, Islamist parties have not fared well in democratic elections. Islamist parties in South and Southeast Asia, for example, have rarely secured more than 10 to 20 percent of the vote. In the eighty-nine instances in which Islamist parties competed in elections around the world from 1970 to 2010, their median share of the vote was 7.3 percent and their share of the available seats was 6 percent. If the votes of all Islamic parties that competed are combined, their median share of the vote rises to 15.5 percent of the vote and 15 percent of the seats.[9] The case studies in this volume of Indonesia, Malaysia, and Pakistan bear that out, with Islamist parties facing a clear upper limit on the size of their electoral support.

Moreover, these parties are often led to moderate their positions as a result of their participation in the political process. In the quest for the support of the median voter, they generally feel pressure to move toward the middle. They begin to feel that they have a greater stake in the democratic process, and the responsibility of participating in governance dims their ideological fervor in favor of greater political pragmatism. The case of Turkey reinforces this point. There, the Islamist stream within politics (from the National Order Party to the National Salvation Party, the Welfare Party, the Virtue Party, and finally today's Freedom and Justice Party) grew increasingly pragmatic and moderate over time as it sought to appeal to a broader political constituency, which now extends well beyond its original Islamist base.

Of course, nondemocratic parties have in certain notable and horrific historical cases exploited democratic processes to achieve power. Adolf Hitler's Nazi Party first gained power through democratic elections, then used force and intimidation to remove any real political competitors. In 1946, Czechoslovak communists won a plurality of the vote and then outmaneuvered their coalition partners to seize complete control of the country the following year. The current fear is that because Islamists are broadly popular at the moment, they could use that popularity and their substantial networks throughout society to capture the political process for themselves.

Unfortunately, it is very difficult to gauge intent ex ante. Most Muslim Brotherhood–affiliated political movements long ago eschewed violence and purport to want to participate in democratic processes. Can they be taken at their word? Both the Egyptian branch of the Brotherhood and Ennahda, Tunisia's moderate Islamist "Renaissance Party," appear to be pragmatists with a program. They have a clear vision for society: its gradual return to the values of Islam, as they interpret them. At the same time, they have demonstrated their willingness to be flexible—to tailor the time frame for the implementation of their program to suit circumstances. They have shown themselves willing to exert as much authority or as little as they are allowed. If there is a political vacuum, they will move to occupy it, as Morsi showed during his brief tenure as president. On the other hand, if they face hard constraints on their power, they will adjust their ambitions accordingly. Ennahda, facing the same kind of constitutional stalemate that the Muslim Brotherhood faced in late

2012 over the text of the new constitution, chose to compromise with its political opponents rather than try to run roughshod over them. Unlike the Muslim Brotherhood–led Freedom and Justice Party in Egypt, they simply did not have the votes to do otherwise.

Second, it would be a mistake for a government to ban all political parties whose views do not coincide with its own and thereby to appear by its own parochial perspective to be outside the mainstream. Doing so would run contrary to the very notion of democracy and provide a very weak foundation on which to build a new one. Islam is an important source of identity in the Arab and Muslim worlds. These very religious societies have become only more so as citizens have come to feel under threat from power-hungry autocratic secular governments at home as well as from globalization and Western cultural and military incursions from abroad. Resistance has been cast in Islamic terms. Like it or not, Islam is going to occupy an important place in the politics of the region for the foreseeable future. Each country is going to have to sort out how and where faith fits into the political sphere. In the West, that issue is resolved through the political process; with luck, the same will be the case in the Arab Middle East. Better to get such issues hashed out through the give-and-take of democratic politics than in more violent ways.[10]

Third, some basic conditions should be stipulated, either through legislation or within a constitution, that all political parties must adhere to if they wish to participate in the political process. They should include requirements to take an oath of allegiance to the state, to respect the outcome of democratic elections, to abide by the rules of the constitution, and to forswear violence. The approach toward Islamist parties should be based on the principle of "innocent until proven guilty." Political parties and movements that agree to the minimum standards should be permitted to participate until their behavior contravenes those standards. At that time, civic and political institutions should be strong enough, one hopes, to enforce their disqualification from office and further participation in the political process. It is an imperfect solution, but democracy is an imperfect system. There is always the risk in a democracy that voters will elect the wrong person—a demagogue, an extremist, or an aspiring dictator.

Fourth, the best hedge against such risks are the people themselves— who, it is hoped, will be enlightened enough to discern the good leader from the bad and engaged enough to impose limits on the power of whomever they elect to office.

Fifth, it is worth reiterating that among Third Wave democratizers, more often than not the greatest threat to democracy was entrenched incumbents, not extreme ideologues. In the most notable cases, Africa and the former Soviet Union, whoever won the first elections—regardless of ideology—did everything possible to ensure that they remained in power and that subsequent elections, if there were any, were tilted heavily in their favor. The real challenge to democratization lay in limiting the power and discretion of those already in office, not in defending it from extremists on the outside.

Defining the Proper Role of the Military in a Democracy

Militaries often play an outsized role in democratic transitions. When citizens take to the streets in opposition to an autocratic leader, whether a country's security forces choose to support or abandon that leader often helps to decide whether the regime survives or perishes. During the Arab Spring, many looked to the military to mediate between opposing factions and help steer their country toward democracy. In Egypt, for example, the Supreme Council of the Armed Forces was initially tasked with overseeing the country's transition to democracy following Mubarak's ouster. More recently, anti-Morsi protesters turned again to the military to intervene to end his brief rule.

The experience of Third Wave democratizers offers many lessons regarding the role of the military in democratic transitions. First, militaries created obstacles to democracy far more often than they enabled it. In many instances, the military was the spoiler, bringing a hasty end to a fragile experiment with democracy (for example, in Argentina, Chile, Nigeria, Pakistan, and Turkey). In Latin America and Africa, it was only after the military heeded the call of the civilian population and retreated to the barracks, surrendering any role in domestic politics, that democracy finally had a chance to take deep root. The cases in which militaries played a positive role in advancing democratic development are few and far between.

In looking to the military to play the role of arbiter, many have cited the example of Turkey. However, chapter 4 shows that the vaunted Turkish model of military guardianship of the democratic process is an inaccurate description of reality. The Turkish military did intervene repeatedly during the twentieth century to defend *secularism,* but its interventions were in fact antithetical to the cause of Turkish *democracy.* The military intervened in an effort to stamp out political movements that deviated from Atatürk's secularist principles; however, those movements, which enjoyed wide support among Turkish voters, became more popular with each intervention. The military wanted to see political parties emerge that reflected its own secular vision for Turkey, but through its actions it ended up inadvertently strengthening the opposition.

Second, for democracy to flourish, the "security state" must be scaled back and put under civilian control. A state requires a national security apparatus to provide for the common defense and maintain public order. A state, by definition, is an entity that possesses a monopoly on the use of force within its territory. If a state is unable to provide its citizens basic security from internal and external threats, it ceases to be a state in the full sense of the word. However, the founders of the United States feared large standing armies—and for good reason. "The means of defense against foreign danger," Madison wrote, "have been always the instruments of tyranny at home."[11] A military's ability to employ lethal force often gives it significant political influence at home (as does an intelligence service's control over a society's secrets). Soldiers trained to inflict harm on foreign foes can also be used to intimidate political opponents on the home front.

Technological advances—in transportation, electronics, and communications—have helped empower citizens, but at the same time they also have augmented the coercive power of the state. As Orwell forewarned, the modern state now possesses the ability to monitor almost every aspect of its citizens' lives and has the lethal force to eliminate those who oppose it. Nowhere is this more apparent than in totalitarian, authoritarian, or semi-authoritarian states, many of which have "upgraded" their coercive capabilities in the face of challenges to their rule from below.[12] They have created "deep states" or "states within a state"—extensive domestic intelligence services and vast military establishments—that are kept out of public view, cloaked in secrecy, and that often operate beyond the control of political leaders (as in, for example, Pakistan, Egypt, and Turkey). The deep state presents an existential threat to democracy's very survival.

The existence of deep states has made it more difficult not only to unseat authoritarian governments (as is now being seen in Syria) but also to undertake a successful transition toward democracy afterward. New political leaders end up inheriting the same powers of repression as their predecessors, and they have strong incentives to employ them to their advantage. Even the most enlightened reformers may find it difficult to undo the structures put in place by their predecessors or even to wrest control over them. Yet establishing civilian control over the military and intelligence services is integral to consolidating democracy.

Third, citizens' most potent weapon for finally corralling security forces under civilian control may be the threat of withdrawing legitimacy from these institutions. Chapter 2 shows how notions of legitimacy—ideas about how citizen and state should relate—are rapidly changing. The events of the Arab Spring have shown how quickly legitimacy can be withdrawn and how dramatically its withdrawal affects the power of an institution or regime.[13] In Latin America, for example, what finally forced the military to retreat to the barracks was the public's widespread dissatisfaction with it. The same will likely be true in the Arab world.

Moving from Civic Protest to Politics

As discussed earlier, civic engagement is critical to the democratization process, not just in ousting an unsavory dictator but also in acting as a counterweight afterward to defend nascent political institutions against executive overreach. The important role that civil society can play in democratic breakthroughs has been widely recognized since Ferdinand Marcos's fall from power in the Philippines in 1986 and the civic revolutions that swept Eastern Europe in 1989. However, the role that citizens can play and have played in later stages of the democratization process has been much less appreciated. There is far less understanding of the part that civic actors can play in the day-to-day struggles of young democracies, long after the old regime has departed and founding elections have been held.

What emerges clearly in the case studies is that while civil society may make many contributions to the democratization process—educating citizens about democracy and teaching them new skills, training new leaders, and serving as mini-laboratories for democracy—its most important contribution is often the sheer force of its numbers. The latent threat of citizens flooding the streets in protest can be a potent force in keeping political leaders in check. It also can give particular civic groups the legitimacy and influence to press elected leaders for greater transparency, accountability, and citizen participation, as these groups are understood to represent a far larger popular constituency.

But public protests are a very blunt instrument for effecting political change. They can be difficult to orchestrate, and they may have myriad unintended consequences. They may force a government to change its course or make it more determined to stay the course; they may topple a repressive leader from power or invite a vicious military crackdown;

they may create a democratic breakthrough or usher in civil war. Once hundreds, thousands, or even millions are massed in the streets, anything can happen—from hooliganism to violence, widespread civil unrest, and revolution. Calling citizens out onto the streets can entail a dangerous roll of the dice.

Democracy activists need to identify other tools with which to engage citizens and try to create change at the political level. As pointed out earlier, a disjuncture exists between the tremendous outpouring of civic energy and activism in Egypt, Tunisia, and throughout much of the rest of the Arab world and the far more limited change that has taken place at the political level. There is a tremendous hunger in the region, particularly among youth, for greater freedom, dignity, and opportunity, but there are few political parties or movements effectively representing that constituency. Democracy activists need to find a way to move from protest to politics. They need to tap the tremendous civic energy of the region's youth to fashion effective political movements for change.

A number of valuable lessons can be drawn from the experience of Third Wave democratizers. First, democracy activists should not shy away from engaging in the messy business of politics. There is a certain moral purity to civic protest —one can condemn what is evil while championing all that is good—and it can be more attractive than the trade-offs and compromises involved in politics. Vaclav Havel and his counterparts in Poland touted the virtues of "living in truth" and the "politics of anti-politics" as means of highlighting the injustices of an evil regime: one's own virtuous behavior can stand as a stinging rebuke to the misbehavior of a repressive regime. But forms of disobedience that are effective in an authoritarian or a totalitarian regime may be less so in a democracy. As mentioned previously, bringing down an authoritarian leader is an act of destruction, while building a democracy afterward is an act of construction. In a new democracy, it may not be constructive to confine one's activities to the realm of symbolic and protest politics. Those living in a democracy have a responsibility to engage in the messy business of politics, wherein the need for consensus and compromise requires trade-offs. In the cases in this book, that was the message that the Romanians and Bulgarians carried to the Slovaks. Civil society has a responsibility to engage in democratic politics, even if solely on a nonpartisan basis.

Second, democracy activists need to find ways to organize civil society. For the vast civic energies of the region's youth to have maximum political impact, they must in some way be coordinated and given structure.

New communication technologies like Facebook and Twitter make it easier to mobilize crowds. However, that very spontaneity may limit the long-term effectiveness of crowd-sourced political movements. As others have observed, the Internet can create instant ties among citizens across a broad area, but often the ties created are weak ties that require only a low level of commitment—just enough to click a button or show up as part of a flash mob. Sustained political movements, on the other hand, require strong ties and long-term commitment.[14] Democracy activists in the Arab world face the challenge of forging effective political movements from dispersed, often spontaneous civic actions that are not part of a coordinated effort. The power of civil society vis-à-vis the state resides in the capacity of civil society to self-organize.

The Slovaks and Serbs provide models of how civic groups can coordinate their activities horizontally to achieve common goals. Both OK '98 in Slovakia and EXIT 2000 in Serbia were loose, nonhierarchical organizations that helped synchronize the myriad election-related activities of diverse civic groups. They united under a common banner, on the strength of common goals, a broad array of organizations that were more accustomed to competing than cooperating. The genius of OK '98 and EXIT 2000 was that they left each member group free to choose and conduct its own activities in working toward those shared goals, while providing a central mechanism for communication and consultation.[15] The two organizations were developed to conduct election-focused civic campaigns, but there is no reason that the same kind of coordinating mechanism could not be employed for broader civic purposes.

Third, civic groups should not wait for political parties that share their values to bring political change. In nascent democracies, political parties typically are organizationally weak. It can take a long time for them to mature and professionalize and to make the transition from personality-driven to ideologically based parties. In the case studies discussed here, often it was civic groups rather than opposition political parties that spearheaded the efforts to oust despotic leaders. The civic groups put pressure on the political parties to overcome their differences and unite under a common political umbrella. In the run-up to the 2000 elections in Serbia that ultimately resulted in the ouster of Milosevic, for example, civic leaders forced opposition leaders Vojislav Kostunica and Zoran Djindjic to join hands at a political rally to demonstrate publicly their political unity. The final chapter discusses the implications of these lessons for the conduct of U.S. policy toward the Middle East.

CHAPTER NINE

POLICY
RECOMMENDATIONS

The preceding chapters illuminate the experience with democratization in various regions of the world during what is commonly referred to as the Third Wave. This concluding chapter attempts to translate those lessons into practical recommendations for U.S. and other policymakers seeking to support activists in the Arab Middle East who are struggling to advance the cause of democracy.

As shown by the survey presented here of democratic transitions in the former Eastern bloc, Muslim-majority Asia, Latin America, and Sub-Saharan Africa, the democratization experience has varied markedly from region to region and even country to country. Because of vast differences in context—in history, culture, economic status, demographics, and class structure—each country's encounter with democracy has been as different from another's as the countries themselves. But what the preceding chapters make clear is that democracy is possible even under some of the most inhospitable conditions. During the Third Wave, countries that were extremely poor, that were sharply divided between rich and poor, that were polarized by ethnic and religious differences, and even that had endured civil war succeeded in becoming electoral, if not liberal, democracies. Their journey was not swift, nor was it without struggle. Many experienced substantial backsliding along the way, and some reverted to authoritarianism. Others remain stuck in a murky gray area between authoritarianism and democracy. But of the ninety or so countries that attempted a transition toward democracy during the Third Wave, the vast majority are now considered electoral democracies and about half are categorized as "free" by Freedom House.

The United States rarely faces easy choices in the Arab Middle East; often its only policy options are those that run from bad to worse. Yet the United States can begin to improve its range of options if it embraces rather than resists change in the region. Across the world, political attitudes are changing dramatically, and as they do, citizens are increasingly clamoring for political systems that accord them greater dignity and rights. For a long time, the Arab Middle East seemed exempt from this broad trend, but that is no longer the case. Through the events of the Arab Spring, citizens of the Arab Middle East have found their voice and are making the same kinds of demands of their governments as citizens elsewhere: for dignity, freedom, opportunity, and just and effective governance.

The United States must recognize that the old Middle East is gone. The Mubaraks and Ben Alis of the region may have been attractive partners in the past because they guaranteed stability, but the region's citizens will no longer accept a return to stability based on authoritarianism and repression. It may take a long time, full of painful and often destabilizing struggles, for the countries of the Arab world to attain a new equilibrium in the form of a more stable order based on democratic governance. But the United States has no choice but to accept that the old order is no longer sustainable. There is no going back.

Accordingly, the United States should throw its support firmly behind the forces of change in the region. It should align itself squarely with those Arab democrats seeking to build more just, participatory, and accountable political systems. In whatever ways possible, it should assist the citizens and countries of the region to make the difficult transition from an order based on coercion to one based on individual choice. That does not mean that the United States should abandon its long-standing allies tomorrow, but it should recognize that the future of the region will be determined by the region's citizens. It should heed their demands and, to the extent feasible, help support and broker the emergence of a new democratic order.

This chapter seeks to outline what that would mean in practice. The central argument of this book is that successful democratization depends over the long term on the emergence of a political constituency for democracy. The United States should make helping to build an effective constituency of this kind the core organizing principle of its assistance to the region. All U.S. investments in the region—public and, it is hoped, also private—in the disparate realms of human rights promotion, development assistance, post-conflict reconstruction, public diplomacy, cultural exchange, and the like should be conducted with that long-term goal in mind. The U.S. government and private philanthropies already undertake a variety of activities that, intentionally or unintentionally, advance that goal. The argument here is that the United States should adopt a grand strategy designed specifically to cultivate effective political constituencies for democracy in the region, one in which all these activities as well as others become part of a single, coherent, long-term approach. That strategy should be the lodestar guiding U.S. development efforts.

Constraints on U.S. Policy

What may seem like a soaring call to action should be tempered with a healthy dose of realism. First, external actors have limited influence on the democratization process in any country. As many have cautioned in recent years, "democracy must come from within."[1] For democracy to flourish, citizens must be willing to claim it as their own and defend it from both domestic and foreign threats. Democracy needs to emerge organically if it is to flourish over the long term. At best, outsiders can only assist at the margins.

Second, the United States faces significant resource constraints that also limit its ability to influence events on the ground. At the time of the Marshall Plan, the U.S. economy was as large as that of all other economies combined; today, it makes up only one-fifth of the global economy. Moreover, the Marshall Plan sought primarily to shore up Europe's existing democracies through economic assistance, not to build new ones from whole cloth. One could argue that nonetheless the moment merits a response of Marshall Plan–sized ambition, although no such response is likely today because there exist neither the financial resources nor the political appetite for it. As was the case with Europe in the first half of the twentieth century, the United States finds itself in the first decades of the twenty-first continually sucked into the conflicts—inter- and intrastate— of the Middle East. However, the Obama administration will not be able to fulfill its oft-stated desire to pivot toward Asia—to direct greater resources and diplomatic attention to the Pacific region—until there is a modicum of stability in the Middle East that allows the United States to reduce its footprint and commitments there.

Third, the ability of the United States to exert influence is limited further by its poor standing in the Arab world. After the end of World War II and the cold war, the United States was highly regarded and its assistance was warmly welcomed by the people living in both Eastern and

Western Europe. The American model of a free-market democracy was respected, and the United States was trusted enough that its advice was heeded as countries restructured their economies and political systems. Not so in the Arab world today. Because of long-standing U.S. support for Israel, military interventions in Iraq and Afghanistan, and longtime backing of dictators like Mubarak and Ben Ali, the United States—or at least U.S. foreign policy—is deeply unpopular in the region. Many Arab citizens perceive the United States as just the latest Western imperial power in the region, following on the French and the British, intent on dominating Arab lands and killing innocent civilians. The U.S. government is therefore widely distrusted and its motives often subject to question. The Egyptian government's raids in late 2011 on U.S. nongovernmental organizations and its arrest and trial of forty-three aid workers epitomize some of the challenges confronting American efforts to promote democracy in the region.[2]

Fourth, more foreign powers are seeking to wield influence than before, diluting U.S. power in the region even further. New actors—from Qatar and the United Arab Emirates to China and Russia—have arrived, dispensing large sums of cash in an effort to advance their own agendas. As can be seen in Egypt, that diminishes American leverage because any cutoff of U.S. assistance in response to undemocratic practices or rights abuses can be made up relatively easily from other sources.

That said, the United States has more tools at its disposal for promoting democracy in the region than it tends to recognize. Americans were surprised by the scenes telecast around the world of hundreds of thousands of Egyptians in Tahrir Square chanting for freedom and democracy. Here were young Arabs courageously taking to the streets and espousing values that Americans too hold dear. American technologies, American music and film, American universities, and the American example of democracy all played some part in bringing about these dramatic cultural and attitudinal changes. Going forward, those assets can be used to help accelerate them.

The Challenge

The challenge that now confronts the United States is how to help broaden the Tahrir Square base: how to expand the changes in culture and perceptions that have brought a new Arab generation into politics and upended political discourse in the region and to build from those changes effective political constituencies for democracy. Ralph Waldo

Emerson once observed: "The wise know . . . that the form of government which prevails, is the expression of what cultivation exists in the population which permits it."[3] The United States should assist with that cultivation.

That does not mean that the United States should abandon the important work that it does in helping to craft effective constitutions, develop democratic political institutions, train government officials to staff those institutions, create vibrant political parties, convene free and fair elections, and ensure civilian oversight of the military. Quite the contrary: if building a political constituency for democracy is the demand side of the democratization equation, those efforts represent the supply side—creating the public institutions through which citizen demands are channeled. They are vital to the proper functioning of a representative democracy, and the United States has developed significant technical expertise in assisting other countries in their creation.

However, institutional design is just one piece of a much larger puzzle. U.S. efforts to build effective political institutions will come to naught unless citizens demand that those institutions function as intended. The best-written constitutions and most perfectly designed democratic institutions amount to nothing but words on paper if political leaders do not feel compelled to abide by them. Human nature being what it is, the rule of law will not take root until political leaders understand that the public demands it. If the United States wants democracy to succeed around the globe, it must help create public demand.

The country case studies in the preceding chapters illustrate how a political constituency for democracy could begin to take shape. It often starts with attitudinal change at the individual level, followed by isolated attempts of citizens at the local level to work together to address communal problems and ultimately by the coming together of diverse networks of engaged citizens to press national governments for meaningful change. Thus, there appear to be three elements in the development of a political constituency for democracy:

—the emergence of an educated population of citizens capable of thinking critically and acting independently

—the banding together to solve communal problems at the local level by citizens, who through that experience learn methods of engaging in collective action and develop networks of like-minded individuals

—the mobilization of disparate networks across the country to push national political leaders for democratic change.

Education and Value Change

In many respects, expanding the Tahrir base will entail helping to open what have been in recent years relatively closed societies in order to cultivate a more informed and engaged citizenry in the Arab world. It will mean providing citizens with the perspective that comes from seeing how other societies function and mediate relations between citizens and the state. As one of the most open societies in the world, the United States should place greater value on openness as a tool for change. Openness promises to speed the cultural and attitudinal changes already under way in the region. The United States should seek to encourage "brain circulation"—the flow of people and ideas in, out, and across the region. It should support initiatives that hasten the movement of people and ideas across borders, regionally and internationally, including by continuing to support greater Internet access and Internet freedom and by finding more ways for Arab and American youth to connect via social and other virtual media.

In addition, the United States should look for ways to get as many Arab youth and professionals as possible out to other parts of the world—through exchanges, study tours, and professional development opportunities—so that they can experience other cultures firsthand and observe how citizens relate to political authority in other settings. And, for the same reasons, the United States should be encouraging as many people as possible from outside the region to come in—as volunteer (or paid) teachers, accountants, managers, entrepreneurs, finance gurus, local and regional government experts, educational administrators, technical advisers, and English-language instructors. One of the most successful initiatives that the European Union devised after the end of the cold war was its Tempus program, a grant program that simply supported the efforts of scholars and educators to move between Eastern and Western Europe to teach, study, and do research.

A step that is even more critical in the long run is for the United States to help develop indigenous educational institutions that are capable of providing a world-class education and nurturing a new generation of informed citizens. Over the long term, the countries of the Arab world need to be able to generate their own human capital rather than sending their best minds abroad to study, sometimes never to return. Citizens who are capable of thinking critically and acting independently are the bedrock of competitive economies and successful democracies. The aim of such endeavors should be to help create a new generation of citizens who are more educated, more open to the world, and more connected to one another.

Grassroots Civic Activism

At the same time, the United States should support local civic initiatives that bring like-minded citizens together for common public purposes. It should develop fast, flexible mechanisms to provide small amounts of financial and technical support to civic initiatives being championed by citizens themselves, not by well-intentioned bureaucrats in Washington. Often very modest funding that targets the right individual or organization can be far more effective than large, expensive top-down programs. During times of rapid change, private foundations and civil society organizations often are more nimble than governments, so they may be better equipped to provide such assistance.

Building a political constituency for democracy requires not only informed citizens but also those who have the skills to work collectively for shared public ends. The United States should help underwrite citizen-inspired initiatives to address pressing political and economic problems, large and small. It not only is the right thing to do—helping others to improve their own societies—it also helps citizens learn how to work together through such initiatives and gain confidence in doing so. From working to halt the construction of a dam to campaigning for better schools, citizens learn effective methods of taking collective action and engaging with political authority while also building enduring cooperative networks. They may become not just environmental or educational activists but also democracy activists. The political learning that takes place and the networks developed through local initiatives become the building blocks for the development of more national political movements.

National Movements for Change

Finally, the United States should assist democracy activists to bring together like-minded networks of citizens to advocate for democratic change. As seen most graphically in Slovakia and Serbia, democratic movements emerge out of countless more local struggles for change—from the networks built and lessons learned over time across the breadth of a country. Such movements begin to have political resonance at the national level when activists succeed in getting diverse groups to coalesce around shared political goals.

One of the most important forms of assistance that the United States can provide may be simply to connect political and civic leaders with their counterparts in other countries who have waged these battles before. As seen in the preceding chapters, many of the strategic and tactical questions with which democratic activists in the Arab world are now wrestling—whether or not to engage in dialogue with an existing authoritarian regime, how to ensure a credible transition, when to write or rewrite a constitution, how to deal with past injustices, how to assert civilian control over the military, how to move from protest to politics—have been confronted in other countries, even if the context has sometimes been much different.

As should by now be clear, the promotion of democracy is as much a political as a technical endeavor. The best-designed institutions will not endure unless they have strong public support. Broad citizen engagement is required not only to oust an authoritarian regime but also to ensure that what comes next is democratic, not just in form but in substance. Well-functioning, liberal democracies are likely to emerge only after a long and highly political struggle between citizens and their leaders. In keeping with its values, the United States should stand squarely behind civic leaders struggling to make the promise of democracy real in their own country.

The building of a political constituency for democracy is a long-term endeavor. In many societies, it may require a commitment not of years but of decades. Tunisia, with its past openness to the outside world, high level of education, and highly networked society, seems more likely to be able to develop such a constituency within a modest span of time than, say, Yemen, which lacks all of those attributes. As suggested previously, it is a political project that outsiders can support and assist with, but ultimately its success depends on indigenous efforts. If the United States hopes to make an impact through assistance, it must plan to be engaged for the long term and prepared to play a supporting, not a leading, role.

The stakes are high. The countries of the Arab world are more open to the world than at any time since their independence, but this window of opportunity may not remain open forever. Already in Egypt, for instance, the security establishment seeks to limit foreign assistance to local nongovernmental organizations and to place restrictions on the media. If the United States is to be of assistance, it needs to act while there is still an opportunity to do so. Two decades ago, Russia experienced a similar opening to the world. The United States did not capitalize on that opening as fully as it could have, thereby missing opportunities to expose more Russians to the outside world, to reform the country's educational system in a more meaningful way, and to nurture a new generation of democracy activists. That made it easier for Vladimir Putin, after coming to power in 1999, to gradually cut off foreign assistance to and impose increasing restrictions on the country's emerging civic sector. Russia under Putin has slid back toward authoritarianism, although it is far from clear that the backsliding is permanent. The point is that no matter what happens at the political level, the United States should seize this unique moment of openness in Arab history to expose as many people of the Arab region as possible to the rest of the world, to help reform educational systems and the media, to nurture networks of change agents, and to acquaint democracy activists trying to steer their country toward democracy with the experience of others who have been through such transitions before.

A Complementary Foreign Policy

Beyond providing material support, the United States—and other external actors that wish to support Arab democracy activists—can help by creating an international and regional environment conducive to democratic development. First, the United States should take a more active role in helping to shape the political future of the Arab Middle East. In doing so, it needs to pursue a foreign policy that reflects its values as well as its interests. It needs to make a leap of faith and align itself with those struggling for democracy in the region, because that is what Arab citizens want and that is where the future lies. The United States should abandon the habit, deeply ingrained in its diplomacy, of always seeking to know and maintain strong relations with whoever is in charge. Repeatedly throughout history, the U.S. government has stood behind long-time dictators because it was afraid that whoever came next would be worse—above all, for the United States. Instead, it should support the democratic process—which means, among other things, that it must accept whoever wins in competitive multiparty elections. That acceptance should be contingent on the winners' abiding by democratic principles once in office—by pledging loyalty to the state, upholding the constitution, enforcing the rule of law, safeguarding the rights of minorities, forswearing violence, and allowing for free and fair elections going forward. At the same time, the United States should engage with all legitimate political forces within a society so that over time it feels less and less as if it has to support "the devil it knows" over "the devil it doesn't know."

Such a policy does not mean abandoning long-standing friends and allies overnight because they fail to live up to U.S. democratic standards. But it does mean continually engaging them in dialogue on issues on which they fall short and making it clear that U.S. support over the long term is conditioned on their opening up their societies and moving in a more democratic direction. They must bring others into the political process, provide guarantees for minority populations, and move toward more participatory and competitive politics if they are to retain U.S. support as an ally. U.S. foreign policy should seek to facilitate such reforms, which are likely to be far less messy than revolution.[4] In places like Bahrain, where majority and minority communities are at loggerheads, the United States should seek to broker agreement on a political road map for the future. A more activist diplomacy that seeks creative solutions to the political conflicts roiling the region may diminish the likelihood of violent conflict.

The United States should also work to help create a security environment in the region that is more conducive to democratic development. Even as it reduces its military footprint, it needs to continue to play a leadership role in the region. Otherwise, Saudi Arabia and Iran, the region's two major powers besides Israel, will be left contending for ascendancy, along with al Qaeda. The resulting sectarian polarization and political violence may jeopardize further democratic experiments in the region, as citizens fearfully come to define their identities even more in religious than national terms.

Good behavior abroad should be matched by good behavior at home. As one of the world's oldest democracies, the United States is looked to as a model. When the government spies on its own citizens, infringes their individual rights in the name of greater security, discriminates against different minority groups, or disregards its own constitutional and legal constraints, it forfeits its credibility in pressing others to refrain from the same undemocratic actions. The United States needs to live up to the values that it espouses abroad. An America that embodies the vision of its Founding Fathers—that fully enables its citizens to "secure the blessings of liberty"—is its own greatest asset in promoting the cause of democracy elsewhere.

Second, the United States should stand squarely behind those struggling to advance democracy in the Arab world. While U.S. influence is limited given the money flowing to the countries of the Arab Spring from wealthy Gulf states, the United States should use what leverage it has to create greater political space for democracy activists in the region.

It should speak out strongly in defense of their right to express their opinions and to organize, associate, and assemble freely. It should provide support and protection to activists and their families when they are imprisoned or their lives are threatened, much as it does for journalists.

Third, because the United States does not have many sticks to wield, it should look for carrots to offer political leaders to encourage them to keep their countries open to the world and allow civic groups to operate freely. One highly cherished carrot would be a free trade agreement, which would significantly reduce the barriers that countries face in exporting goods to the United States. Over the short term, such agreements are unlikely to be politically realistic: in most instances, they would meet with stiff congressional opposition. However, country-by-country agreements that define a road map toward an eventual free trade agreement might be more politically feasible and would provide incentives for countries to move forward on the path to political and economic reform.[5]

In looking for positive incentives, the United States also should think creatively with Arab leaders about the design of regional institutions. The Arab Middle East lacks the regional institutional infrastructure found in Europe, Latin America, East Asia, and even, arguably, Africa. In each, regional institutions are in place that encourage greater cross-border trade and investment, both of which are lacking in the Middle East. These institutions often have built-in democratic norms that uphold the basic rights of citizens, competitive elections, and the non-interference of the military in politics. Other regional mechanisms, like the Helsinki Process in Europe and the Stability Pact in the Balkans, have encouraged countries, through peer pressure of a kind, to make aspirational commitments on issues of political rights, then established peer review mechanisms for assessing how well the countries lived up to their commitments.

Above all, if the United States wants to promote democracy in the Arab world, it needs to be patient. Building political constituencies for democracy will require not a year or two but decades, if not generations. If the United States is to help the citizens of the Arab world succeed in their quest for democracy, it must be committed for the long term.

The Case of Egypt

No discussion of U.S. assistance to the Arab world would be complete without delving more deeply into the case of Egypt. As the most populous country in the Arab word, one with broad cultural influence in the region and a location of considerable strategic importance, Egypt is a bellwether for the region as a whole. If Egypt can somehow navigate a successful transition to democracy, its success will have positive repercussions across the entire region. If it fails, the negative consequences will be significant.

Egypt is at a critical juncture. The Tamarood petition campaign and the ensuing protests on June 30, 2013, may have halted the Muslim Brotherhood's gradual consolidation of state power, but the military's ouster of President Mohamed Morsi four days later unseated a democratically elected government. The military is back in the business of governing. More than 1,000 Muslim Brotherhood members have been killed in clashes with the police and military and many more have been jailed. Tensions run deep between Islamists and secularists. In late December 2013, the interim government banned the Brotherhood, designating it a terrorist organization. A fifty-member constitutional committee approved a new draft constitution—which, among other things, outlaws religious-based political parties and further entrenches the power of the security forces—which was overwhelmingly approved by voters in a referendum in mid-January 2014 (although only 38 percent of the electorate participated). Presidential and parliamentary elections are expected to ensue in the months ahead, almost certainly without the participation of the Brotherhood. General Abdel Fattah el-Sisi seems all but certain to put his name forward as a candidate for president, and in the current environment, he likely will win.

The military is once more in the driver's seat and shows few signs of being willing to relinquish the wheel anytime soon. It has sidelined the Brotherhood, temporarily though likely not permanently. It also has jailed a number of secular political activists—the very activists who helped bring Egyptians to the streets in the June 30 protests against the Morsi government—and passed laws restricting protests and the media. Meanwhile, the secular political parties are weak and divided, and it is not clear that they would be prepared to take the helm even if it were on offer.

These events have presented the U.S. government with an unenviable dilemma. With the ouster of former president Mohamed Morsi and his government on July 3, 2013, the United States was forced to choose between its support for the Egyptian military, the key guarantor of the long-standing peace agreement with Israel, and its support for Egyptian democracy. The Obama administration, refraining from calling the military's action a coup, equivocated on the issue. It then belatedly linked delivery of elements of the U.S. assistance package (military weapons systems in particular) to progress made on the democratic road map, only to have Secretary of State John Kerry, on a visit to Cairo, downplay those conditions and suggest that democracy was on track in Egypt.

One can quibble over the semantics, but Morsi's removal from power was for all intents and purposes a military coup: an elected civilian government was replaced by the military with a government of its own choosing. The military may have had justification in doing so: President Morsi, though popularly elected, overstepped his constitutional powers with his November 2012 emergency decree and rammed through his own constitution over the strong objections of the political opposition. The military could justifiably claim to be acting in accordance with the will of the Egyptian public, which showed its deep dissatisfaction with the Morsi regime through the millions of signatures on the Tamarood petition and its overwhelming presence on the streets in subsequent protests (although it was dissatisfied with the government as much for its incompetence in addressing the country's vast socioeconomic problems as for exceeding its constitutional mandate). Many Egyptians saw Morsi and the Muslim Brotherhood as an existential threat to the country, akin to the communists in Czechoslovakia in 1947, who won a plurality in popular elections and then used their newfound power to take over a democratic government. Morsi's opponents judged, rightly or wrongly, that the only way to remove him and the Brotherhood from power was with the help of the military. The reality is that international law is vague when it comes to the rights of citizens vis-à-vis a government that was freely elected but oversteps the existing constitutional rules. With the prevalence around the globe of so many hybrid regimes that hold elections but fail to work within the established constitutional framework or to respect basic individual and civil rights, the international community probably requires clearer rules of the road regarding when and how an elected government can be removed legitimately.

Regardless of how one interprets the events of July 3, 2013—whether one considers it a coup or not—there is no denying that the military now controls Egyptian politics. As earlier chapters of this book show, that is unlikely to be good for Egypt or its prospects for democracy. Militaries, once they wade into political waters, tend to stay, yet rarely are they well suited to govern. Commanding a military brigade is very different from managing a modern economy or responding to the demands of newly empowered citizens. As it showed in the year after Mubarak's ouster, the Egyptian military is not up to the task of directly governing Egypt. It is not capable of improving Egypt's moribund economy or addressing its myriad social challenges.

The U.S. government must recognize that military rule is no longer a sustainable solution to the problem of governance in Egypt. The Egyptian people, who have repeatedly taken to the streets over the last three years in pursuit of greater dignity and personal freedom, are unlikely to stand for long for the kinds of infringement of personal liberty and freedom of assembly that accompany military rule. It is only a matter of time before Egyptians take to the streets once again, in large numbers, against the military. Although they may be frustrated and disillusioned because the Arab Spring has not yet brought about fundamental change, in the current highly polarized environment, with security forces firmly in control, few Egyptians dare stick their neck out. But the idea of democracy is not dead in Egypt. Egyptians will not allow General el-Sisi to become the next Hosni Mubarak. Whether in three months or three years, there will be a confrontation—this time between secularists and the military—over whether Egypt will be a democracy. The military will ensure that the planned presidential and parliamentary elections bring an acceptable outcome; it will continue to control political life, whether directly or indirectly; and the public will eventually take to the streets to challenge the military once again.

The U.S. government should gear its assistance efforts to support that upcoming struggle and all that will follow. It should begin by abandoning its long-standing ambivalence and wholeheartedly embrace democracy in Egypt as its overriding policy goal. To do otherwise is to risk being left once again on the wrong side of history, as it was to its great detriment with regard to its support for Mubarak. A democratic Egypt would in no way conflict with other U.S. interests in the region. As became clear during President Mohamed Morsi's tenure in office, none of the major political forces in Egypt has an interest in abrogating the peace treaty or renewing hostilities with Israel. Nor does the Egyptian military, for all its bluff and bluster, have an alternative to continuing its strategic partnership with the United States—its force capability depends on access to U.S. military parts and equipment.[6] Over the long term, a democratic Egypt is likely to be a more stable and reliable ally in the region.

Along with the rest of the international community, the United States should seek to act as a guardian of the democratic process. It should press the Egyptian military to respect not only the letter but also the spirit of its democratic road map. It should strongly discourage General al-Sisi or any other military official from running for political office. It should speak out forcefully against any and all infringements of individual and civil rights, including freedom of speech and assembly. And it should insist on a political reconciliation with the Muslim Brotherhood that leads to the group's re-incorporation into the democratic process. The

Egyptian military needs to understand that it cannot eradicate an idea by force. The Brotherhood and the sizable constituency that it represents will not go away, and if democracy is to succeed, they must be given a place in the political process.

At the same time, the United States should support civic activists as they seek to forge a third alternative to the military and the Islamists. These brave individuals need to be given the freedom and the resources to organize. They face a daunting challenge. Egyptians took to the streets against Mubarak in 2011, they did so repeatedly against the Supreme Council of the Armed Forces (SCAF) the following year, and they did so a third time against Mohamed Morsi in June 2013. However, on each occasion what they got was far different from what they had demanded. Egypt does not lack civic energy—as the millions of signatures on the Tamarood petition and the massive crowds that have time and again filled Tahrir Square attest—but activists have never been able to translate that energy into concrete political gains. Their efforts to oust Mubarak led not to democracy but rule by the SCAF. Their protests against the SCAF brought the election of a Brotherhood-dominated government. Their mass demonstrations against Mohamed Morsi's government resulted in the return of military rule. In the age of social media, it is far easier to spontaneously generate crowds on the streets than it is to harness that energy in a manner that produces meaningful political change.

The crowds that have repeatedly flooded Tahrir Square and myriad other public spaces in Egypt suggest that there is an emerging political constituency for democracy in the country. How wide and deep it is remains to be seen. Democracy activists face the challenge of expanding the Tahrir constituency to include Egyptians other than the well-educated, upwardly mobile, cosmopolitan denizens of Cairo. In particular, activists need to extend their reach into the hinterlands, particularly Upper Egypt, the more remote and rural southern region of the country. This region, which is poorer and has less access to quality education, is a stronghold of the Muslim Brotherhood. Democracy activists also face the challenge of expanding their activism beyond street protests, which have often led to bloody confrontations with the police and are increasingly unpopular with the broader Egyptian public. They need to find other ways to make the collective will of the Egyptian people clear to political leaders. For all its flaws, the Tamarood petition drive was a step in that direction.

Still another challenge that democracy activists face is to strengthen their role in organized politics. They need to cobble together a more formal political movement from the diverse civic groups advocating for true democracy in Egypt. They need to pressure secular political parties—which remain highly personality based, poorly organized, and largely untested politically—to listen more to the voices of the street, to incorporate the new generation of youth activists into their ranks, and to overcome their internal squabbling to unite in a common political front. In short, to have a larger impact on democratic development, the civic sector needs to become greater than the sum of its parts. A civic sector that is politically effective must consist of more than just an array of successful human rights and government watchdog groups each pursuing its own independent mission; it requires close coordination among them. If Egyptian democracy activists are finally to succeed in channeling the tremendous civic energy on the streets into lasting political change, they need greater structure and strategy to support their efforts.

Neighboring Tunisia may help point the way forward. There, a larger and determined political opposition and an engaged civil society forced the ruling Ennahda party to compromise. When political violence flared in 2013, citizens took to the streets, citing the inability of the government to provide basic security and govern competently and calling for it to resign. In the end—conscious of the fate of the Brotherhood in Egypt—the Ennahda-led government responded with an attempt at reconciliation rather than confrontation. The trade union movement brokered a deal between the country's two leading political figures that put in place a nonpartisan caretaker government to oversee forthcoming primary and presidential elections. The constitution that emerged is a consensus document that addresses the needs of both Islamists and secularists.

Regardless, in today's highly charged political climate in Egypt, with the military exercising tight control, the United States and other outside actors can assist only at the margins. Ultimately, the struggle over whether Egypt will be a democracy is a political one that Egyptians themselves must wage. The U.S. government and others can help democracy activists expand their base by using this window of opportunity to expose more Egyptians to the wider world through study opportunities at U.S. universities (the number of Egyptian students currently studying in the United States is shockingly low[7]), two-way professional exchanges, education reform efforts, creative television and film programming, and social media. Outside actors can provide activists with the resources and expertise to enhance their institutional capabilities and strengthen their networks within Egyptian society. They can make available to them the expertise of democratic activists elsewhere who have played a part in making successful transitions to democracy. They can assist the secular political parties to become more professional, more unified, and more deeply rooted in Egyptian society. They can help prepare those likely to serve in the country's next democratically elected government, should it come to pass, for the difficult task of governing, so that they meet with more success than Mohamed Morsi's government did in its first year.

But much of the rest is up to Egyptians themselves. They must engage their compatriots in debate over what kind of Egypt they want to live in and what political values they want to support. They must organize and forge networks of like-minded Egyptians. They must find creative ways to challenge the military if and when it deviates from the democratic path. And they must be prepared to continue that struggle for some time to come, potentially even long after a new, truly democratic government is ultimately elected. Only then will the spirit of Tahrir prevail.

NOTES

Chapter 1

1. The Third Wave occurred between the mid-1970s and the late 1990s.

2. See Anne Applebaum, "In the Arab World, It's 1848—Not 1989," *Washington Post*, February 22, 2011.

3. See, for example, Raymond Ibrahim, "Parallel Betrayals: Iranian Revolution and Arab Spring," Middle East Forum, June 18, 2012 (www.meforum. org/3264/iranian-revolution-arab-spring).

4. "Ambassador Anne W. Patterson's Speech at the Ibn Khaldun Center for Development Studies," June 18, 2013 (http://egypt.usembassy.gov/mobile/pr061813a.html).

5. Larry Diamond, *The Spirit of Democracy: The Struggle to Build Free Societies throughout the World* (New York: Henry Holt, 2008), pp. 6, 54. That number includes newly independent states.

6. Ralf Dahrendorf, *Reflections on the Revolution in Europe*, rev. ed. (Brunswick, N.J.: Transaction Publishers, 1995), p. 100.

7. This section draws on a typology developed in Kenneth M. Pollack and Daniel Byman, *The Arab Awakening: America and the Transformation of the Middle East* (Brookings, 2011).

8. Ivan Krastev, "The Transparency Delusion," *Eurozine*, February 2, 2013 (www.eurozine.com/articles/2013-02-01-krastev-en.html).

9. Sheri Berman, "The Promise of the Arab Spring: In Political Development, No Gain without Pain," *Foreign Affairs*, January/February 2013 (www.foreign affairs.com/articles/138479/sheri-berman/the-promise-of-the-arab-spring).

10. Robert Alan Dahl, *Polyarchy: Participation and Opposition* (Yale University Press, 1971), p. 20.

11. In a similar vein, Marina Ottaway writes of the importance of a "popular constituency" for political reform in "The Missing Constituency for Political Reform," in *Uncharted Journey: Promoting Democracy in the Middle East*, edited

by Thomas Carothers and Marina Ottaway (Washington: Carnegie Endowment for International Peace, 2005), pp. 151–70.

12. Zbigniew Brzezinski, *Second Chance: Three Presidents and the Crisis of American Superpower* (New York: Basic Books, 2007), pp. 201–04.

13. Pippa Norris, *Critical Citizens: Global Support for Democratic Government* (Oxford University Press, 1999); "World Publics Say Governments Should Be More Responsive to the Will of the People," World Public Opinion, May 12, 2008 (www.worldpublicopinion.org/pipa/articles/governance_bt/482.php?nid=&id=&pnt=482).

14. The term "deep state" refers to well-entrenched groups within a state, such as the military, intelligence agencies, and the police, whose interests may diverge from those of political leaders or the general public. See, for example, Merve Kavakci, "Turkey's Test with Its Deep State," *Mediterranean Quarterly*, vol. 20, no. 4 (2009), pp. 83–97.

15. Edwin S. Corwin, *The President: Office and Powers, 1787–1957*, 4th ed. (New York: New York Press, 1971), p. 171.

16. James Madison, "Letter to George Thomson, June 30, 1825," *Letters and Other Writings of James Madison*, vol. 3 (Philadelphia: J.B. Lippincott, 1865), p. 492 (http://archive.org/stream/lettersandother01madigoog#page/n8/mode/2up).

17. Philip B. Kurland and Ralph Lerner, *The Founders' Constitution*, vol. 1, chap. 13, doc. 36 (University of Chicago Press) (http://press-pubs.uchicago.edu/founders/documents/v1ch13s36.html).

18. "Jefferson to Richard Price," January 8, 1789, Paris (Library of Congress) (www.loc.gov/exhibits/jefferson/60.html).

Chapter 2

1. The late political scientist Samuel Huntington introduced the notion of three historical waves of democratization. See Huntington, *The Third Wave: Democratization in the Late 20th Century* (University of Oklahoma Press, 1991).

2. See Stephen Grand, "Starting in Egypt: The Fourth Wave of Democratization?" Brookings Opinion, February 10, 2011 (www.brookings.edu/research/opinions/2011/02/10-egypt-democracy-grand).

3. Larry Diamond, *The Spirit of Democracy: The Struggle to Build Free Societies throughout the World* (New York: Henry Holt, 2008), appendix, table 2.

4. See Seymour Martin Lipset, "Some Social Requisites of Democracy," *American Political Science Review*, vol. 53 (1959), pp. 71–85; and Adam Przeworski, *Democracy and the Market: Political and Economic Reforms in Eastern Europe and Latin America* (Cambridge University Press, 1991).

5. See "Independent Countries," *Freedom in the World 2013: Democratic Breakthroughs in the Balance*, p. 15 (www.freedomhouse.org/sites/default/files/FIW%202013%20Charts%20and%20Graphs%20for%20Web_0.pdf).

6. Diamond, *The Spirit of Democracy*, p. 27.

7. CIA, "Field Listing: Government Type," *The World Factbook* (www.cia.gov/library/publications/the-world-factbook/fields/2128.html); and Pippa Norris, Research: Data, John F. Kennedy School of Government, Harvard University (www.pippanorris.com/).

8. Ronald Inglehart and Christian Welzel, "Changing Mass Priorities: The Link between Modernization and Democracy," *Perspectives on Politics* (June 2010), p. 553.

9. Ibid.

10. Ibid., pp. 560–61; and Christian Welzel, "Theories of Democratization," in *Democratization*, edited by Christian W. Haerpfer and others (Oxford University Press, 2009). These include the World Bank's Social Accountability Index, Noncorrupt and Lawful Governance Index, Government Effectiveness Index, and Voice and Accountability Index and Freedom House's Freedom in the World Index.

11. Inglehart and Welzel, "Changing Mass Priorities," p. 561.

12. Ronald Inglehart and Christian Welzel, "Development and Democracy: What We Know about Modernization Today," *Foreign Affairs* (March-April 2009), pp. 33–41.

13. Ibid., p. 35.

14. Derived from "Country Comparison: Telephones: Mobile Cellular per Capita," CIA, *The World Factbook* (www.indexmundi.com/g/r.aspx?v=4010).

15. Derived from International Telecommunication Union data in "Internet Users by Country," *Global Finance* (www.gfmag.com/tools/global-database/ne-data/11942-internet-users.html#axzz2eVL0iusH).

16. See Pippa Norris, *Making Democratic Governance Work: How Regimes Shape Prosperity, Welfare, and Peace* (Cambridge University Press, 2012), chap. 5.

17. Pippa Norris, *Critical Citizens: Global Support for Democratic Government* (Oxford University Press, 1999); "World Publics Say Governments Should Be More Responsive to the Will of the People," World Public Opinion, May 12, 2008 (www.worldpublicopinion.org/pipa/articles/governance_bt/482.php?lb=btgov&pnt=482&nid=&id=).

18. The Arab Barometer survey was conducted in 2010–11. The data can be found at www.arabbarometer.org/?q=content/arabbarometer-i-spss-data-file.

19. Amaney Jamal and Mark Tessler, "The Democracy Barometers: Attitudes in the Arab World: 2008," in *Public Opinion in the Middle East: Survey Research and the Political Orientations of Ordinary Citizens*, edited by Mark Tessler (Indiana University Press, 2011), p. 108.

20. See Mark Tessler, "Islam and Democracy in the Middle East: The Impact of Religious Orientations on Attitudes toward Democracy in Four Arab Countries: 2002," in *Public Opinion in the Middle East*, edited by Tessler, p. 68; Jamal and Tessler, "The Democracy Barometers," in *Public Opinion in the Middle East*,

edited by Tessler, p. 120; and John Esposito and Dalia Mogahed, *Who Speaks for Islam? What a Billion Muslims Really Think* (New York: Gallup Press, 2007).

21. Shibley Telhami, *The World through Arab Eyes: Arab Public Opinion and the Reshaping of the Middle East* (New York: Basic Books, 2013), p. 148.

22. See *Freedom in the World 2013* (www.freedomhouse.org/sites/default/files/FIW%202013%20Charts%20and%20Graphs%20for%20Web_0.pdf).

23. See Steven Heydemann, "Upgrading Authoritarianism in the Arab World," Saban Center Analysis Paper Series, October 2007 (www.brookings.edu/research/papers/2007/10/arabworld).

24. Ibid.

25. Barrington Moore Jr., *Injustice: The Social Bases of Obedience and Revolt* (New York: M.E. Sharpe, 1978).

26. See Amy L. Freedman, *Political Change and Consolidation: Democracy's Rocky Road in Thailand, Indonesia, South Korea, and Malaysia* (New York: Palgrave Macmillan, 2006).

27. Samuel Huntington employs the term "snowballing" for this phenomenon in *The Third Wave*.

Chapter 3

1. See, for example, John O. Koehler, *Stasi: The Untold Story of the East German Secret Police* (Boulder, Colo.: Westview Press, 1999), chap. 1.

2. The early literature on democratization, drawing on the transitions in Portugal and Spain as examples, emphasized the importance of elite bargains. See, for instance, Guillermo O'Donnell and Philippe C. Schmitter, *Transitions from Authoritarian Rule: Tentative Conclusions about Uncertain Democracies* (Johns Hopkins University Press, 1986).

3. Vaclav Havel and others, *The Power of the Powerless: Citizens against the State in Central Eastern Europe* (New York: M.E. Sharpe, 1986), chap. 1.

4. As quoted, for example, in Anthony Lewis, "'As If We Were Free,'" *New York Times*, December 2, 1986 (www.nytimes.com/1986/12/02/opinion/foreign-affairs-as-if-we-were-free.html).

5. The protesters' demands included the right to form independent trade unions, the release of political prisoners, and the expansion of political rights.

6. Norman Davies, *Europe: A History* (Oxford University Press, 1996), p. 1108.

7. Timothy Garton Ash, *History of the Present: Essays, Sketches, and Dispatches from Europe in the 1990s* (New York: Random House, 2000), p. 8.

8. They included the Rose Revolution in Georgia, the Orange Revolution in Ukraine, and the attempted Denim Revolution in Belarus, which were largely nonviolent civic movements that aimed to unseat authoritarian or semi-authoritarian governments.

9. "GDP Growth Rate," based on data from the World Bank, Google Public Data (www.google.com/publicdata/explore?ds=d5bncppjof8f9_&met_y=ny_gdp_mktp_kd_zg&idim=country:SVK&dl=en&hl=en&q=slovakia%20gdp%20growth).

10. Freedom House, *Freedom in the World 2011: The Authoritarian Challenge to Democracy* (Washington, 2011), p. 585.

11. "GDP Growth Rate," based on data from the World Bank, Google Public Data (www.google.com/publicdata/explore?ds=d5bncppjof8f9_&met_y=ny_gdp_mktp_kd_zg&idim=country:SRB&dl=en&hl=en&q=serbia%20gdp%20growth).

12. Ibid.

13. Dan Bilefsky, "Next Premier of Serbia Is from Party of Milosevic," *New York Times,* July 25, 2012 (www.nytimes.com/2012/07/26/world/europe/new-serb-leader-stokes-fears-of-return-to-nationalism.html?ref=serbia&_r=0).

14. Ibid.

15. Andrew Wilson, *Belarus: The Last European Dictatorship* (Yale University Press, 2011), x.

16. Rodger Potocki, "Dark Days in Belarus," *Journal of Democracy* (October 2002), p. 146.

17. Ronald J. Hill, "Post-Soviet Belarus: In Search of Direction," in *Post-Communist Belarus,* edited by Stephen White and others (Oxford: Rowland and Littlefield, 2005), pp. 4–5, and Wilson, *Belarus: The Last European Dictatorship,* p. 145.

18. Hill, "Post-Soviet Belarus," p. 5.

19. Ibid., p. 6; Potocki, "Dark Days in Belarus," p. 143.

20. Wilson, *Belarus: The Last European Dictatorship,* p. 168.

21. Ibid., p. 170.

22. Hill, "Post-Soviet Belarus," p. 7.

23. Stephen White and Elena Korosteleva, "Lukashenko and the Postcommunist Presidency," in *Post-Communist Belarus,* edited by White and others, p. 61.

24. Wilson, *Belarus: The Last European Dictatorship,* p. 192.

25. Potocki, "Dark Days in Belarus," p. 147.

26. Ibid., pp. 148–51.

27. Ibid., pp. 150–52.

28. Ulazdimir Padhol and David R. Marples, "The Dynamics of the 2001 Presidential Election," in *Post-Communist Belarus,* edited by White and others, p. 86.

29. Wilson, *Belarus: The Last European Dictatorship,* p. 202.

30. Rodger Potocki, "Belarus: A Tale of Two Elections," *Journal of Democracy* (July 2011), p. 51.

31. Wilson, *Belarus: The Last European Dictatorship,* p. 199.

32. Potocki, "Dark Days in Belarus," p. 155.

33. Potocki, "Belarus: A Tale of Two Elections," p. 52.

34. Wilson, *Belarus: The Last European Dictatorship,* p. 207.

35. Ibid., pp. 211–13.

36. As quoted in Wilson, *Belarus: The Last European Dictatorship*, p. 209.

37. Ibid., p. 214.

38. Ibid., pp. 215–19.

39. Ibid., pp. 219–21.

40. Potocki, "Belarus: A Tale of Two Elections," p. 54

41. Ibid., pp. 54–55.

42. Ibid., p. 62.

43. Paul Kubicek, *The History of Ukraine* (Westport, Conn.: Greenwood Press, 2008), p.100.

44. Ibid., pp. 101–05.

45. Ibid., pp. 114–15.

46. Bohdan Nahaylo, *The Ukrainian Resurgence*, pp. 57–58, as quoted in Kubicek, *The History of Ukraine* pp. 122–23.

47. Kubicek, *The History of Ukraine*, pp. 124–26.

48. Ibid., pp. 126–27.

49. Ibid., pp. 128–30.

50. Ibid., pp. 131–32.

51. Ibid., pp. 133–34.

52. Ibid., pp. 136–37.

53. Anders Aslund, *How Ukraine Became a Market Economy and Democracy* (Washington: Peterson Institute for International Economics, 2009), pp. 34–35; Kubicek, *The History of Ukraine*, pp. 141–43.

54. Comecon (Council for Mutual Economic Assistance) was established in 1949 to coordinate trade and development policies among the centrally planned economies of the Eastern bloc.

55. Aslund, *How Ukraine Became a Market Economy*, p. 35; Kubicek, *The History of Ukraine*, pp. 143.

56. Kubicek, *The History of Ukraine*, pp. 144–45.

57. Aslund, *How Ukraine Became a Market Economy*, pp. 4–5.

58. Kubicek, *The History of Ukraine*, pp. 146–51.

59. *Freedom in the World 2011*, pp. 702–03; Kubicek, *The History of Ukraine*, p. 148.

60. Kubicek, *The History of Ukraine*, pp. 151, 149.

61. Ibid., pp. 160–61.

62. Adrian Karatnycky, "The Fall and Rise of Ukraine's Political Opposition: From Kuchmagate to the Orange Revolution," in *Revolution in Orange: The Origins of Ukraine's Democratic Breakthrough*, edited by Anders Aslund and Michael McFaul (Brookings, 2006), pp. 36–37.

63. Ibid, p. 39.

64. Nadia Diuk, "The Triumph of Civil Society," in *Revolution in Orange*, edited by Aslund and McFaul, pp. 78–83; Kubicek, *The History of Ukraine*, pp. 170–73.

65. Kubicek, *The History of Ukraine*, pp. 173–74.

66. Aslund, *How Ukraine Became a Market Economy and Democracy*, pp. 204–09; Kubicek, *The History of Ukraine*, pp. 173–75.

67. Kubicek, *The History of Ukraine*, pp. 176–77; Aslund, *How Ukraine Became a Market Economy and Democracy*, pp. 214–15.

68. Kubicek, *The History of Ukraine*, p. 178; Aslund, *How Ukraine Became a Market Economy and Democracy*, pp. 216–18.

69. Aslund, *How Ukraine Became a Market Economy and Democracy*, pp. 222–32.

70. *Freedom in the World 2011*, p. 704.

71. Daryna Krasnolutska, Olga Tanas, and Ilya Arkhipov, "Ukraine Protesters Want Answers on $15 Billion Russia Aid," *Bloomberg News*, December 18, 2013 (www.bloomberg.com/news/2013-12-17/russia-commits-15-billion-to-ukraine-bonds-as-gas-price-reduced.html); "Putin's Expensive Victory: Under Its Current Government, Ukraine May Be a Prize Not Worth Winning," *The Economist*, December 21, 2013 (www.economist.com/news/europe/21591897-under-its-current-government-ukraine-may-be-prize-not-worth-winning-putins-expensive-victory).

72. *Freedom in the World 2011*.

73. Marina Ottaway, *Democracy Challenged: The Rise of Semi-Authoritarianism* (Washington: Carnegie Endowment for International Peace, January 2003).

Chapter 4

1. They were protesting development plans for Taksim Gazi Park, Istanbul's central park. The demonstrations, which were brutally suppressed by the government, soon burgeoned into larger protests against the government's restrictions on personal freedoms.

2. Ergun Ozbudun, *Contemporary Turkish Politics: Challenges to Democratic Consolidation* (Boulder, Colo.: Lynne Rienner Publishers, 2000), p. 6.

3. Henri J. Barkey, "The Struggles of a Strong State," *Journal of International Affairs* (Fall 2000).

4. Ömer Taşpınar, "Turkey: The New Model?" in *The Islamists Are Coming: Who They Really Are*, edited by Robin Wright (Washington: Woodrow Wilson International Center for Scholars and U.S. Institute of Peace, 2012), at www.brookings.edu/research/papers/2012/04/24-turkey-new-model-taspinar, p. 3.

5. Ozbudun, *Contemporary Turkish Politics*, p. 5.

6. As quoted in Ozbudun, *Contemporary Turkish Politics*, pp. 33–34.

7. Ibid., p. 35.

8. Barkey, "The Struggles of a Strong State," p. 99.

9. Ibid., p. 100.

10. Ibid., p. 103.

11. Taşpınar, "Turkey: The New Model?" p. 4.

12. Ibid., p. 5.

13. Henri J. Barkey and Yasemin Congar, "Deciphering Turkey's Elections: The Making of a Revolution," *World Policy Journal* (Fall 2007), p. 64.

14. Ibid., pp. 64–65.

15. Taşpınar, "Turkey: The New Model?" p. 6.

16. Ibid., pp. 7–9.

17. Barkey and Congar, "Deciphering Turkey's Elections," p. 68.

18. Larry Diamond, "Indonesia's Place in Global Democracy," in *Problems of Democratisation in Indonesia: Elections, Institutions, and Society,* edited by Edward Aspinall and Marcus Mietzner (Singapore: Institute of Southeast Asian Studies, 2010), p. 21.

19. Harold Crouch, *Political Reform in Indonesia after Soeharto* (Singapore: Institute of Southeast Asian Studies, 2010), p. 16.

20. Ibid., p. 17; Edward Aspinall, "Indonesia: The Irony of Success," *Journal of Democracy* (April 2010), p. 25.

21. Aspinall, "Indonesia: The Irony of Success," p. 23.

22. Crouch, *Political Reform in Indonesia after Soeharto,* p. 16.

23. Ibid., p. 1.

24. Ibid., pp. 17–18.

25. Aspinall, "Indonesia: The Irony of Success," pp. 24–25.

26. Ibid.

27. Edward Aspinall, *Opposing Suharto: Compromise, Resistance, and Regime Change In Indonesia* (Stanford University Press, 2005), p. 87.

28. Most governments allow some level of associational activity out of pure pragmatism. They cannot ban everything, and they want to be seen as operating within a legal framework, if only for appearance's sake. These groups may have been allowed to provide legal aid, but that does not necessarily mean that they won the cases in Suharto's courts.

29. Ibid., pp. 87–96.

30. Aspinall, "Indonesia: The Irony of Success," pp. 24–25, 32.

31. Aspinall, *Opposing Suharto,* p. 40.

32. Ibid., pp. 154–68.

33. Ibid., pp. 175–89.

34. Ibid., pp. 182–93.

35. Crouch, *Political Reform in Indonesia after Soeharto,* pp. 18–19.

36. Ibid., pp. 19–20; Aspinall, *Opposing Suharto,* pp. 209–11.

37. Crouch, *Political Reform in Indonesia after Soeharto,* pp. 19–20; Aspinall, *Opposing Suharto,* pp. 209–11.

38. Crouch, *Political Reform in Indonesia after Soeharto,* pp. 20–21; Aspinall, *Opposing Suharto,* pp. 232–37.

39. He was described in the *New York Times* as "eccentric" and "disorganized and improvisational in style and enigmatic in speech"; see Seth Mydans,

"Abdurrahman Wahid, 69, Is Dead; Led Indonesia for 2 Years of Tumult," *New York Times*, December 30, 2009 (www.nytimes.com/2009/12/31/world/asia/31wahid.html?ref=indonesia&_r=0)]

40. Crouch, *Political Reform in Indonesia after Soeharto*, pp. 28–32.

41. Ibid., pp. 32–35.

42. Ibid.

43. Ibid., pp. 35–38.

44. *Country Report: Indonesia*, Economist Intelligence Unit, January 2013 (www.eiu.com).

45. For a more elaborate argument along these lines, see Aspinall, "Indonesia: The Irony of Success."

46. A phrase famously used by the political scientist Guillermo O'Donnell to describe Brazil's transition to democracy, as quoted in Aspinall, "Indonesia: The Irony of Success," p. 21.

47. Meredith L. Weiss, *Protest and Possibilities: Civil Society and Coalitions for Political Change in Malaysia* (Stanford University Press, 2006), p. 35.

48. CIA, *The World Factbook*, "Malaysia" (www.cia.gov/library/publications/the-world-factbook/geos/my.html).

49. Harold A. Crouch, *Government and Society in Malaysia* (Cornell University Press, 1996), pp. 22–23.

50. Ibid., pp. 23–24; Weiss, *Protest and Possibilities*, p. 84.

51. Weiss, *Protest and Possibilities*, pp. 86–87; Crouch, *Government and Society in Malaysia*, pp. 24–27.

52. Calculation based on World Bank and OECD national accounts data, as found at Index Mundi, "Malaysia: GNI Growth" (www.indexmundi.com/facts/malaysia/gni-growth).

53. "The Exotic Doctor Calls It a Day," *The Economist*, November 3, 2003 (www.economist.com/node/2172673?story_id=2172673).

54. Weiss, *Protest and Possibilities*, pp. 104–14.

55. Ibid., p. 116.

56. Crouch, *Government and Society in Malaysia*, p. 20.

57. Amy L. Freedman, *Political Change and Consolidation: Democracy's Rocky Road in Thailand, Indonesia, South Korea, and Malaysia* (New York: Palgrave Macmillan, 2006), p. 108.

58. Ibid., pp. 22–23, 108.

59. Ibid., p. 109.

60. Weiss, *Protest and Possibilities*, pp. 127–61; Freedman, *Political Change and Consolidation*, pp. 111–12.

61. The *reformasi* movement was given the formal name the Social Justice Movement (ADIL) in December 1998 by Wan Azizah, but it had difficulty registering as a party. See Freedman, *Political Change and Consolidation*, p. 111.

62. Weiss, *Protest and Possibilities*, pp. 143–48; Freedman, *Political Change and Consolidation*, pp. 112–13.

63. "Malaysia," *Freedom in the World 2011* (New York and Washington: Rowman & Littlefield and Freedom House, 2011), pp. 416–17.

64. The charges, which accused him of sodomizing a former political aide, were brought by state prosecutors following the opposition's strong showing in the 1998 general elections (www.nytimes.com/2012/01/09/world/asia/malaysia-court-acquits-anwar-ibrahim-of-sodomy-charge.html).

65. As of January 2014, its final report had yet to be released. See G. Vinod, "Too Much Info Bogs People's Tribunal Report," *Free Malaysia Today News*, December 17, 2013 (www.freemalaysiatoday.com/category/nation/2013/12/17/too-much-info-causing-bersih-report-delay/).

66. Bruce O. Riedel, *Deadly Embrace: Pakistan, America, and the Future of the Global Jihad* (Brookings, 2011), p. 4.

67. Figure from Mohammad Waseem, "Patterns of Conflict in Pakistan: Implications for Policy," Brookings Project on U.S. Relations with the Islamic World Working Paper (January 2011), p. 4 (www.brookings.edu/research/papers/2011/03/01-pakistan-waseem).

68. Ibid., p. 4.

69. Ibid., pp. 3–5.

70. Philip Oldenburg, *India, Pakistan, and Democracy: Solving the Puzzle of Divergent Paths* (New York: Routledge, 2010), p. 21.

71. Ibid., pp. 17–27.

72. Thanks to Mohammad Waseem for this insight.

73. Riaz Ahmed Shaikh, "A State of Transition: Authoritarianism and Democratization in Pakistan," *Asia Journal of Global Studies* (2009).

74. Riedel, *Deadly Embrace*, pp. 8–9.

75. Ibid., pp. 9–10.

76. Oldenburg, *India, Pakistan, and Democracy*, pp. 132–36; Riedel, *Deadly Embrace*, p. 19.

77. World Bank Development Indicators, "GDP Growth Rate" (www.google.com/publicdata/explore?ds=d5bncppjof8f9_&met_y=ny_gdp_mktp_kd_zg&idim=country:PAK&dl=en&hl=en&q=pakistan+gdp+growth+rate).

78. Thanks to Bruce Riedel for this metaphor. See Riedel, *Deadly Embrace*, p. xviii.

79. Thanks to Mohammad Waseem for this insight.

80. See Benedict Anderson, *Imagined Communities: Reflections on the Origin and Spread of Nationalism* (New York: Verso, 1983).

Chapter 5

1. When Uruguay first became an electoral democracy and how democratic it was in its early history are open to dispute. See "Uruguay," *Encyclopaedia Britannica* (www.britannica.com/search?query=uruguay); Peter Smith, "Cycles

of Electoral Democracy in Latin America: 1900–2000," Working Paper 6, Center for Latin American Studies, University of California, Berkeley, 2004; and "Uruguay Profile," BBC News, December 11, 2013 (www.bbc.co.uk/news/world-latin-america-20043130).

2. Arturo Valenzuela, "Latin American Presidencies Interrupted," in *Latin America's Struggle for Democracy,* edited by Larry Diamond (Johns Hopkins University Press, 2008), p. 3.

3. Ibid., p. 4. General Augusto Pinochet in Chile was a prominent exception.

4. See Integrated Network for Societal Conflict Research (INSCR), Polity IV, Coups d'Etat 1946–2012 dataset (www.systemicpeace.org/inscr/inscr.htm).

5. Valenzuela, " Latin American Presidencies Interrupted," p. 4.

6. Jorge I. Dominguez, "Constructing Democratic Governance in Latin America: Taking Stock of the 1990s," in *Constructing Democratic Governance in Latin America,* 2nd ed., edited by Jorge I. Dominguez and Michael Shifter (Johns Hopkins University Press, 2003), p. 356.

7. Guillermo O'Donnell, Philippe Schmitter, and Laurence Whitehead, *Transitions from Authoritarian Rule: Tentative Conclusions about Uncertain Democracies* (Johns Hopkins University Press, 1986), pp. 6–14.

8 Valenzuela, " Latin American Presidencies Interrupted," p. 4.

9. Ibid., pp. 3–16.

10. Ibid., pp. 6–7.

11. "Gini Back in the Bottle: An Uequal Continent Is Becoming Less So," *The Economist,* October 13, 2012 (www.economist.com/node/21564411).

12. Juan J. Linz, "Presidential or Parliamentary Democracy: Does It Make a Difference?" in *The Failure of Presidential Democracy,* edited by Juan J. Linz and Arturo Valenzuela (Johns Hopkins University Press, 1994), pp. 18–19.

13. Valenzuela, " Latin American Presidencies Interrupted," p. 11.

14. Dominguez, "Constructing Democratic Governance in Latin America," pp. 351–83; and Javier Corrales, "Constitutional Rewrites in Latin America: 1987–2009," in *Constructing Democratic Governance in Latin America,* 4th ed., edited by Jorge I. Dominguez and Michael Shifter (Johns Hopkins University Press, 2013) .

15. Michael Shifter, "Emerging Trends and Determining Factors in Democratic Governance," in *Constructing Democratic Governance in Latin America,* 3rd ed., edited by Jorge I. Dominguez and Michael Shifter (Johns Hopkins University Press, 2008), p. 5.

16. Ibid., pp. 5-6. "Horizontal accountability" refers to internal oversight exercised by government bodies over one another.

17. Scott Mainwaring, "The Crisis of Representation in the Andes," in *Latin America's Struggle for Democracy,* edited by Diamond, p. 23.

18. Calculated using data from World Bank, "GDP Growth (Annual %) in Latin America and Caribbean" (www.tradingeconomics.com/latin-america-and-caribbean/gdp-growth-annual-percent-wb-data.html).

19. Javier Corrales, "The Backlash against Market Reforms in Latin America in the 2000s," in *Constructing Democratic Governance in Latin America,* 3rd ed., edited by Dominguez and Shifter, p. 39.

20. Matthew F. Cleary, "Explaining the Left's Resurgence," in *Latin America's Struggle for Democracy,* edited by Diamond, p. 62–65.

21. Ibid., p. 69.

22. Ibid., p. 65.

23. Christopher Sabatini and Eric Farnsworth, "The Transformation of the Labor Arena," in *Latin America's Struggle for Democracy,* edited by Diamond, p. 92.

24. Mainwaring, "The Crisis of Representation in the Andes," p. 21.

25. Ibid., p. 25.

26. Robert J. Barro and Jong-Wha Lee, "A New Data Set of Educational Attainment in the World: 1950–2010," Working Paper 15902 (Cambridge, Mass.: National Bureau of Economic Research, April 2010) (www.nber.org/papers/w15902).

27. Shifter, "Emerging Trends and Determining Factors in Democratic Governance," p. 9.

28. Lourdes Sola, "Politics, Markets, and Society in Brazil," in *Latin America's Struggle for Democracy,* edited by Diamond, p. 125.

29. Arturo Valenzuela and Lucia Dammert, "Problems of Success in Chile," in *Latin America's Struggle for Democracy,* edited by Diamond, p. 143.

30. Ibid., p. 144.

31. Ibid., p. 140.

32. Ibid., p. 142.

33. Ibid., p. 146.

34. "Chile Profile," BBC News (www.bbc.co.uk/news/world-latin-america-19356356).

35. "Argentina," in *Freedom in the World 2011* (Freedom House), pp. 38–42.

36. Abente Brun, "Introduction," in *Latin America's Struggle for Democracy,* edited by Diamond, p. xviii.

37. Steven Levitsky and Maria Victoria Murillo, "Argentina: From Kirchner to Kirchner," in *Latin America's Struggle for Democracy,* edited by Diamond, pp. 113–14.

38. Ibid., p. 101.

39. Ibid., p. 108.

40. Steven Levitsky, "Argentina: Democracy and Institutional Weakness," in *Constructing Democratic Governance in Latin America,* 3rd ed., edited by Dominguez and Shifter.

41. Ibid.

42. "Argentina Profile," BBC News, November 13, 2013 (www.bbc.co.uk/news/world-latin-america-18712378).

43. At various times since the Dirty War, the military has enacted or put pressure on civilian governments to enact amnesty for crimes committed during that

period. Those amnesties had to be repealed (most recently by the supreme court in 2005) for prosecutions to go forward.

44. Javier Corrales and Michael Penfold, "Venezuela: Chavez and the Opposition," in *Latin America's Struggle for Democracy*, edited by Diamond, p. 185.

45. David J. Myers, "Venezuela: Delegative Democracy or Electoral Autocracy?" in *Constructing Democratic Governance in Latin America*, 3rd ed., edited by Dominguez and Shifter, p. 318.

46. Ibid.

47. Ibid., p. 285.

48. Corrales and Penfold, "Venezuela: Chavez and the Opposition," p. 186.

49. World Bank, "World Development Indicators" (www.google.com/public-data/explore?ds=d5bncppjof8f9_&met_y=ny_gdp_mktp_kd_zg&idim=country: VEN&dl=en&hl=en&q=venezuela%20gdp%20growth).

50. Corrales and Penfold, " Venezuela: Chavez and the Opposition," p. 189; and Myers, "Delegative Democracy or Electoral Autocracy?" p. 310.

51. "Bolivia," in *Freedom in the World 2012* (Freedom House) (www. freedomhouse.org/report/freedom-world/2012/bolivia).

52. Ibid.

53. "Bolivia," *New York Times* (http://topics.nytimes.com/top/news/international/countriesandterritories/bolivia/index.html).

54. "Bolivia," in *Freedom in the World 2012*.

Chapter 6

1. Steven Radelet makes this argument most powerfully in *Emerging Africa: How 17 Countries Are Leading the Way* (Washington: Center for Global Development, 2010).

2. Michael Bratton and Nicolas Van de Walle, *Democratic Experiments in Africa: Regime Transitions in Comparative Perspective*, pp. 3–7, as cited in Radelet, *Emerging Africa*, pp. 53–54.

3. Radelet, *Emerging Africa*, pp. 51–53.

4. Ibid., pp. 54–55.

5. As noted previously, the lonely democratic exceptions in 1989 were Botswana, the Gambia, and Mauritius. The total of seventeen electoral democracies in contemporary Sub-Saharan Africa is derived from data in *Freedom in the World 2011* (Freedom House), Appendix: Table of Electoral Democracies, pp. 836–37.

6. Figures adjusted for purchasing power parity. CIA, *The World Factbook* (www.cia.gov/library/publications/the-world-factbook/rankorder/2004rank. html).

7. In *Emerging Africa*, Radelet identifies seventeen of Sub-Saharan Africa's fifty countries as "emerging countries," which he defines as African countries that

since the mid-1990s have experienced "dramatic changes in economic growth, poverty reduction, and political accountability"; he identifies another six as not far behind. See Radelet, *Emerging Africa,* p. 12.

8. Ibid., pp. 12–13; and Michael Lewin Ross, "Does Oil Hinder Democracy?" *World Politics* (April 2001), pp. 325–61.

9. Thomas Carothers, "Democracy without Illusions," *Foreign Affairs* (January-February 1997), pp. 85–89.

10. Richard Joseph, "Africa, 1990–1997: From *Arbetura* to Closure," in *Democratization in Africa: Progress and Retreat,* edited by Larry Diamond and Marc F. Plattner (Johns Hopkins University Press, 1999), p. 11.

11. Kate Baldwin, "Zambia: One Party in Perpetuity?" in *Democratization in Africa,* edited by Diamond and Plattner, p. 295.

12. Richard Joseph, "Challenges of a 'Frontier' Region," in *Democratization in Africa,* edited by Diamond and Plattner, p. 8.

13. Lise Rakner and Nicolas van der Walle, "Democratization by Elections: Opposition Weakness in Africa," *Journal of Democracy* (July 2009), p. 108.

14. Larry Diamond and Marc F. Plattner, "Introduction," in *Democratization in Africa,* edited by Diamond and Plattner, p. xv.

15. H. Kwasi Prempeh, "Presidents Untamed," in *Democratization in Africa,* edited by Diamond and Plattner, p. 18.

16. See Michael Bratton and Carolyn Logan, "Voters but Not Yet Citizens: The Weak Demand for Political Accountability in Africa's Unclaimed Democracies," Working Paper 63 (Afrobarometer, September 2006).

17. Terrence Lyons, "Ghana's Elections: A Major Step Forward," in *Democratization in Africa,* edited by Diamond and Plattner , p. 158.

18. Ibid.

19 The final Carter Center report recognized that there were numerous irregularities and inconsistencies in the vote but found no systematic attempt to skew the vote one way or another. However, it conceded that because the process was so flawed, others might believe that there had been such an attempt (www. google.com/url?sa=t&rct=j&q=&esrc=s&source=web&cd=2&ved=0CDYQFjA B&url=http%3A%2F%2Fwww.cartercenter.org%2Fdocuments%2Felectionrep orts%2Fdemocracy%2FFFinalReportGhana1992.pdf&ei=rgOmUtyIHPDNsQTF j4L4BQ&usg=AFQjCNGtzJvn0KGhtAmFBsVPA0dWNj7zBw&sig2=dU03kpvS 4reYgbGlL2y62A&bvm=bv.57752919,d.cWc).

20. E. Gyimah-Boadi, "Ghana's Elections: The Challenges Ahead," in *Democratization in Africa,* edited by Diamond and Plattner, pp. 171–75; and Lyons, "A Major Step Forward," in *Democratization in Africa,* edited by Diamond and Plattner, pp.163–65.

21. Gyimah-Boadi, "Ghana's Elections," p. 172.

22. E. Gyimah-Boadi, "Another Step Forward for Africa," in *Democratization in Africa,* edited by Diamond and Plattner, p. 145.

23. Ibid., p. 147.

24. Calculated from data from United Nations Development Program, "Human Development Index (HDI) Value" (https://data.undp.org/dataset/Human-Development-Index-HDI-value/8ruz-shxu).

25. Gyimah-Boadi, "Another Step Forward for Africa," p. 147.

26. Baldwin, "Zambia: One Party in Perpetuity?" p. 297.

27. Ibid., p. 299.

28. Ibid., p. 300.

29. Ibid., p. 295; and *Freedom in the World 2011*, p. 746.

30. Baldwin, "Zambia: One Party in Perpetuity?" p. 295.

31. Resentment has arisen because of the way that the Chinese treat their workers and the low wages that they pay as well as Zambians' sense that the nation's patrimony of mineral resources is being expropriated by the Chinese and the politicians with whom they cut corrupt insider deals. See, for example, Alexis Okeowo, "China, Zambia, and a Clash in a Coal Mine," October 10, 2013 (www.newyorker.com/online/blogs/currency/2013/10/china-zambia-and-a-clash-in-a-copper-mine.html).

32. "Country Report: Zambia," Economist Intelligence Unit, February 2013.

33. Nse Udoh, "Sata Faces Call for Impeachment," Zambia Reports, March 12, 2013 (http://zambiareports.com/2013/03/12/sata-faces-calls-for-impeachment/).

34. CIA, *The World Factbook*, "Population below Poverty Line" (www.cia.gov/library/publications/the-world-factbook/fields/2046.html#ni).

35. Rotimi T. Suberu, "Nigeria's Muddled Elections," in *Democratization in Africa*, edited by Diamond and Plattner, p. 122.

36. Peter M. Lewis, "Nigeria: An End to the Permanent Transition," in *Democratization in Africa*, edited by Diamond and Plattner, p. 231.

37. Ibid., p. 232.

38. Ibid., pp. 233–34.

39. Ibid., pp. 238–44.

40. Suberu, "Nigeria's Muddled Elections," p.122.

41. Ibid., p. 123.

42. Lewis, "An End to the Permanent Transition," p. 204.

43. Ibid., p. 208.

44. Ibid., p. 233.

45. Ibid., p. 236.

46. "Uganda," *Freedom in the World 2012* (www.freedomhouse.org/report/freedom-world/2012/uganda).

47. "Country Report: Uganda," Economist Intelligence Unit, January 2013 (www.marketresearch.com/Economist-Intelligence-Unit-v458/Country-Uganda-January-7283482/).

48. Derived from data from Uganda Bureau of Statistics, "Uganda GDP Annual Growth Rate" (www.tradingeconomics.com/uganda/gdp-growth-annual).

49. On the ripple effects of the Arab Spring throughout Africa, see "Africa and the Arab Spring: A New Era of Democratic Expectations," Africa Center for Strategic Studies Special Report, November 2011 (http://africacenter.org/2011/11/africa-and-the-arab-spring-a-new-era-of-democratic-expectations-2/).

Chapter 7

1. That figure is based on counting as liberal democracies those countries categorized by Freedom House as "free." See *Freedom in the World 2012* (Freedom House), appendices, "Combined Average Ratings," p. 834, and "Electoral Democracies," pp. 836–37.

2. Laurel E. Miller and others, *Democratization in the Arab World: Prospects and Lessons from around the Globe* (Santa Monica, Calif.: RAND, 2012) (www.rand.org/pubs/monographs/MG1192).

3. Larry Diamond, *The Spirit of Democracy: The Struggle to Build Free Societies throughout the World* (New York: Henry Holt, 2008), pp. 48–50.

4. Samuel Huntington, *The Third Wave: Democratization in the Late Twentieth Century* (University of Oklahoma Press, 1991), pp. 266–67.

5. While that statement generally is attributed to Jefferson, historians debate whether he ever actually said it. See "Quotations" (www.monticello.org/site/jefferson/eternal-vigilance-price-liberty-quotation).

6. Acton Institute, "Lord Acton Quote Archive" (www.acton.org/research/lord-acton-quote-archive).

7. Speech in the Virginia Constitutional Convention, December 2, 1829 (www.constitution.org/jm/18291202_vaconcon.txt).

8. Thanks to Ivan Vejvoda for his insights on this issue.

9. George Orwell, *1984* (New York: New American Library, 1949), p. 263.

10. For a good summary of the World Bank's gradual philosophical shift from an emphasis solely on market incentives toward an emphasis on good governance and mechanisms of vertical and horizontal accountability, see "State-Society Synergy for Accountability: Lessons for the World Bank," World Bank Working Paper 30 (2004).

11. For an overview and bibliography of the extensive literature on civil society, see Michael Edwards, *Civil Society* (Malden, Mass.: Blackwell, 2004).

12. Meanwhile, scholars like Sheri Berman pointed out that countries can have a rich associational life yet still fall prey to dictatorship, as was the case in Weimar Germany. See Berman, " Civil Society and the Collapse of the Weimar Republic," *World Politics,* April 1997.

13. Michael Bratton and Carolyn Logan, "Voters but Not Yet Citizens: The Weak Demand for Political Accountability in Africa's Unclaimed Democracies," Working Paper 63 (Afrobarometer, September 2006).

Chapter 8

1. See John Rawls, *A Theory of Justice* (Harvard University Press, 1971).

2. See Sheri Berman, "The Promise of the Arab Spring: In Political Development, No Gain without Pain," *Foreign Affairs* (January/February 2013), pp. 64–74.

3. See, for instance, Amartya Sen, *Identity and Violence: The Illusion of Destiny* (New York: W.W. Norton, 2007).

4. See Benedict Anderson, *Imagined Communities: Reflections on the Origin and Spread of Nationalism* (Verso, 1983).

5. See William Antholis and Stephen Grand, "Inside Out: The Double Minorities: An Interdisciplinary Study of Ethnic Conflict in Cyprus and Northern Ireland," unpublished honors thesis, University of Virginia, April 1986.

6. See Arend Lijphart, *Democracy in Plural Societies: A Comparative Exploration* (Yale University Press, 1977).

7. George Santayana, *The Life of Reason* (Amherst, N.Y.: Prometheus Books, 1998), p. 82.

8. For more on issues of justice in times of transition, see the work of the organization Beyond Conflict (www.beyondconflictint.org/).

9. Charles Kurzman and Ijlal Naqvi, "Do Muslims Vote Islamic?" *Journal of Democracy* (April 2010), pp. 50–63 (http://search.proquest.com/docview/195 557470/139E0C9812F15218245/9?accountid=26493)

10. See Nader Hashemi, *Islam, Secularism, and Liberal Democracy: Toward a Democratic Theory for Muslim Societies* (Oxford University Press, 2009).

11. James Madison, speech to the Constitutional Convention, June, 29, 1787, in *The Records of the Federal Convention of 1787,* vol. 1, edited by Max Farrand (Yale University Press, 1911), p. 465.

12. Steven Heydemann, "Upgrading Authoritarianism in the Arab World," Analysis Paper 13 (Saban Center for Middle East Policy, Brookings, October 2007); and William J. Dobson, *The Dictator's Learning Curve: Inside the Global Battle for Democracy* (New York: Anchor Books, 2013).

13. Thanks to Khaled Elgindy for this observation.

14. One variant of this argument can be found in Malcolm Gladwell, "Small Change: Why the Revolution Will Not Be Tweeted," *New Yorker,* October 4, 2010 (www.newyorker.com/reporting/2010/10/04/101004fa_fact_gladwell? currentPage=all).

15. This is in keeping with the recent findings in what has been referred to as "collective impact theory." See John Kania and Mark Kramer, "Collective Impact," *Stanford Social Innovation Review* (Winter 2011) (www.ssireview.org/ articles/entry/collective_impact). They identify five conditions that enable organizations that collaborate to have the maximum social impact: common agenda; shared measurement systems; mutually reinforcing activities; continuous communication; and backbone support organizations. Thanks to Barbara Ibrahim for bringing this research to my attention.

Chapter 9

1. As former secretary of state Hillary Clinton observed with regard to building the foundations of democracy in the region: "None of this can—or should—be imposed from the outside. It must emerge from citizens themselves." Speech at the U.S.-Islamic World Forum, February 14, 2010, Doha, Qatar (www.state.gov/secretary/rm/2010/02/136687.htm).

2. Ben Hubbard, "Egypt Convicts Workers at Foreign Nonprofit Groups, Including 16 Americans," *New York Times,* June 4, 2013.
(www.nytimes.com/2013/06/05/world/middleeast/in-egypt-guilty-verdicts-for-employees-of-foreign-nonprofits.html?_r=0).

3. Ralph Waldo Emerson, "Politics," *Essays,* 2nd series (1844).

4. See Kenneth M. Pollack, "Introduction: Understanding the Arab Awakening," in Kenneth M. Pollack and others, *The Arab Awakening: America and the Transformation of the Middle East* (Saban Center for Middle East Policy, Brookings, 2011), p. 8.

5. See Meredith Broadbent, "The Role of FTA Negotiations in the Future of U.S.-Egypt Relations," Center for Strategic and International Studies, December 2011 (https://csis.org/publication/role-fta-negotiations-future-us-egypt-relations).

6. Shadi Hamid and Peter Mandaville, "Bringing the United States Back into the Middle East," *Washington Quarterly* (Fall 2013), pp. 95–105.

7. According to a study by the Institute of International Education, only 2,201 Egyptians were studying in the United States, at all levels of higher education, during the 2011–12 academic year, while there were 72,295 students from South Korea, which has less than two-thirds the population of Egypt. See Institute of International Education, "Open Doors Report on International Educational Exchange," Fact Sheets by Region: 2012 (www.iie.org/Research-and-Publications/Open-Doors/Data/Fact-Sheets-by-Region) and Fact Sheets by Country: 2013 (www.iie.org/Research-and-Publications/Open-Doors/Data/Fact-Sheets-by-Country/2013).

Index

Abacha, Sani, 148, 162–64. *See also* Nigeria

Abdülmecid (Sultan; Turkey), 83

Abiola, Moshood K.O., 162, 163, 164

Abkhazia, 73

Abubakar, Abdulsalami, 164

Act of Union (1977, Belarus, Russia), 58

Acton, Lord. *See* Dalberg-Acton, John, 1st Baron Acton

Afghanistan, 113, 114, 117, 205

Africa: Arab Spring and, 170; citizenry in, 181; democracy in, 21, 150–54, 175; elections in, 174, 175; imperial presidencies in, 170; incumbents in, 197; independent media in, 152–53; military in, 197; political power in, 150–52; politics in, 170; societal polarization in, 190; "strong man" and "big man" regimes in, 147, 149, 153, 157, 159, 161, 165, 170, 177, 178. *See also* Lessons; Recommendations; *individual countries*

Africa, South. *See* South Africa

Africa, Sub-Saharan: civil society in, 159–60, 161; democratic ferver in, 15; economic issues in, 148, 149–50; human development in, 158; military in, 147; positive changes in, 12–13, 146; term limits in, 152, 156, 157, 159, 168; Third Wave of democratization in, 146–50. *See also* Lessons; Recommendations; *individual countries*

Africa, Sub-Saharan—elections: as a focal point for political life, 169–70; founding elections, 148, 151; multiparty elections, 149, 150, 151–52, 153, 155, 161; Third Wave of democratization and, 147, 150–51, 153, 155–56

Africa, Sub-Saharan—elections in specific countries: in Ghana, 154, 155–56, 158, 169; in Liberia, 149; in Nigeria, 162, 164; in Sierra Leone, 149; in Uganda, 166, 167, 168–69; in Zambia, 158–60, 161

Afrobarometer surveys, 153, 158

Albania, 24

Alfonsín, Raúl, 133–34

Algeria, 18

al Qaeda. *See* al Qaeda under Q

Ali, Chaudhary Rahmat, 109–10

Ali Khan, Liaquat, 112

Aliyev, Heydar, 38